THE WINTER
SOLSTICE

THE WINTER SOLSTICE

THE SACRED TRADITIONS
OF CHRISTMAS

JOHN MATTHEWS

With contributions from CAITLÍN MATTHEWS

Thorsons

An Imprint of HarperCollins *Publishers*

for
Martin & Jessica Ruby Simpson
Who know how to Celebrate

and

For David
who is Santa

Thorsons
An imprint of HarperCollins *Publishers*
77-85 Fulham Palace Road, Hammersmith, London W6 8JB

Copyright © 1998 Godsfield Press

Text © 1998 John Matthews

Originally published by Thorsons 1998

1 3 5 7 9 10 8 6 4 2

Picture research by Vanessa Fletcher

Write to: Godsfield Press
Laurel House, Station Approach
New Alresford, Hants
SO24 9JH, UK

John Matthews asserts the moral right to be identified
as the author of this work.

A catalogue record for this book is available
from the British Library.

ISBN 0-7225-3738-7

Printed in the United States

CONTENTS

INTRODUCTION

*W*elcome everything! Welcome all alike what has been, and what never was, and what we hope may be, to your shelter underneath the holly, to your places around the Christmas fire, where what is sits open-hearted! CHARLES DICKENS, 1851

LEFT: The modern Western celebration of the Winter Solstice has become inextricably linked with the celebration of the birth of Christ.

The Solstice and Christmas

In our own time the Solstice is indissolubly linked with the festival of Christmas, though it was not always so. The myths of the festival are so deeply imbedded within us that we no longer ask why we decorate a fir tree at this time, or why we place green boughs and candles in our home. We take these things for granted, as we plunge into the whirlwind passage of preparations that lead up to the all-too-brief day of Christmas itself. Yet even here we forget the season is really twelve days in length – we sing the carol "The Twelve Days of Christmas," but have little understanding of its origin.

Today the festival is most often known simply as Christmas, and it has been celebrated for nearly two thousand years. During that time, it has taken many forms, changed direction several times, absorbed the influence of many cultures, and developed into a modern industry. Yet the simplicity of the Christmas message has continued to ring through the ages, and despite the commercialism and nonliturgical appropriateness of many aspects of Christmas today, it continues to exert a powerful effect upon everyone who celebrates it, adults and children alike.

There is a moment of silence that occurs every year, somewhere between the dawn of Christmas Eve and the setting of the sun on Christmas Day itself – a moment we have all experienced at least once in our lives, maybe more than once. It can silence a great city like London or New York, and it can bring stillness to our hearts, whoever and wherever we may be. That moment of is unlike any other. It offers the promise of new beginnings, of the clean slate of new year, and it incorporates the breathless expectancy of Christmas night itself, when a familiar figure enters our lives and changes them briefly. It is a moment such as this that lies at the heart of the Midwinter Solstice, and it is in celebration of this that this book is written.

Alternative Patterns

Every one of us in the West is familiar with the Christian story of Christmas. For many, irrespective of their actual religious persuasion, the celebration is still concerned with cribs and carol singers, churches, and Christmas bells. But as well as marking the wondrous birth of the Christ Child, December 25th is also the date on which the birthday of the Roman God Mithras is celebrated.

In the same way, several of the more familiar customs originate in surprisingly different places and times. For example, the Yule Log, originating in pagan Scandinavia, once celebrated the turning of the magical year in a very different fashion from its use today. The Christmas Tree began life as the Solstice Evergreen, being adapted in medieval and Victorian times to the tinsel-decked image of today. Even the ancient carol, "The Holly and the Ivy," derives from a pre-Christian age when the Lord and Lady of the Greenwood were honored by the hanging of green garlands from ridge poles of houses.

The Alternative Santa

Once we begin to consider the alternative history of Christmas, all kinds of readily accepted images come into question. Take the spirit of Christmas himself – Santa Claus, Father Christmas, Saint Nicholas, Old St. Nick, Syre Christemas, Sinter Class – his names are legion and his true origins almost as old as history. Have you ever wondered why he climbs down the chimney, why he is dressed in red, and why he gives gifts at all? You may be surprised by the answers. The last point is supposed to be because of the birthday of the Christ Child. In fact, it has more to do with the life of a medieval bishop, one Nicholas by name. This kindly churchman, saddened by the poverty of his parish, took to delivering gifts to poor children, at night and in secret. He would slip into houses and leave gifts in the shoes of his parishioners – not only at Christmas time but at other times in the year also. Gradually the legend grew and developed, as legends will, and the generous and pious Bishop Nicholas became the first Saint Nicholas.

This is not Santa's sole point of origin, nor his earliest, as we shall see. For Santa really derives from an even earlier set of figures – the shamans who were the first priests and magicians of the human race. The very notion of a gift giver descending from a high place bearing gifts can be traced back to the shaman's habit of climbing up the world tree to reach the otherworld, and then climbing back down with the gifts of prophecy and wisdom to give to the rest of us.

LEFT: The nativity scene is a familiar focus of Christmas celebrations.

The Green Guest

Another, at first more sinister, bringer of Christmas fare, is the Green Knight. In Arthurian tradition he came to King Arthur's hall as the Christmas festivities were getting under way, offering a strange game – that someone should strike him with his great axe, on the understanding that he will give back such a blow in a year's time. Only Gawain is brave enough to accept the challenge, and he undergoes many trials before the tale ends. For once his head has been severed, the Green Knight is able to pick it up, and await the coming of his challenger – a trick that Gawain is not able to do. The story is a wonderful one, and very ancient. The Green Knight is the incarnate spirit of Winter, able to present his frightening challenge as the prelude to a battle for the hand of the Spring Maiden.

> *It is only in the past three hundred years or so that a "rational" civilisation has turned its back on both the Christian and Pagan traditions and remembered the Solstice by custom and habit rather than by an instinctual involvement with the turning seasons.*
>
> SHIRLEY TOULSON: A WINTER SOLSTICE

This was written in 1980, and there has been no significant return toward a less secular celebration of Christmas. Indeed, people everywhere seem less and less concerned with the celebration of anything other than the holiday itself and its ever more commercially strident accompaniment.

It is partly to redress this trend that the present book has been written. Not that I believe that thousands will return to the true celebration of Midwinter: rather that a shift in emphasis away from the celebration, as it is currently perceived, and back toward a tradition which existed for centuries before Christianity may put us in touch more firmly with the roots of the Solstice itself and with the high mystery of the Christmas Revels. After all, the Solstice is, as much today as ever, about the rebirth of Wonder – something which has never really gone away, but has become much occluded in recent times.

The Alternative Christmas

In this book we shall consider the origins of the customs surrounding the Solstice, including such matters as the significance of the timing of Christmas, the origin of the strange and barbarous custom of the Wren Boys of St. Stephen's (Boxing) Day, and the presence of Old Father Christmas in the Mummers' plays of the Middle Ages (many still performed to this day). We shall look at the tradition of the Feast of Fools, at the Boy Bishop Nicholas, and at much more that was once current but is now largely forgotten.

"Celebration" sections can be found at the end of each chapter. These contain suggestions for ways to celebrate the period extending from a little before the actual date of the Solstice (December 20/21st) throughout the Christmas season and on to Twelfth Night (January 6th). Included here are ceremonies, ways to prepare for the season, recipes for everything from Eggnog to a Solstice Animal Cake, and many other suggestions to make the Solstice tide a memorable occasion.

The Winter Solstice has been celebrated in different places and at different times throughout history; today we can still acknowledge it with an ever deepening awareness of its antiquity and sacredness.

JOHN MATTHEWS.
OXFORD, THE FESTIVAL OF YULE, 1997

ABOVE: The Arthurian story of the Green Knight carries many of the ideas of the Winter Solstice: death and loss followed by restoration and renewal.

Chapter 1

THE SOLSTICE DREAM

Here at the gateway of the year,
may we strive to make good cheer.
In our revels shall joy abound
and sorrow be cast underground.

CAITLÍN MATTHEWS: SUN STILL; SUN RETURN

I*t is just before sunrise on a cold December day some three thousand years before the coming of Christ. For those crouched at the heart of the mound it must seem as though light has been banished forever. Then, suddenly, a tiny sliver of sunlight strikes the stone slab at the back of the chamber. Slowly it widens, climbs upward, illuminating a number of mysterious carvings – circles and spirals, zigzag patterns. For the people crouched in the center of the great mound of Brug na Boine (also known as New Grange) every symbol has meaning. But by far the greatest significance is the return of the sun itself. The light that enters the dark womb of the earth brings with it the promise of warmth and life to come.*

LEFT: The Great Passage at New Grange, along which the Winter Solstice sunrise brings its promised rebirth.

Darkness and silence...

It has been celebrated and honored in this way for generations and will continue to be so for many more; for the celebration of Midwinter, of the demise of the old year and the birth of the new, has always held a deep fascination for humanity. Long before the coming of Christianity, with which this time of year has become inextricably linked, people all over the world celebrated the rising of the Midwinter sun and the birth of the gods who held out to them the promise of a New Year with new hopes. They celebrated in many ways, most often with fire – a symbol of hope – and with boughs of greenery that symbolized the eternal circle of creation. Images of deities were restored also, repainted, decorated with special hangings or flowers, a clear indication of the importance of the season at all levels and in all walks of life. As E.C. Krupp so elegantly puts it in his study of the patterns of ritual and celebration around the year:

[T]he Winter Solstice was the turning point of time and the birthday of the sun, the moment of new beginnings. All of nature was poised then to step over the border of the year. When it became the birthday of Christ, Christmas night became the hinge of the year. It commemorated the timeless moment when heaven…came in contact with earth, and each year the anniversary... re-created once again the circumstances of that first Christmas.

KRUPP: BEYOND
THE BLUE HORIZON

ABOVE: *The traditional figure of Santa Claus may have originated as a bear-clad shaman.*

Nativity

The earliest date to which any sign of a celebration of the nativity of Christ can be traced is A.D. 336, in Rome. Before this it is possible that the birth of the Holy Child was celebrated on January 6th – the present Twelfth Night – in line with the Eastern Orthodox Church. This is mentioned in a document known as the Philocalian Calendar, which dates from A.D. 354, but contains information contained in an earlier, now lost, document dating from A.D. 336.

The choice of the 25th for the birthday of Christ is complex and will be more fully discussed in Chapter 2, but as the learned eighteenth-century Jesuit, Antonio Lupi, remarked, "There is not a single month in the year to which the nativity has not been assigned by some writer or another." (quoted in Miles)

From this point the celebration of the Nativity spread throughout the Roman world, arriving in Britain with the Celtic saints in the early fifth century. In A.D. 567 the Council of Tours declared the twelve days from Christmas to Epiphany (January 6th) a festal tide, thus drawing both the dates of the birth and baptism of Christ into a single celebration.

The Epiphany, celebrated as early as the second century by an obscure Christian sect known as the Basilidans (after their founder Basilides), was a celebration of both the baptism and the birth of Christ. It is more than likely, as we shall see in Chapter 2, that this festival originated in the celebration of more than one "Child of Wonder," among them Mithras (Rome), Aion (Greece), and Attis (Syria). By the time Christianity had established itself throughout the Roman Empire, however, the emphasis had shifted, with a greater importance placed on the baptism as the true birth of Christ – as announced by the angel: "On this day I have begotten Thee." Hence the festival of the baptism may have come first, with the celebration of the Stable at Bethlehem being added later, partly as a result of the passage in St. Luke's Gospel that implied that Jesus was baptized on his thirtieth birthday. However, as the doctrine of the Incarnation became increasingly emphasized, it may have been felt that the celebration of the birth and the baptism on the same day (January 6th) smacked of heresy. Probably as a result of this, the separate dates for the celebration of the birth on December 25th, and the baptism on the January 6th, came into being, though in the Eastern Orthodox Church they continued to be celebrated on the same day until as late as the fourth and early fifth centuries.

In the Ozark Mountains the Christmas holiday retained the traditional date of January 6th rather than December 25th until as recently as the 1900s. The mountain people of the region not only spurned the later date but began their celebrations on the evening of the 5th, just as their ancestors would have done. Thus, while in Europe the older traditions began to die out or be forgotten, the

ABOVE: The exact date of the birth of the Child of Wonder has been the subject of fierce controversy over the centuries.

folk traditions of the United States still retained numerous aspects that had their origins in a far earlier time.

Long before the appearance of an obscure wonder-worker in Palestine, the celebration of the Midwinter sun held a central place in civilizations throughout the ancient world. It is to these that we must turn now in order to be able to understand something of the continuity of belief and celebration that has attended the rising and setting of the sun from the earliest days of humanity.

RIGHT:The Magi found their way to the birthplace of Jesus by observing the stars.

To Summon the Sun

Fire and light. These are the two poles around which the festival of Midwinter revolves. From the time of the first Neolithic farmers, through to the Celtic tribes, and later the Romans who invaded the land of Britain in A.D. 43 and remained until A.D. 436, the common practice was the celebration of the Midwinter sun (a god whose necessary power was sovereign). Thus ceremonies were almost always based around the need to preserve light and to ensure the return of the sun.

The movement of the earth around the sun creates the Solstices – Winter and Summer – when the two hemispheres of the globe stand at opposite extremes in relationship to the solar body. From around the beginning of October to the end of March, reaching a period of darkness and cold around December 22nd, the northern hemisphere experiences the night of Midwinter; at the same time the southern hemisphere faces the warmth of the sun. On or around June 21st the situation is reversed: it is cold in the south and warm in the north.

These basic astronomical facts have stood at the heart of the human observance of the seasons for as long as we have knowledge of our spiritual and religious practice. The Neolithic farmers and hunters, who left their marks on the land in the form of earth temples and standing stones, watched the skies constantly, and possessed an intimate and detailed knowledge of the passage of sun, moon, and stars. The reason for this is obvious; their lives depended on their knowledge. When the sun was at its highest point (Midsummer), their crops grew tall and their animals thrived. At the other extreme (Midwinter) they suffered the effects of cold, damp, and darkness, and all the ailments of the body and soul that derived from these.

The Returning Sun

It seemed to these ancient peoples that when the sun went below the horizon it might never return, and in order to prevent this they first practiced rites that would summon it back. They also sought to capture its light, and to this end fire itself became of central importance in the majority of these rites – if harbored and protected, fire would remain alive, as a symbol of the hidden sun.

Sometimes it was enough to celebrate the return of the sun, at others it was necessary to make sacrifices to the god (or goddess) who was the source of its light, to insure that he (or she) returned. It is the legacy of these now long-forgotten ceremonies that lies at the heart of our own acknowledgment of the Solstices. Virtually every festival that was celebrated, or which still takes place today, owes something to these ancient celebrations of the year's turning.

The word *solstice* itself comes from the Latin *sol stetit*, literally "sun stands still," which recognizes that for approximately six days in June and again in December, the sun appears to rise and set at more or less the same point on the horizon, appearing to stand still in the sky. For the people of the old world, the solstices effectively divide the year in two, a dark half and a light half; six months of waxing sun and six months of waning. The points where intersection occur, the borderlands between Summer and Winter, were of tremendous importance to these people, governing the round of their lives and serving as anchor points in the natural as well as agricultural and pastoral year. They have always been recognized as mysterious, shadowy, uncertain times, when the conviction that the sun would return becomes doubtful, and when the gates between the worlds stand ajar.

At these times the coming and going of other-worldly beings, communications between the dead and the living, happen all the more easily, and there is a need to propitiate them, and to watch closely to see that things return to "normal" once the Solstice tide has passed.

This was above all a time of celebration, of ritual acts designed to align the individual with the cosmos. Dances were devised to enact the movement of the seasons, the fertility of land and people. The masked dancers and shamans of the Bronze Age and the Neolithic people are still reflected in the masked "guisers," who tour the outlying villages of Britain and Ireland to this day; while the shamans, who descended a ladder or tent pole into the smoky fires of the ancestral world, recall a more familiar red-suited figure who descends our chimneys every year at Midwinter. (*See Chapter 4.*)

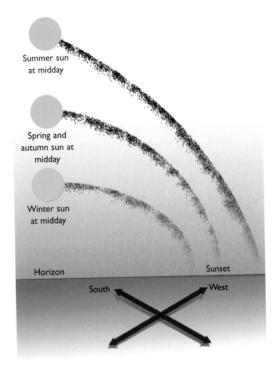

Summer sun at midday

Spring and autumn sun at midday

Winter sun at midday

Horizon

Sunset

South

West

Chambers of the Sun

Throughout northern Europe a huge number of prehistoric and Neolithic sacred sites are oriented to capture the rays of the sun and moon at certain specific points in the year – generally these coincide with either the solstices or the equinoxes, which mark the subdivision of the year into quarters. The most famous of these sites is New Grange in Ireland, as its original name, *An Liamh Greine*, the "Cave of the Sun," testifies. For about a week before and after the Winter Solstice, the light from the rising sun passes through a narrow slot above the doorway and sweeps down the 80-foot-long passageway into the heart of the central chamber. Striking the back wall, it illuminates a series of intricately carved spirals and solar discs. For approximately seventeen minutes the light illuminates the chamber, then slowly retreats until all is dark again...

A similar arrangement is found at sites such as Gavranis in Brittany (aligned with both sun and moon), Loch Crew in Ireland (sun and moon), Long Kennet in Wiltshire, England (sun), and at a number of stone circles that mark out the landscape of Britain from the Hebrides to Land's End.

Nor is this phenomenon found only in Europe. Throughout the ancient pre-classical world of the Mediterranean, as well as in the continents of Australia and North and South Americas, similar structures designed around the movement of the sun and moon have survived. One of the most striking can be found at Chaco Canyon in New Mexico, where the Solstice sunrise creates the shape of two daggers flanking a spiral carved into the cliff face. Another impressive monument is the pyramid at the Mayan site of Kukulkan in Chichen Itza, Mexico. Here the light of the rising sun crawls down the steps of the pyramid, forming the shape of a serpent (a sacred animal to the Mayans) that eventually seems to join onto the head of the serpent that is carved into the pyramid at the foot of the steps.

Sun-Rites of the Zuñi and Hopi

Further evidence for the celebration of the Solstice in ancient America is to be found among the Zuñi and Hopi peoples, who are themselves the descendants of the more shadowy Anasazi. The Zuñi celebrated Shalako, a ceremony extending through the night, on Midwinter's Day. The *Pekwin*, or "Sun Priest," after fasting and prayer, and having observed the rising and setting of the sun for several days before, announced the exact moment of *itiwanna*, the rebirth of the sun, with a low, mournful call. This was a signal for general rejoicing, and the appearance of twelve kachina clowns in elaborate masks, accompanied by 12-foot-high bird headed effigies that were seen as the messengers of the gods. Extraordinarily, many of the Zuñi houses contained plates fixed to their walls that were lit by the rays of the sun passing through a small window. This only happened on this one day out of the 365.

The Hopi have similar ceremonies. For them the rising of the sun was announced by the Sun Chiefs, who sat on the rooftops of the houses throughout the winter evenings, observing the setting and rising of the sun, finally

LEFT: A Hopi snake priest in dance regalia, bearing a traditional feather fan.

proclaiming the precise moment at which the all-night ceremony was to commence. Another important task allotted to the sun-watcher was to calculate the times of planting through the seasons and to assure the correct observance of the year-long cycle of ceremonies. As the noted anthropologist Edmund N. Nequatewa wrote in 1931:

ABOVE: The sun icon appears in stories and art of all ages and all across the world as testimony to its importance and life-giving powers.

> *The cycle of Hopi ceremonies begins in the Winter... The first is in November. When the sun sets over a particular hump of the north side of the San Francisco Peaks, the ceremony, Wu-Wu-che-ma, takes place... After this ceremony is over they again watch the sun on the Western horizon. They just know on a certain day that it will take the sun eight days to reach its southernmost point, and so they announce the ceremony eight days ahead. Thus Sol-ya-lang-eu, the Prayer-offering ceremony, is the Winter Solstice Ceremony, and takes place in December. This is one of the most sacred ceremonies of the Hopi. It is a day of good will, when every man wishes for prosperity and health, for his family and friends...*

Though we can only speculate as to the exact nature of the ceremonies that took place in the more ancient sacred sites of the Americas, the common factor in all of them is the rebirth or capture of the sun. This makes it clear that the setting and rising of the Midwinter or Midsummer sun were observed as sacred events within these cultures.

The Celtic Wheel

For the Celtic peoples of northern Europe the year began with the Festival of Samhain, on or around October 31st. The Winter period extended until Imbolc at the beginning of February. Between these two poles, the celebration of the Midwinter season was seen as a time when the dead came close to warm themselves at the hearthfires of the tribe, and when the health of the people, and its animal stock, had to be maintained at all costs.

This was a period when sacrifices and offerings were made to the *Cailleach*, the "Old Woman," who ruled over the Winter season. The rituals of Samhain were concerned primarily with the dead, with divination, and with storytelling. Offerings were put out for the ancestors of the tribe, divinations were made to explore the status of the coming year, and the dead ancestors were remembered in story and song.

The depths of Winter were called *an dudlach* or "the gloom," and the seasonal revels were presided over by a "king" with a blackened face, whose emblem of office was a sword, scythe, or sickle, representing the sudden curtailment of life that could happen at this time. It is probably from this threatening figure that stories such as the medieval "Gawain and the Green Knight" derive. The more recent character of the "Turkish Knight" in the European Mummer plays has many of the same attributes. (*See Chapters 5 and 7.*)

ABOVE: This detail from the Gundstrup cauldron found in Jutland shows various mythical beasts surrounding the central figure of a Celtic god.

Mischief Night and Halloween

Many features of Celtic traditions have been carried over into modern festivals and traditions, surviving in the festival of Halloween, also known as "Mischief Night" or "Punky Night." The modern pursuits of "trick or treating" has resonances of a time when such games would have been played out at the doorways, not of houses, but between the worlds.

The Christian feast of All Souls on November 2nd has drawn upon many levels of these ancient customs, particularly the Festival of Samhain. Many Roman Catholics in Europe and the Americas visit cemeteries on this day to light candles on the graves of their dead. In Britain, this occurs a few days later on Armistice Day, when the fallen of two world wars are honored. The bonfires of Samhain are now more likely to be lit, in Britain at least, on November 5th, when Guy Fawkes is remembered for his abortive attempt to blow up the Houses of Parliament in 1605. This figure has, indeed, taken over the sacrificial aspect of this feast.

Imbolc marks the loosening of Winter's grip. At this time, new lambs are born and ewes are in milk, hence the name of the festival, which may be translated as "Ewes Milk." In an age that depends on the production of foodstuffs by modern farming methods, it is hard to imagine what Winter would have been like without fresh milk. Yet neither ewes nor cows will lactate unless they have given birth. The protein from new milk, butter, cheese, and whey, not to mention the pies made from the docked tails of lambs, would very often make the difference between life and death for both the very old and the very young during the hard frosts of February. Little celebration was observed at this time of year, but the women would have met together to celebrate the return of the maiden aspect of the goddess at the time when the Cailleach's Winter was beginning to retreat. Many folk songs and customs have survived from this time relating to the reenactment of the age-old battle between Winter and Summer. (*See Chapter 5.*)

Celtic Calendars

The general nature of the Celtic seasonal observance is reflected in the names given to the months in the ancient Coligny Calendar, a sophisticated system of astronomical observation discovered on bronze tablets in 1897 near Bourge in France. Much work is still being carried out in the interpretation of these tablets, which date from at least as early as the first century A.D., but it is clear that they relate to important lunar–solar notation.

The calendar is both seasonally and agriculturally oriented, with each month relating to the events that take place at that time, both in the natural life of the year, as well as that of the tribe. The titles given to the months of November/December and December/January (they do not exactly equate to our own modern division of the months) are *Dumannios*, "The Darkest Depths," and *Riuros*, "Cold Time." The months of January/February were given the name of *Anagantios* or "Stay-Home Time."

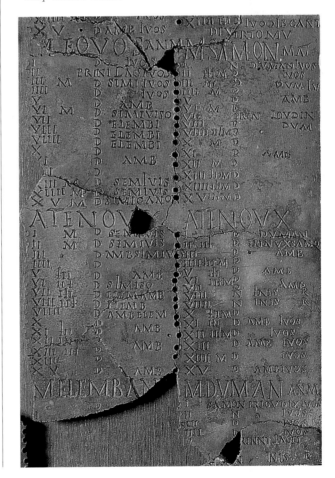

RIGHT: One of the bronze tablets of the Coligny calendar, an important source of information on Celtic seasonal observance.

The Living Sun

In ancient Egypt the sun was valued as a symbol of life. Re, or Ra, the Sun, was the chief of the gods, and the heretical Pharaoh Amenhotep IV made him, under the name Aton, the central figure of a reformed religion. Amenhotep then took the name Akhenaton.

A hymn to Aton, probably composed by a royal poet, expresses this ancient attitude to the sun as a purveyor of light and life:

ABOVE: The return of the sun is celebrated in many ancient artefacts, like this Bronze Age wheeled model of a horse drawing a golden sun.

> *Thou dost appear beautiful on the horizon of heaven,*
>
> *O living Aton, thou who wast the first to live.*
>
> *When thou hast risen on the eastern horizon,*
>
> *Thou hast filled every land with thy beauty...*
>
> *When thou dost set on the Western horizon,*
>
> *The earth is in darkness, resembling death...*
>
> *At daybreak, when thou dost arise on the horizon,*
>
> *Dost shine as Aton by day,*
>
> *Thou dost dispel the darkness And shed thy rays.*

TRANS. E.A. WALLACE BUDGE

The importance of the Solstices to the Egyptian culture is expressed in the architecture of the great temples at Karnac, Thebes, and Abydos, each of which focuses the rays of the Midwinter/Midsummer sun into the heart of the temple enclosure. This clearly echoes the construction of the earth temples and stone circles of Europe.

The Old New Year

In ancient Egypt, at the start of the New Year, a festival celebrating the return of the sun was held along the Nile delta. As the rising waters brought agriculture to a halt, there was time to celebrate the Festival of Opet, held at Thebes and Karnac for a period of twenty-four days. The ceremonies began with offerings to the god Amon, his consort Mut, and their son Knonsu. Their boat-shaped shrines were carried out of the temple. Followed by the Pharaoh himself, they proceeded to the tributary that led into the Nile. There, the shrines were placed aboard ceremonial barges, elaborately decorated and manned by priests. They were towed by soldiers down to the main stream of the river, where a small flotilla of craft escorted them downstream to Luxor, where they would remain for the next twenty-four days. People lined the banks along the barge's route, joining in the singing, dancing, and music.

At Luxor the festival really got under way, with banquets in honor of the gods, and the reenactment of episodes from the life of the deities. The procession made its way back upstream, and the shrines were once again restored to the temple precincts. The festival celebrated the return of the sun and the inundation of the Nile, and restored the rule of the Pharaoh for another year.

ABOVE: An ancient limestone carving showing the Pharaoh Amenhotep offering a gift of lotus flowers to the sun god Aton, a central figure of worship in ancient Egypt.

ABOVE: *This decorated plate from an Ancient Greek tomb shows the signs of the zodiac with a procession of animals.*

The Sun in Jerusalem

Even in the earliest period of the developing Judaic religion, the entry of the rising sun at the equinoxes played a significant part in the celebrations in Solomon's great temple at Jerusalem. While there is no specific evidence of any formal observance of either solstices or equinoxes later on, Richard Heinberg, in his excellent book on the solstices, *Celebrate the Solstice: Honoring the Earth's Seasonal Rhythms through Festival and Ceremony*, quotes from a fifteen hundred-year-old Jewish commentary on the Babylonian Talmud. It tells how Adam, shortly after his expulsion from Paradise, notices the shortening of the days and prays and fasts for eight days in the hope of calling back the lost light. As this took place at Midwinter, the days soon grew longer again, and thereafter Adam repeated the ritual every year.

Saturn's Games

The ancient festival from which we derive many of the traditional celebrations associated with Midwinter is the Roman Saturnalia. The Roman presence in Britain and other parts of Europe from the second century B.C. to the fourth century A.D. probably accounts for this. During this time the Romans suppressed many of the older practices of the Celts.

Saturnalia itself developed from the older rituals of Midwinter into a riotous assemblage of fun, laughter, and gift giving. It is, indeed, from this festival that we receive the idea of giving gifts at Christmas and not from the gifts of the Magi as commonly supposed. As its name suggests, the celebration was in honor of Saturn, the Roman god of agriculture and time, who is thought to have received his name from the Latin *satus*, "to sow." His feast was celebrated from December 17th to the

ABOVE: Saturnalia celebrated the overthrow of the old father-god Saturn, by the new, Jupiter, continuing the theme of renewal and continuation as the New Year dawned.

24th, during which time the normal patterns of social behavior were abandoned. Masters served their slaves (who dined with their usual masters wearing the badge of freedom known as the *pillius*), the law courts and schools were closed, and the whole community gave itself up to feasting, gambling, and drinking. Indeed, so noisy were the celebrations, that the author Pliny built himself a soundproof room so that he could work during the holiday.

The festival began with the *sacrificium publicum* in which a young pig was sacrificed in the temple of Saturn in the Forum. Senators put aside their togas and assumed less formal attire, and gifts were exchanged, among them wax tapers called *cerei*, symbolic of the eternal light, and terracotta dolls known as *signillaria*, which may well refer back to a time when human sacrifices were offered to the gods of Midwinter. Certainly Saturnus was known to have had a consort, Lua Mater, who governed baneful influences (*lares*) and to whom soldiers' weapons were offered.

Midwinter in the Fields

Apart from Saturn, three other deities were remembered and celebrated around the Midwinter period in Rome. The feast of Consus was celebrated on December 15th, and that of his consort Ops on December 17th. Consus was the god of the corn-bin or storeroom. His subterranean altar, which symbolically stood at the entrance to the Otherworld, was uncovered only on his feast days, which fell not only in December but also during harvest time in August. Ops was a mother goddess, and is often portrayed sitting with loaves in her lap. In later times she became associated with Saturn as well as with Consus, and her presence was acknowledged at the Saturnalia festival.

At the same time that the festival of Saturnalia was in progress, devotees of the woodland goddess, Strenia, gave each other twigs cut ritually from a sacred grove. These were believed to bring good luck for the whole year and they were carried in procession along the Via Sacra in Rome at the end of the festival.

The festival of Saturnalia continued to be celebrated every year right up until the end of the fourth century, when it was moved to the New Year and became amalgamated with the Kalends of January. Kalends was itself a significant part of the Roman Midwinter celebrations, and has lent its name to Midwinter festivals all over the Western world. For example, in Provence in France the festival is known as *Calendas*, in Poland it is called *Kolenda*, and in Russia, *Kolyada*. In the Czech Republic it is called *Koteda*, in Lithuania, *Kalledos*, and in Wales and Scotland, *Calenig* and *Calluinn* respectively – all these names derived from the Latin *Kalendae*, and all referring to the festival of Midwinter.

The New Year Dawns

Initially the Kalends followed Saturnalia, beginning a few days of rest to allow aching heads and stomachs to recover! At this time new consuls were inducted into office, and for at least three days a high festival took place. Houses were decorated with lights and greenery and gifts were exchanged. It was also the custom to give special presents to the emperor. These, called *Votae*, were left in the porch of the imperial palace, and it is recorded that the Emperor Caligula not only demanded these gifts from everyone, but also stood in the porch to collect them personally! It may have been the memory of this that prompted the fourth-century writer Libanius to

24

describe the festival in terms that might as easily be applied to the modern celebration of Christmas as to the celebrations in ancient Rome:

The impulse to spend seizes everyone...

People are not only generous themselves, but also towards their fellow men. A stream of presents pours itself out on all sides...

The Kalends festival banishes all that is connected with toil, and allows men to give themselves up to undisturbed enjoyment.

From the minds of young people it removes two kinds of dread: the dread of the schoolmaster and the dread of the pedagogue.

The slave also it allows, as far as possible, to breathe the air of freedom...

Another great quality of the festival is that it teaches men not to hold too fast to their money, but to part with it and let it pass into other hands.

TRANS. C. MILES

*ABOVE: In the Middle Ages the Kalends of January
were celebrated with colorful mumming performances.*

The Masked Dancers

Elsewhere the same author writes of the Kalends in detail. Few people go to bed he says, preferring to go about the streets singing and dancing. In the morning they decorate the houses and then fall into bed to sleep off the indulgence of the previous night. On January 1st money was distributed to the poor, on the 2nd everyone stayed at home and played dice, masters and slaves together. It is also said that during the festival people would dress up in animal skins, and that men would put on women's clothes, while all would wear masks. This may date back to very early times indeed, when the Neolithic shamans put on masks and danced the hunt and the kill, or it may be a residue of the Kalends' custom of "guising," which still continues to the present time. It was, of course, much condemned in later times, especially by Christian priests, as the following diatribe, probably written by Caesarius of Arles in the sixth century A.D. reveals:

*On those days the heathen... put on
counterfeit forms and monstrous faces...
Some are clothed in the hides of cattle;
others put on the heads of beasts, rejoicing
and exulting that they have so transformed
themselves into the shapes of animals that
they no longer appear to be
men...furthermore, it is those who have
been born men are clothed in women's
dresses... and effeminate their manly
strength by taking on the forms of girls,
blushing not to clothe their warlike arms in
women's garments; they have bearded faces,
yet they wish to appear women... Also there
are some who on the Kalends of January
practise auguries...*

Such descriptions could as well be applied to practices which, as we shall see later on, are still very much alive to this day, and with much the same purpose – to distract the mind from the serious fear that the New Year might not actually dawn, to placate the gods, and to call back the sun.

*ABOVE: The masked sun dance of the
Hopi Indians of New Mexico is just one of the
many sun rites performed worldwide.*

ABOVE: *The sole charge of the King of Fools was to behave as foolishly as possible.*

The Feast of Fools

Feast of Fools –
Feast of Buffoons –
Feast of the ass –

Feast of Fools –
Feast of the sub-deacons –
Feast of the Fool's Bishop –
Feast of the lower clergy.

LA FÊTE DE L'ÂNE

The Kalends were not the only celebrations that earned the condemnation of the Church. In the eastern provinces of the Empire, during Saturnalia, it was customary to choose and crown a mock king, who ruled over chaos rather than the order that was such a central aspect of Roman rule. Lots were cast and the chosen person became the *Saturnalicus Princeps*, who assumed the role of Saturn throughout the festival. His task was to behave as foolishly as possible, insulting guests, chasing women and girls, and wearing outlandish clothing. Even the hiding of coins in puddings dates from this period, as this was one of the methods used to select the kingly fool.

The origins of this part of the Roman festival are obscure, though it may have been adopted by legionaries stationed along the Danube from an older, local tradition. If this is the case, it may be that the King Fool originated from a time when, in much of the ancient world, kings reigned for a year and were then ritually slaughtered to ensure good fortune for the coming year. In Scotland during this time barley bannock cakes were baked and one deliberately burned. These were passed around in a bag, and the person who chose the black bannock was designated as the Fool. At one time this may have decided his fate as the Year King marked for sacrifice, his death ensuring the return of light and fertility to the world.

Wild Disports and Merry

In later times this aspect of the festival gave rise to an extraordinary medieval phenomenon known as the Feast of Fools, which owed its nature as much to the Saturnalia as to the need for ordinary people everywhere to escape from the iron control imposed on them by the Church. Essentially this was a riotous assemblage of clergy in lower orders, canons, and sub-deacons (the festival is also sometimes called The Feast of Sub-Deacons). It took many forms, ranging from mock masses to the crowning of the Boy Bishop (see Chapter 2). But it is the foolishness of the celebration, the enjoyment of what various medieval churchmen described as "wild disports," "silly pranks and gesticulations," and "disorderly laughter and illicit mirth." In all, a general aura of chaos gave this feast its peculiar quality, and made it seem such a threat to the order and sobriety of the medieval Christian foundation.

A description found in a letter addressed to the Bishops and Chapters of France from the Paris Faculty of Theology in 1445 gives a telling account of the Feast:

*Priests and clerics may be seen
wearing masks and monstrous visages
at the hours of the office.*

*They dance in the choir dressed as
women, panders, or minstrels.*

They sing wanton songs.

*They eat black puddings at the horn of the
altar while the celebrant is saying Mass.*

They play at dice there.

*They cense with stinking smoke from
the soles of old shoes.*

*They run and leap through the church,
without a blush at their own shame.*

*Finally they drive about the town and
its theaters in shabby traps and carts,
and rouse the laughter of their fellows
and bystanders in infamous performances,
with indecent gesture and verses scurrilous
and unchaste.*

E.K. CHAMBERS: THE MEDIEVAL STAGE

The letter goes on to speak of false bishops, archbishops, and even popes, all wearing a mixture of fool's attire with vestments, and carrying crosiers and pastoral staffs.

Perhaps the most extraordinary ceremonies were those that aped the normal proceedings of the Church, as, for example, at Beauvas in France when a girl on an ass rode into the cathedral on January 14th, carrying a child in her arms. In the mass that followed, the congregation responded by braying at the Inroit, Kyrie, Gloria, and Credo. At the conclusion of the service the priest, instead of saying *"Ite Missa Est"* (Mass is ended) had to bray three times, to which the people responded by braying back.

ABOVE: *The riotous celebration of the Feast of Fools*
pays homage to the greatest reveler of them all, Bacchus.

The Ass's Turn

This extraordinary event, which owes so much to the Saturnalia, was carried even further in such cities as Bourges and Sens. There, on New Year's Day, the exact time of the Kalends, a *Festum Asinorum* or Feast of the Ass took place in which very different words were substituted for the usual text of the Mass. Here the priest invited the congregation to approach the altar of Bacchus and to be blessed in wine:

Introibo ad altare Bachi –
Ad eum qui letificat cor hominis
(Let us go up to the altar of Bacchus:
To him who gives joy to man's heart.)

Potemus. Aufer a nobis, quesumus, Bache,
cuncta vestimen'ta nostram, ut ad taberna
poculorum nudis corporibus mereamur
introire, Per omnia pocula poculorum.
Stramen.
(Let us drink: take from us, we beseech thee,
Bacchus, all our clothes, that we may be
worthy, with naked bodies, to enter into the
tavern. Unto us all, drink without end.)

ABOVE: Mockery and buffoonery
have always been an essential
feature of Mummer plays.

Later in the same text we find the following proclamation:

Let the trumpet of the new moon sound
And proclaim the celebration of games
In our land to mark
Our solemn feast day.
We have a Bishop!

The Fool's Bishop!
The Lord of the Feast!
Here is the Lord of the Feast!
The Staff of the New Year!
We have the Staff of the New Year!
Overthrown, overthrown!

The Fool's Abbot!

And ends with the wonderful statement:

Omnia tempus habent!
(There is time for everything!)

Misrule's Day

It is scarcely surprising that these wild extremes were condemned by the Church. Yet despite constant reproof and orders to stop, the Feast of the Fools continued in its various forms well into the seventeenth century. A similar celebration occurred in England throughout the Middle Ages, in the form of the Lord of Misrule, who was appointed by the royal and noble households to oversee the Christmas Revels. After this the practice fell into disuse, though it is to this particular form of celebration that we owe many of the aspects of the Mummer plays, which are still performed to this day. In these we can see so many echoes of an older time, just as through the medieval mockery and buffoonery, we can look back to an earlier period still, when the dark time of the year was brightened by ritual, comic obscenity, and sacrifice in equal measure.

LEFT: *The traditional Morris dance, still widely practiced in Britain, developed from the Mummer plays that were performed during the Solstice tide.*

Dancers in the Green

...a merry crew,
Bedeck'd in masks and ribbons gay,
The "Morris Dance," their sports renew,
And act their Winter evening play.

The clown turned king, for penny-praise,
Storms with actor's strut and swell;
And Harlequin, a laugh to raise,
Wears his hunchback and tinkling bell.

JOHN CLARE:
THE SHEPHERD'S CALENDAR

The drama of Midwinter is played out in many different ways, and these are often remembered in folk customs and beliefs the world over. The so-called "Mummer plays" are performed throughout Britain during the Solstice tide, enacting the ritual slaying and rebirth of the year as has been the case for as long as anyone can remember. The phenomenon of these plays, despite being much written about and commented upon, remains something of a mystery.

Involving a team of varying numbers of men, who carry sticks or kerchiefs and dance a broad variety of complex steps to the accompaniment of fiddle or accordion, the Morris is preserved in various forms to the present time, though its origins are still vague. Even the derivation of the name has never been agreed upon. "Morisco" says one early authority, "a Moor; also a dance, so called, wherein there are usually five men, and a boy dressed in a girl's habit, whom they call the Maid Marion, or perhaps Moron, from the Italian Moraine, a head-piece, because her head was wont to be gaily trimmed up (sic). Common people call it a Morris-dance."

This derivation of Morris, frequently repeated since the eighteenth century, has been brought into question recently. Douglas Kennedy, the late director of the English Folk-Song and Dance Society, in his book *England's Dances*, suggests that the confusion arose from the tradition of the Morris teams blacking up their faces, which they did because of the prohibition against wearing masks, but which gave rise to an association with the Moors and possibly even the renaming of an older dance. "A still simpler explanation," Kennedy continues, "is that the word 'Moorish' was used in the sense of 'Pagan,' and that the Morris was a pagan dance." This explanation seems eminently sensible in the light of the probable antiquity of these traditions.

In the United States, throughout much of the 1800s and the beginning of the nineteenth century, masking, guising, and Mummer plays continued to be performed. In Savannah, there were the Fantastics and the Callithumpians; while in the Carolinas, the Negro slaves dressed themselves in false beards, masks, and horns and danced through the streets. They referred to the custom as "John Canoing" or "John Kunering" – an obscure term that may have referred to the mask itself – known as a "Kuner-Face." It has also been suggested that this name goes back to a character known as John Connu, who lived on the African Guinea Coast, but it is hard to be sure of this.

The important factor is that this ancient form of Solstice games survived at all, and flourished in the New World. In Baltimore these traditions became so riotous that episodes of looting took place and the police were called out to stop the celebration from becoming a riot – a veritable modern Saturnalia! Despite this, in Philadelphia to this day there is a huge procession of Mummers every New Year's Day. The procession is so large that it takes most of the day to pass by City Hall, and includes every imaginable kind of costumed performer.

ABOVE: Groups of players would travel from house to house during the festive season.

33

The Jolly Old 'Oss

The Hobby Horse or 'Oss undoubtedly originated in pagan times, possibly during the very earliest era of human occupation, the first stirrings of shamanistic practice. In present times you can see the 'Oss at most Morris or Mummers' performances. It is usually a man dressed in a strange costume that includes a horse-skull mask, a wide hooped skirt, and sometimes a hobby-horse stick with mask or skull attached. The sole purpose of this strange and sometimes sinister character is to play tricks and chase people – especially young women – whom he covers with his wide skirt. He also makes gestures that are generally of a sexual nature, so that it is not difficult to recognize both a type of ancient Trickster and a potent fertility figure. We may also recall at this point the description of the Roman Saturnalia described by Caesarius in the fourth century and quoted earlier.

Francis Douce, an earlier investigator of the origins of the Morris, recalls that:

It has been supposed that the Morris-dance was first brought into England in the time of Edward the Third, when John of Gaunt returned from Spain... but it is much more probable that we had it from our Gallic neighbours, or even from the Flemmings. Few, if any, vestiges of it can be traced beyond the time of Henry the Seventh, about which time, and particularly that of Henry the Eighth, the churchwarden's accounts in several parishes affords materials that throw much light on the subject...

A DISSERTATION ON THE ANCIENT ENGLISH MORRIS DANCE, 1807.

The accounts referred to concern themselves with money allocated to various players for their costumes, which include those for Robin Hood, Maid Marion, and Friar Tuck – all consistent participants in the Morris.

RIGHT: *Animal disguise is part of many ritual Solstice dances and performances.*

34

ABOVE: Fire, music, costume, and masks are all aspects of ancient Solstice festivals that still form a part of our modern celebrations.

ABOVE: Elements of the familiar Morris dancers and Mummer plays can be found in shamanic traditions from across the world.

The Animal-Men

As to the suggestion that the Morris originated in Europe, this is somewhat supported by the description of a dance that is still current in Romania. Here the dancers are called *Calusari*, a name that is often translated as "Fairies" (though it means literally "Little Horses," a term not unconnected perhaps with the 'Oss). Their remarkable dance, which is clearly shamanistic in content, consists of a kind of contest between the "Fairies" themselves and the "Animal-Men." The former are beautifully dressed in ribbons and bells that glitter in the sun, while the latter are roughly clad in animal skins. They carry a short pole, possibly phallic in origin, garlanded with wild garlic. From the early morning the whole team goes through a kind of initiation rite, involving each and every man being beaten with staves. A ring is then formed by the Fairies in which a symbolic wedding ceremony takes place, occasionally interrupted by the Animal-Men who attempt to thrust their way "into the house." Finally women whose children are sick bring them out and the "Fairies" dance around and over them. The day ends with a general dance in which the whole village joins – those girls who manage to touch one of the dancers are assured of fertility and a happy marriage.

The dance in which the symbolic wedding is interrupted by the Animal-Men bears many similarities to the healing dance of the shaman in which spirits invade his charmed circle. These would then be driven out and the sick person – whether adult or child – is healed. As the following verse from Witt's *Recreations* of 1640 says:

> *With a noise and a din,*
> *Comes the Morris-dancer in,*
> *With fine linen shirt, but a buckram skin.*
>
> *Oh, he treads out such a peale*
> *From his pair of legs of veal,*
> *The quarters are idols to him.*

As we shall see further in Chapter 6, the tradition that is represented here is far older than the Middle Ages, dating back in fact to the most primitive level of ritual celebration. In our own time, this particular form of honoring the Solstice has undergone a revival, both in Europe and, more recently, in the United States. Morris dancers and Mummer plays can now be seen all over the United States and many parts of Britain, celebrated with all the vigor and enthusiasm of the older time in which they were born (*see Resources p. 242*).

RIGHT: The costumes of the Morris vary from place to place, with some dancers carrying staves and others handkerchiefs.

The Solstice in China

Solstice celebrations are by no means limited to the West. In China, under the old monarchy, December 22nd was the day on which the Emperor led the annual sacrifices to the gods in the Temple of Heaven in Peking. Since no foreigners were ever permitted to view these rites, little is known of them. Not even the ordinary citizens were allowed into the temples at this time, and curtains were hung over the doors and windows of the houses, so that no one would accidentally catch a glimpse of the sacred procession that passed by on the way to the temple.

When the monarchy fell in 1912, the old rites ceased to be observed, but in Hong Kong people still treat the day as a holiday. They make offerings to their ancestors, who are regarded as sacred, and generally serve a large family feast. Even in the New Territories of Communist China, rituals still take place at the ancestral temples, and gifts of pork are given to all who attend. Roadside shrines to specific ancestors are still maintained, and at this time of year one can often see offerings of flowers and fruit laid upon them.

LEFT: *In Asia, celebrations at the turning of the year also emphasize fire and light to welcome back the returning sun.*

The Solstice in Japan

In Japan the Solstice is also observed. This period, known as *Toji*, marks the time when the days grow longer and the nights shorter. It is particularly sacred to the farmers, who welcome the return of the sun to help quicken their crops after the long germinating period of the cold Winter. At this time people take holidays, light huge bonfires to encourage the return of the sun, and attend ceremonies to celebrate their ancestors. Pumpkins, more familiar in Europe and the United States at Halloween, are also eaten at this time and are believed to bring luck. But as in the West the celebrations revolve around the return of the sun and the ripening of crops with the onset of Spring. To this day huge bonfires burn on Mount Fuji around December 22nd, welcoming back the rising sun, which is, of course, the national emblem of Japan.

The Solstice in Taiwan

Here the Solstice gets an even bigger reception. As well as making offerings at ancestral shrines, something the Taiwanese share with both Japan and China, they make a dish called *Tang choeh i* or "Winter Balls." These consist of rice dough rolled into balls the size of small marshmallows, which are then boiled in sugar syrup. Half are dyed red and the rest left white, so that when they are served up in a bowl they look like red and white cherries. Twelve (one for each month in the year) are made larger than the rest, and are called *Ibu* or "Mother Balls." When the Midwinter feast has been prepared, three bowls are placed on a table in front of the house shrine to the ancestors in such a way that the place of guest of honor is offered to the ancestors. (This is astonishingly similar to customs all over Northern Europe.) Dishes consisting of three or five kinds of meat are prepared: usually pork, chicken, duck, or goat, but almost never beef, which is considered less lucky. Incense is then lit, and paper money burned while the oldest member of the family offers prayers to the gods asking for protection in the coming year. The red Winter Balls are then taken around and stuck over doorways and on the walls of animal shelters as tokens of the returning sun, and as an invocation of good luck.

In recent years these customs have tended to be scaled down, and as most people now count the turning of the year from the Chinese New Year (usually the first new moon in January), the ceremonies are less extravagant. The ancestors are still honored, however, and in most parts of Taiwan the day is still a public holiday.

LEFT: *Mount Fuji is central to many Solstice celebrations in Japan, and enormous fires are lit on its slopes.*

The Gates of the Solstice

The importance of the Solstices from classical times to well into the Middle Ages is seen in the belief that the human soul entered and exited life through the gates of the Solstices. The medieval scholiast Macrobius, writing in *A Commentary on the Dream of Scipio*, says the following:

> *The Milky Way girdles the zodiac, its great circle meeting it obliquely so that it crosses it at the two tropical signs, Capricorn and Cancer. Natural philosophers named these "the portals of the sun" because the Solstices lie athwart the sun's path on either side... Souls are believed to pass through these portals when going from the sky to the earth and returning from the earth to the sky. For this reason one is called the portal of men and the other the portal of gods: Cancer the portal of men, because through it descent is made to the infernal regions; Capricorn, the portal of gods, because through it souls return to their rightful abode of immortality, to be reckoned among the gods.*

Capricorn, then, the time of the Winter Solstice, admits the soul into life and then allows it to return to its former god-like state. This was also the time when the gods became incarnate as mortals, and they too are said to have journeyed through the solstitial gates.

Although we have come a long way in time since the cave dwellers and Neolithic farmers looked to the heavens for answers to their need for continuance, for the return of the sun, it is really no distance at all to a time and place where the gates of the Solstices opened upon all the immensity of the soul's great journey. This echoes the voyage of the gods in ancient Egypt, as well as the desire to capture the sun that we saw behind the great stone monuments of our ancestors. At the Solstice tide the gods were close, and the wheel of the year turned once more. Portents of new blessings were everywhere, and all around the word was whispered of the coming of new wonders. Somewhere on a dusty road, a group of wise travelers were in search of one such wonder – a child of light who held the future of the world in its hands.

BELOW: The impact of the seasonal movements of the sun on agriculture is fundamental.

ABOVE: During the Middle Ages the heavens were studied carefully during the Solstice tide when the influence of the constellations was especially potent.

CELEBRATION

Many things happen to us and to the world in which we live as the Solstice approaches. The days grow shorter, there is less light, the weather is cold (which tends to make us stay indoors more often), the trees become bare and show their skeletons; the bones of the land show through their tattered coat and we ourselves put on more clothes, looking for colors to tone with the light, the season, and the weather.

OBSERVING THE SOLSTICE

The Solstice is a time of quietude, of firelight and dreaming, when seeds germinate in the cold earth and the cold notes of church bells mingle with the chimes of icicles. Rivers are

stilled and the land lies waiting beneath a coverlet of snow. We watch the cold sunlight and the bright stars, maybe go for walks in the quiet land. Sometimes we go carol singing – even those who would normally never think of lifting their voice in song. Attending Midnight Mass, even for those without Christian beliefs, can become a special event. All around us the season seems to reach a standstill – a point of repose. Then, as the Solstice sun moves across the heavens, the new year wakens, the darkness is dispelled, the days grow longer, and we prepare for new beginnings. There are many ways to celebrate this event. Here are just a few suggestions that reflect an older way of honoring Midwinter.

THE FIRE OF THE GODS

Lighting a fire is, as we shall see, one of the oldest and best ways of honoring the return of the sun. We can also create a shrine to the gods of the Solstice – to Jesus, Mithras, Attis, even to the old thunderer Odin, god of the Norse Yuletide – or we can make a shrine to the heart of Winter itself. We can meditate on aspects of the holiday: on fire, on the cold, on snow, on darkness, on silence, on making mischief, and on giving gifts. We can look at the stars and consider their beauty and power to move us, and we can celebrate the return of the sun by painting it, photographing it, carving its likeness in wood and painting it gold. There are so many things we can do, and some will be outlined in detail throughout this book.

ABOVE: *Lighting a simple candle can be a good way of starting your Winter Solstice celebration.*

To begin, however, let us consider going out into the natural world and looking – really looking – at what there is to see all around us. In every direction there is something special: a tree, a star, a bird or beast, an icy spider's web, or the simple shape of the land.

HONORING THE DIRECTIONS

To help focus on the unique nature of the Solstice and the wonders that open to us on every side, go out into the landscape, into nature, on four consecutive days and on each occasion face a different direction and focus on its particular qualities.

Every land has its own lore about the qualities of each direction. From these directions come different gifts and opportunities. Although there are many books that list these qualities, only you can discover these for yourself. Even within one continent, the qualities of directions are different depending upon how land features shape the land, and from which direction the winds blow. Inland areas will be different from coastal regions, low-lying districts different from mountainous ones. The trick is to attune yourself to the winds that blow. Each of the winds brings a different kind of weather, mood, disposition, and quality.

You can make this celebration as formal or as casual as you like, and you can do it alone or with friends. If the weather is cold you might wish to light a fire (but be sure to get permission before you do so if it is anywhere but on your own land, and don't forget to cover the fire with water or earth when you are done! Remember that peaty soil can hold fire even after the actual flames are out.) Sit by the fire and contemplate the Solstice and all that it means to you. Then stand and face whichever one of the directions you have decided to focus upon that day. Close your eyes and think of the qualities which that direction brings to you every moment. Throughout the world the qualities of directions are honored by the native peoples, just as they have been for generations. The examples here suggest general qualities associated with the directions within the northern hemisphere; if you live in the southern hemisphere you may need to look for others.

ABOVE: Sharing a fire is a fundamental ritual to bind any community.

◎ the north is generally associated with cold, with earth, with challenge and endings. It is the place of ice and snow, of things waiting to germinate and be born.

◎ the east brings with it the idea of awakening, of the new life that spreads through the world in Springtime. It is the direction of air, of peace, and of triumph of the spirit.

◎ the south is the direction of fire, of the heat of life burgeoning and ripening in the earth. It is where we seek the roots of our lives, the stability that the hearth fire brings.

◎ the west is the area of water, of restless seas and wandering spirits. It brings the blessing of movement, emotions, seeking new direction as the year begins its journey through Fall into Winter.

These are only some of the qualities associated with the directions. Consider which you would add and think about them individually. If you are doing this simple ceremony with friends you can each take a different direction or else contemplate the same one and compare notes, discussing the different aspects that you each perceive. When contemplating the gifts of the directions, the four cardinal directions of north, south, east, and west will suffice, but you can also include the north-eastern, south-eastern, south-western, and north-western points as well if you have time.

Then, sitting by the fire, or in the simple light of the half-hidden sun, make a litany of praise to the thing that you hold most precious about this season and the great festival in which you are taking part. Gather your friends about you in the open air, or in front of a roaring fire, and say the words aloud. Here are a few suggestions to get you started. Once you begin, ask other family members to add their own lines – and remember, this can be fun as well as serious – witty lines are just as much a part of the litany since laughter is essential to any celebration.

ABOVE: Observe the four directions in your celebration. Respect the different qualities associated with each.

A LITANY FOR THE WINTER SOLSTICE

For the return of the sun – blessing and praise!

*For the gifts we give – and receive –
blessing and praise!*

*For all the gift-givers – blessings
and praise!*

*For the Children of Wonder – blessings
and praise!*

*For children everywhere – blessings
and praise!*

For sunsets and starlight – blessings and praise!

For fabulous feast days – blessings and praise!

For those who cook them – blessings and praise!

For the tree in the corner – blessings and praise!

*For the candles in the window –
blessings and praise!*

For the icicles on the trees – blessings and praise!

For light on the snowfields – blessings and praise!

For the gifts of friendship – blessings and praise!

For hand-bell ringers – blessings and praise!

For the robin and wren – blessings and praise!

For animals everywhere – blessings and praise!

You can continue with this litany for as long as you like and as many things as you can think of. In this way nothing gets forgotten (hopefully!) and the things that mean most to each one of us are acknowledged and honored.

ABOVE: Honor the Old Woman of Winter by appreciating and celebrating the harsh beauty of this time.

45

RENEWAL OF THE SOLSTICE

At this time of year we become closed to the outside world. And yet, to be out in the snow or the wind is to feel renewed. In the poem that follows, which can be sung to the old Irish tune of the Wexford or Ennisciorthy Carol, the bonds of life and love are celebrated.

THE WINTER WEDDING

Good people all this happy tide,
Consider well and bear in mind,
All that strong love for us can do
When we remember our promise true.

Now love itself stands in this place
With glorious beauty and pleasant grace;
To welcome us with open heart
And riase up welcome in every hearth.

Whatever life on us bestows,
Love's mantle round our shoulders goes
Remembering this day's delight,
To bring us help and mercy bright.

When darkest winter draweth near,
The light is kindled without fiear;
Love sparks at Midwinter so deep,
This blessed time in our hearts keep.

When coldest winter draweth near,
Turn we to joy and make good cheer;
Remembering our vows so strong,
We raise our voices in this song:

Drive darkest want and need away,
Remember we this happy day.
Call love to witness, everyone,
And dance beneath the winter sun.

CAITLÍN MATTHEWS

HONORING THE OLD ONE

In the Celtic world she is the Cailleach, the Old Woman, who brings frost and snow and the bitter winds of Winter. Among the Mandan Indians of North America she is "The Old Woman Who Never Dies," who offers bowls filled with earth and sky, which are of great sacred significance to the tribe. Elsewhere she is the Mountain Mother, who carries great boulders in her apron, occasionally letting them fall, and who is perhaps a creatrix from the beginning of time.

In each instance she personifies the cold dark days, and brings the snow, which is seen as feathers emptied from her pillow. What follows is a modern invocation that expresses our own feelings at the arrival of the Cailleach.

Welcome to you, Old One
Welcome to the snow and ice,
The bitter cloud of your breath,
The pillow-feathered snow
Welcome you in, this Winter day.

May your blessing hold us,
May your chills avoid us,
May the bright promise
Of each clear day
Remind us of your gifts.

Old One, cold one,
Though we fear your storms,
Yet we welcome you
Into our winter hearts,
With your cleansing breath,
To blow away the old year
And usher in the new.

JOHN MATTHEWS:
INVOCATION TO THE OLD ONE

MAKING A WINTER SHRINE

1. *Gather some items that represent the season for you: stones, leaves, and twigs from the hedgerow or the yard for earth's bounty; carved animals to represent the wonder of the animal world;*

2. *You might choose to make a model of your street or neighborhood… whatever you feel evokes the spirit of the Solstice for you.*

3. *You might want to spread some cotton batting or a piece of white blanketing over the area of your shrine, placing pieces of scrap cardboard underneath it to create a molded snowy landscape into which things can be placed.*

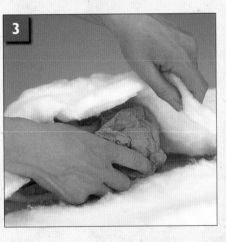

4. *Place a candle in the shrine to represent the undying flame of the sun. You should make sure, of course, that your candle is in a metal or heat-resistant glass container with a well to catch any drips.*

5. *When the shrine is complete, spend a few moments in quiet contemplation of its beauty.*

6. *Standing before this special place of focus and invocation, speak aloud the words that welcome and acknowledge the Old Woman of Winter. (You may wish to salute a figure from your own tradition, or hold such a being in your thoughts as you speak.)*

FOLLOWING PAGES: The Lord of Misrule, the jester, and two bird-headed hobby-horses.

Chapter 2

CHILD OF WONDER

Was it because the cold weather came that we sit around in our lodges
and feast and give honor to each other...
or it is because this is when the white man's god was given to all people...
born to this man and woman, a baby boy...?

MOUNTAIN CHIEF, LAST WAR-CHIEF OF THE BLACKFOOT NATION, 1896

The Winter Solstice has always been a time of celebration – whether it is the return of the sun, the promise of the evergreen boughs, or the birthday of the Midwinter King. This wondrous child, celebrated in so many ways and throughout such an extended period of time, has had many names, though he (and it seems always to be a male child) shares characteristics despite the different cultures and periods in which he has come into being.

A surprising number of the gods of the ancient classical world shared nativity stories that would later influence the development of the story of the birth of Jesus. Among those recorded are Tammuz (Mesopotamia), Attis (Asia Minor), Apollo and Dionysus (Greece), Mithras (Rome), and Baal (Palestine). All are Wonder Children, born under extraordinary circumstances and conditions, at or near to the time of the Winter Solstice.

LEFT: The celebration of the birth of a Child of Wonder at the time of the Winter Solstice features in many traditions and seems to transcend both time and culture.

ABOVE: The birth of the Greek sun god Apollo was celebrated at the time of the Winter Solstice, many years before the birth of Christ.

The Birthday of the Unconquered Sun

Today we celebrate the birthday of Christ on December 25th without thinking. Yet it was four hundred years after the birth of Jesus that the date was fixed. The Church Fathers did not institute the festival until the fourth century – later even than good old St. Nicholas himself. And, having no exact references to the birthday of Jesus, they borrowed a festival from another great Midwinter event, the Roman celebration of the Birth of the Unconquered Sun, which was declared to fall on December 25th by the Emperor Aurelian in A.D. 274. In fact there had been a cult of Sol in Rome from very early times – possibly even from the time of the Etruscans, who predate the Romans by several hundred years and are seen as the foundation of much of the culture of the Classical world. Then, in about 10 B.C., another Roman emperor, Augustus, replaced Sol with the Greek Apollo and instituted celebratory games in the god's honor.

The Birthday of Apollo

In fact, Apollo may not have been a solar deity originally, but the representation of him with a halo probably influenced the way in which he came to be regarded. Born in a cave on the island of Delos at the time of the Midwinter Solstice, he was the son of Zeus and the mortal woman Leto. He grew to full manhood in only three days and set off at once for Delphi, where he slew the serpent that Zeus's jealous wife, Hera, had sent to plague his mother. The serpent, or python, was held to be sacred to the gods of the underworld, and, after slaying the serpent, Apollo established his own shrine in a temple built for him by bees out of feathers and wax. This story has been said to describe a religious takeover by the followers of Apollo who ousted the more ancient mysteries of Pythia, the oracular priestess of Delphi. As well as the time and nature of his birth, which made him half mortal and half god, Apollo was also seen as a shepherd and is often represented as a youth with a sheep draped around his shoulders – a fact that offers a further resonance of Jesus, "the Good Shepherd." Indeed, to this day, Greek Orthodox iconographers still depict Christ's birth as taking place in a cave.

Mithras, God of the Morning

In time another figure superseded Apollo – Mithras, originally an Iranian/Persian deity who dates back to the sixth century B.C., and whose mysteries were imported into Rome around the second century A.D. by legionaries who had served in the east of the Empire. The religion was an important aspect of Roman spiritual life until as late as the fifth century A.D., and it has been said by some commentators that but for the accident of history that popularized Jesus, the Western world could well have adopted Mithraism as its religion, and still be following an ancient Middle Eastern god to this day. It is this figure who is celebrated in Kipling's well-known poem, *A Song to Mithras*:

Mithras, God of the Morning,
our trumpets waken the Wall!
Rome is above the Nations,
but Thou art over all!
Now as the names are answered,
and the guards are marched away,
Mithras, also a soldier,
give us strength for the day!

Mithras, God of the Noontide,
the heather swims in the heat,
Our helmets scorch our foreheads,
our sandals burn our feet.
Now in the ungirt hour,
now ere we blink and drowse,
Mithras, also a soldier,
keep us true to our vows!

Mithras, God of the Sunset,
low on the Western main,
Thou descending immortal,
immortal to rise again!
Now when the watch is ended,
now when the wine is drawn
Mithras, also a soldier,
keep us pure till the dawn!

Mithras, God of the Midnight,
here where the great bull dies,
Look on Thy children in darkness.
Oh, take our sacrifice!
Many roads Thou hast fashioned:
all of them lead to the Light!
Mithras, also a soldier,
teach us to die aright!

Like Apollo, Mithras was a solar deity who had been sent to earth by the supreme God of Light to slay a huge bull whose blood was the source of all fertility on earth. Worshipers underwent extremely rigorous rites of baptism and self-sacrifice that ended when they reached a semidivine status. The central event of the cult was the slaying of the bull, which was seen as a cosmic parable of creation and redemption. Sculptures are found all over the Roman world depicting this dramatic event. Typically Mithras perches on the back of the great bull, cutting its throat from which flows either wine or grain.

Mithras's birth was attended by shepherds, and at the end of his time on Earth, when Mithras returned to his father, he took a last supper with his followers, later remembered by believers in a communion of bread and wine. At the end he was believed not to have died but ascended to heaven, whence it was believed he would return at the end of time to raise the dead from their tombs for a final judgment. The parallels between this and the orthodox teachings of Christianity are too close to mistake.

RIGHT: The slaying of the bull by Mithras is symbolic of the releasing of the blood of fertility onto the land.

Mithras's feast day was Sun-Day, a fact which was no doubt noted by the Emperor Aurelian who declared December 25th to be not only the birthday of Sol, but of Mithras as well.

And, perhaps not surprisingly given such striking parallels, when the fourth-century Christians sought a day to celebrate the birth of Jesus, they chose December 25th also. In fact it was the Emperor Constantine, himself a follower of Mithras until he adopted Christianity as the state religion around A.D. 360, who declared the date to be the birthday of Jesus, thus successfully amalgamating the old festival and the new. We have continued to celebrate this festival ever since, despite the fact that the 25th is no longer Midwinter in calendrical terms. (Though it is indeed the feast of the returning sun that is being celebrated, so the shift in the calendar does not really matter in this instance.) Once again, gift-giving and general celebrations took place, further reinforcing a trend that has continued ever since.

The Reborn God

By far the oldest of the Wonder Children is the Egyptian god Osiris, whose mysteries were also celebrated around the time of Midwinter. Born to the primal gods Geb and Nut, he took Isis for his consort and set about bringing peace, order, and the arts and crafts to the world. Much beloved and worshiped throughout the ancient Mediterranean word, as well as in Greece, Osiris was later murdered by his jealous brother Set, who dismembered his body and hid it in various parts of Egypt. Isis, frantically searching for the remains, restored Osiris to life on December 25th – thus marking his second nativity at the time of the Solstice. The story of his death and resurrection came to be seen as a representation of the rising and setting of the sun, which was believed to be intimately connected with the rising and falling of the Nile River, and hence with the fertility of Egypt. Horus, the son of Isis and Osiris, is often iconographically represented as sitting on the knee of his mother Isis in a pose later transferred to images of the Virgin Mary and Jesus.

ABOVE: There are many parallels between the cult of Mithraism and Christianity, not least the shared birthday on December 25th.

The God of the Pine

Another youthful god, born in a cave at around the turning of the Winter Solstice, was the Phrygian Attis, sometimes said to be the son of the Goddess Isis, sometimes the son of Cybele, who may well be one and the same. As the Great Mother Goddess of Anatolia (modern Syria), Cybele was known throughout the classical world for a considerable time before the third century B.C., at which time she became part of the Roman pantheon. Formally welcomed into Rome in the year 204 B.C., she virtually became their national goddess, and, after the Emperor Claudius adopted her as a personal deity in the first century A.D., she was widely honored under the title of Magna Mata (Great Mother).

Rites celebrating the story of her son, Attis, took place throughout the agricultural year, reaching a climax at the Vernal Equinox. The central story of the religion concerned Cybele's passionate and forbidden love for her own son, who was said to have been driven mad by his mother's desire for him. As a result Attis castrated himself under a pine tree, which consequently became a symbol of his sacrifice.

Attis's followers called him "Father," and Cybele "Mother," and worshiped him in an annual festival at the Vernal Equinox in which a pine tree was first decorated and then cut down (a tradition that may well have a distant echo in the decoration of pine trees during the Solstice) in memory of the god's act of self-mutilation. His priests were called *Galloi* and were themselves eunuchs. They would often slash their own arms or whip themselves during the festival in a frenzy of adulation.

Although little is known of the precise content of the rites of Cybele and Attis, a fragment of a prayer believed to originate in the celebration of the wounded God suggests something of their nature:

> *I have eaten from the drum*
> *I have drunk from the cymbal;*
> *I have carried the sacred dish;*
> *I have stolen into the inner shrine.*
>
> TRANS. BY M.W. MEYER

As one of the "vegetation" gods (others include the Mesopotamian Tammutz and the Greek Adonis), Attis is perceived as growing to full strength with the sun, then dying or being cut down, to return again each year. In this way he shares the attributes of many of the youthful wonder gods, who bring with them the promise of the returning Midwinter sun and the blessing of the New Year.

RIGHT: The Egyptian goddess Isis, nursing the young Horus, reminds us of later images of the Virgin and Child.

The Cave and the Grotto

Both Mithras and Attis are said to have been born in a cave, an idea that later became transferred to the Christian nativity. In the writings of the third-century Platonist, Porphry, we find a detailed description of the practices that evolved from this idea. According to Porphyry, the Persians taught their initiates the shape and meaning of the universe by taking them into an underground grotto, decorated with flowers and with a spring running through it. This rep-

ABOVE: Attis was worshiped by the Romans, and here is being presented with a torch and sacrificial offerings.

resented "an image of the cosmos that Mithras created, and the things arranged symmetrically within were symbols of the cosmic elements and regions." This idea was taken up throughout the classical world, with subterranean temples dedicated to the gods of the underworld being found throughout Greece and Italy. Porphyry adds:

not only... [is] ... the cave a symbol of the [generated], perceptible cosmos, but ...also ... a symbol of all the unseen powers, since the caves are dark, and that which is the essence of the powers is invisible.

TRANS. M.W. MEYER

There is, then, a mystery that is hidden in the caves. The birth of the Child of Wonder takes place in darkness as does the symbolic rebirth of the initiate. As we have seen, the coming forth into bright day, enacted in all of the stories concerning these mighty births, is emblematic of the rising of the sun and the birth of the New Year (*see Chapter 1*).

This is wonderfully depicted in an ancient Mithraic text known as the *Mithras Liturgy*. In this, a number of images of the god are invoked. At one point the initiate, having invoked the god under a number of sacred titles, sees the deity approaching, out of the light of the risen sun:

you will see a youthful god, beautiful in appearance, with fiery hair, and in a white tunic and a scarlet cloak, and wearing a fiery crown.

TRANS. M.W. MEYER

This is Mithras himself, and the initiate must at once greet him with an invocation of fire and light. The experience must have been one of tremendous import to the initiate. Here he was literally face to face with his god – even if only in a visionary state – standing before the risen sun at the dawn of the New Year, which was also the beginning of his own "new" life. The parallels between this and the Christian idea of baptism (from where it in all probability stemmed) is striking. The imagery is rich in the imagery of the New Sun and the Midwinter birth of the young god.

ABOVE: *In Celtic myth, Culwch's quest to release the child god Mabon from his dark prison is symbolic of the release of light at the Solstice.*

It is also strikingly reminiscent of another story, from across the world in the cold lands of Wales, where another young god is born in similar circumstances. But this god, the Mabon, must be actively sought before he can come fully into manifestation.

Mabon, Son of Modron

The medieval Welsh myth-book known as the *Mabinogion* (Tales of Youth) gathers together a number of ancient Celtic stories, among them a vast compilation of tales arranged by a master story-teller under the title *Culhwch and Olwen*. This story, one of the earliest surviving accounts of King Arthur and his heroes, tells of a number of impossible tasks set by the giant Yspaddaden in order to prevent Culhwch from marrying his daughter, Olwen. Helped by Arthur and his warriors, the young hero sets out to accomplish all the tasks that he has been set. One of these is to get the comb and shears that are behind the ears of the giant boar Twrch

Trwyth. The only way he can accomplish this is with the help of the finest hunter in the land – Mabon son of Modron. But Mabon, whose name literally means "The Mother's Son," has been lost, stolen from his mother's side while he was only two nights' old. Culhwch, helped by the war-band that accompanies him, must find him and release him.

The story of how this is accomplished is a fascinating and deep one, and has much to do with the releasing of the child that is a part of us all. Culhwch is helped by a number of animals in his quest. These animals are both extensions of the Mabon's soul and also represent those of the animal kingdom who recognize the young god, just as the animals are believed to have witnessed the birth of Mithras and Christ and to have acknowledged their nascent deity.

The story tells of the search to find Mabon, who is imprisoned in a cave beneath a rocky outcrop named Echymynt. Unable to discover the whereabouts of the lost god, Culhwch is helped by a blackbird, an owl, a stag, an otter, and a salmon, – all of which are sacred creatures in the Celtic tradition – each one older than the last, until finally the ancient salmon of Llyn Llaw carries him on its back to the place where Mabon is imprisoned. There they hear the young god lamenting, and with the help of Arthur's warriors, set him free.

A whole mythology lies behind this mysterious tale: Mabon is the child god, the *puer eternis* of the Celts. He carries within him the promise of youth and the energy of the sun – as all the Children of Wonder, he is born at the time of the greatest darkness and is, after many years of imprisonment, released into light. Perhaps we should say that Mabon brings back the light that has been missing throughout the time that he has been hidden in the cave beneath the rock of Echymynt.

*ABOVE: It has been suggested that Stonehenge
was in fact erected as a circular
temple to the sun god Apollo.*

The British Apollo

This may, indeed, be referred to in a classical account that speaks of the visit by Apollo to his temple in "Hyperborean lands" (generally identified with Britain) every nineteen years. Diodorus Siculus, who wrote about this in his *Library of History*, says:

> Leto [the mother of Apollo] was born on this sland, and for that reason Apollo is honored... above all gods; and the inhabitants are looked upon as priests of Apollo... And there is also on the island both as magnificent sacred precinct of Apollo and a notable temple which is adorned with many votive offerings and is spherical in shape... The account is also given that the god visits the island every nineteen years, the period in which the return of the stars to the same place in the heavens is accomplished... At the time of this appearance of the god he both plays on the cythera and dances continuously the night through from the vernal equinox until the rising of the pliades, expressing in this manner his delight...

BOOK II. CH. 47.
TRANS. BY C.H. OLDFATHER

This circular temple to Apollo has been tentatively identified with Stonehenge. Furthermore, the nineteen-year cycle has been identified with a calendrical adjustment called the Metonic Cycle, which was first introduced in Athens in 432 B.C. in order to reconcile both the solar and lunar cycles. Among the Romano-Celts in Gaul, Apollo was worshiped under the name of Maponus, which is itself a variation of Mabon. Hence it is possible see in this that Mabon was very closely associated with the solar Apollo, and, by extension, with the cycle of Solstices.

Mary's Mabon

In Wales, from early to late Middle Ages, Christ was known as "Mary's Mabon," and in the thirteenth century a Welsh poet named Madawg ap Gwallter wrote a wonderful song celebrating the nativity of Jesus. However, instead of "Christ" he wrote "Mabon," and instead of the Magi it is the Druids who are traveling to visit the Child of Wonder.

> To the house they went, no rampart,
> no door,
> Wind-battered doorways:
> The Son, [Mabon] there He was, the One
> who was born
> Under its shelter,
>
> Mother on the ground with her
> precious breast
> Held next to His lips.
> A man they beheld, they believed Him God,
> Good was their credence.

TRANS. J.P. CLANCY

We need not be surprised by this: the Druids were an exact equivalent to the Magi, and Mabon bears all the hallmarks of a Wonder Child in Celtic dress.

The Babe of Bethlehem

> We must follow the star.
> Even on godless nights
> when there is no star
> we must follow the star.

JOHN MORIARTY:
TURTLE WAS GONE A LONG TIME

Whatever point of origin we take in our examination of the Solstice, it is to the Christian tradition that we are drawn, since it is this which has left its mark most clearly on the face of the festival by subsuming so much that was older under its umbrella of ritual and belief. When we look back to that distant time when the Magi set forth in search of a Child of Wonder, however, we find the familiar picture breaking down. To begin let us look at an old Latin carol to the King:

> Sing of desert and forest
> and far distant places;
> Sing of all nations and sing of all races;
> Sing of the light that now shines
> on all faces;
> Cum Virgine Maria
>
> Sing of the Ear of the World –
> what it heareth;
> Sing of the Heart of the World –
> what it feareth;
> Sing of the Soul of the World –
> what it bareth;
> Cum Virgine Maria
>
> Sing, Eastern Monarchs,
> ye Chaldeans three;
> Sing of thy gifts which ye bear in plentee;
> Sing, while ye worship on bended knee;
> Cum Virgine Maria
>
> Sing of this Maid who
> hath born the Messiah;
> Sing of the purity, faith, and the fire
> Which burns in Her heart for the Son
> and the Sire;
> Haec Virgine Maria.

The scene is a familiar one over half the world: the Magi, the Three Wise Men, travel in search of a wonder whose coming they have read in the stars. They bring gifts of gold, frankincense, and myrrh to honor the child, and declare that his future will affect the history of humankind – a prophecy that is demonstrably true.

Wise Men from the East

Yet, who are these mysterious wise men? And, more importantly, who is the child that is the cause of such celebration and prophecy? Most people would answer with confidence, at least about the second question. But, would they be right? If we look beyond the biblical testimony, and at some of the less familiar texts, we will find a different story.

To look at the question of the wise men first, many would know them as Caspar, Melchior, and Balthasar. But even in the carol quoted before there is a suggestion of something more. Why "Chaldeans" for instance? If we look to the writings of an early Christian sect known as the Gnostics ("those who know"), we can see how these names might have evolved. However, we may be surprised at the number of the wise men who followed the star in the East.

In the *Book of Adam* the kings are called Hor, King of Persia, Basantar, King of Saba, and Karsundas, King of the East. These names, though different, are still within a recognizable parameter. But in another Gnostic text, *The Book of the Bee*, the Magi are twelve in number, and their names are recorded as:

Zarwendad, the son of Artaban.
Hormizdad, the son of Sitaruk.
Gushnasaph, the son of Gundaphar.
Arshakh, the son of Miharok.
(These four brought gold.)

Zarwandad, the son of Warzad.
Iryaho, the son of Kesro.
Artahshesht, the son of Holiti.
Ashtonabodan, the son of Shishron.
(These four brought myrrh.)

Meharok, the son of Hunam.
Ahshiresh, the son of Hasban.
Sardilah, the son of Baladan
Merodach, the son of Beldaran.
(These four brought frankincense.)

THE GNOSTIC BOOK OF ADAM

So here we have twelve wise men – all of them kings – rather than the usual three. They are, in fact, representatives of the twelve months of the year and the twelve zodiacal signs, powerful cosmic influences gathered in this place and this time to bear witness to the birth of an extraordinary being, a Child of Wonder who will change the course of history forever.

These, then, are our wanderers, who come from distant lands in pursuit of a star. In the familiar biblical account we read:

Now when Jesus was born in Bethlehem of Judea in the days of Herod the king, behold there came wise men from the east to Jerusalem, saying, "Where is he that is born King of the Jews? For we have seen his star in the east, and are come to worship him..." Then Herod, when he had privily called the wise men, enquired of them diligently what time the star had appeared. And he sent them to Bethlehem... When they heard the king they departed; and lo, the star, which they saw in the east, went before them, till it came and stood over where the young child was... And when they were come into the house, they saw the young child with Mary his mother, and fell down, and worshiped him: and when they had opened their treasures, they presented unto him gifts: gold, frankincense, and myrrh.

THE GOSPEL OF MATTHEW

*ABOVE: The story of the three wise men may be a familiar one, but on closer
scrutiny their identities, and even their purpose, become less so.*

Following the Star

By looking further into Gnostic texts we find a somewhat different account of these events.

Now, it was two years before Christ was born that the star appeared to the Magi. They saw the star in the firmament of heaven, and the brilliancy of its appearance was brighter than that of every other star. And within it was a maiden carrying a child, and a crown was set upon his head. Now it was the custom of the ancient kings, and the Magi of the Chaldeans, to consult the Signs of the Zodiac about all the affairs of their lives. And when the Magi saw the star they were perturbed, and terrified, and afraid, and the whole land of Persia was disturbed.

THE BOOK OF THE CAVE OF TREASURES

This is still not so far from the basic outline of the biblical account, despite its interesting variants. The account given in *The Book of the Bee*, however, begins to take us further into unfamiliar territory:

As touching the nature of that star, whether it was a star in its nature, or in appearance only, it is right to know that it was not as other stars, but a secret power which appeared like a star; for all the others that are in the firmament, and the sun and moon, perform their course from east to west. This one, however, made its course from north to south, for Palestine lies thus, over against Persia. This star was not seen by them at night only, but also during the day, and at noon; and it was seen in the time when the sun is particularly strong, because it was not one of the stars...Sometimes it appeared, and sometimes it was hidden entirely. It guided the Magi as far as Palestine...This was not an ordinary movement of the stars, but a rational power. Moreover, it had no fixed path. It did not always remain in the height of heaven, but sometimes it came down, and sometimes it mounted up."

THE BOOK OF THE BEE

+SCS BALTHASSAR +SCS MELCHIOR +SCS GASPAR.

LEFT: *The meaning behind the Magi's gifts of gold, frankincense, and myrrh has been much disputed by scholars.*

RIGHT: Most texts agree that the Magi undertook a historic journey to visit the newborn Christ child.

The Great Journey

After they had read the signs that pointed to the great and miraculous event that was about to occur, the Magi started to make all the various preparations that were necessary for their momentous journey.

> *Straightway, according to what they had received from the tradition which had been handed down to them by their fathers, they left the East, and went up into the mountains of Nodh...and they took from them gold, and myrrh, and frankincense... the gold was for a king, the myrrh for a physician, and the frankincense for a priest, for the Magi knew who He was, and that He was a king, and a physician, and a priest.*

THE BOOK OF THE CAVE OF TREASURES

Thus the gifts themselves are seen to be appropriate to the Child of Wonder – though they are, perhaps, not the gifts of the simple, wise men of biblical tradition. Nor are they, indeed, that simple, as we can see from the following extract from *The Book of the Chaldeans*:

> *Now the Magi are called "Magi" because of the garb of Magianism in which they arrayed themselves whensoever they offered up a sacrifice and made offerings to their gods. They made use of two different kinds of apparel; that which appertained to royalty they wore inside, and that which appertained to Magianism they wore outside. And thus it was with those who went up prepared to make offerings to Christ, and they were arrayed in both kinds of apparel.*

THE BOOK OF THE CHALDEANS

ABOVE: The Gnostic accounts of the nativity may bring us to a closer understanding of this profound event.

The Gnostic Heretics

The Gnostics have been considered as heretics by the Church of Rome almost from the beginning of established Christianity. This is primarily because they did not fit into the evolving canon of commentary and scripture upon which the Church had begun to impose its will. There was too much of the esoteric, too many echoes of older mystery teachings to be acceptable to the fathers of orthodoxy. But in disallowing the writings of the Gnostics, they closed the door on a rich and literate source of wisdom which has only begun to be explored in recent years with the discovery of the so-called "Dead Sea Scrolls," which are largely Gnostic in content.

When we look at these alternate visions of the events leading up to the birth of the wondrous child, we find that they bring us closer to the accounts of those other beings – Mithras, Attis, Dionysus, or Apollo – who are all protectors of the world sent into manifestation at the darkest time of the year.

The Age of Gold

Much of this had to do with the belief in a coming Age of Gold (or a return to an earlier, more perfect time) and to the annunciation of the arrival that age by the coming of a divine child. Thus the Roman poet, Virgil, in his fourth Eclogue says:

> Come are those last days
> that the Sybil sang:
> The Ages mighty march begins anew.
>
> Now comes the Virgin,
> Saturn reigns again:
> Now from high heaven
> descends a wondrous race.
>
> Thou on the new-born babe
> – who first shall end
> That age of iron, bid a golden dawn
> Upon the broad world...

TRANS. T.F. ROYDS

This has been taken to refer to the coming of Christ, but it equally refers back to the birth of Apollo, as well as to the many other child gods born at the Winter Solstice. The greatest of these must be Aion (from whose name we derive the word "aeon"). Born at the Winter Kalends, to the virgin Kore (daughter of the mother goddess Demeter), the mystery of this Midwinter birth was still celebrated as late as the second century A.D. The Christian writer Epiphanius describes the celebration that took place on the night of January 5th/6th, at which time there was a great festival.

> They stay up the whole night singing songs and playing the flute, offering these to the images of the gods; and, when the revelries of the night are over, after cock-crow, they go down with torches into a subterranean sanctuary and bring up a carved wooden image, which is laid naked on a litter. On its forehead it has the sign of the cross, in gold, and on both its hands two other signs of the same shape, and two more on its knees; and the five signs are all fashioned in gold. They carry this carved image seven times around the middle of the temple precincts, to the sound of flutes and tambourines and hymns, and after the procession they carry it down again into the crypt. But if you ask them what this mysterious performance means they answer: Today, at this hour, the Kore, that is to say the virgin, has given birth to the Aeon.

TRANS. C.G. JUNG

LEFT: The story of Mithras offers an alternative vision of the story of the birth and life of the Child of Wonder.

The Birth of Brimo

It is fairly clear that this ceremony has been influenced by Christian iconography, but behind it lies a far older celebration, one that dates back to at least the eighth century B.C.. At this time, in the mysteries celebrated at Eleusis, there is evidence of the enactment, by a priestess of Demeter and a priest representing the human initiate, of a Sacred Marriage. The result of this was, either symbolically or actually, a child whose coming is announced from the steps of the temple in bright torchlight by the heirophant (the guardian of the mysteries), who declared: "Holy Brimo, has born a sacred child, Brimos." Brimo is thought to be a northern name for Demeter, represented as a dark goddess, even as Queen of the Dead, though at the same time referred to as "the Nursing Mother." Of Brimos we know nothing more, though like the Celtic Mabon and Modron, Brimo and Brimos may well be titles applied to the sacred mother and child.

Out of this conflicting pattern of myths emerges the idea of the virgin goddess bearing a son, in the darkness, whose coming is then announced in bright light. Like Mithras, Attis, and Dionysus, Brimos is born from the darkness of the Midwinter into the light of the New Year. He brings that light with him and is welcomed as the bringer of hope and renewal, just as Jesus is said to do more than five hundred years later.

LEFT: Native American myths often involve communication with animal spirits.

A Native American Jesus

Jesuit missionaries, as well as bringing a darker legacy of cruelty, sickness, and intolerance to the Native American people of America, also brought the traditions of the babe of Bethlehem. This underwent a curious reshaping among some of the peoples, who, as the quotation from the Blackfoot Mountain Chief that heads this chapter shows, were well aware of the significance of the Wonder Child. The Huron Indians made Jesus the child of Gitchimanitou, and, in this remarkable carol, the babe is worshiped by chieftains instead of kings, and wrapped in rabbit skins rather than swaddling bands:

The Huron Indian Carol

T'was in the moon of wintertime
when all the birds had fled,
That mighty Gitchimanitou
Sent angel choirs instead.
Before their light the stars grew dim
And wand'ring hunters heard the hymn:

Jesus your king is born,
Jesus is born,
In exchelsis gloria.

Within a lodge of broken bark
The tender babe was found,
A ragged robe of rabbit skin
Enwrapped his beauty round.
The chiefs from far before him knelt
With gifts of fox and beaver pelt.

O children of the forest free,
O sons of Manitou,
The holy child of earth and heav'n
Is born today for you.
Come kneel before the radiant boy
Who brings you beauty, peace, and joy.

The Peacemaker

ABOVE: *The Native American myth of Deganawidah has many astonishing parallels with the story of Christ.*

The influence of the Christian myths may well have affected another story from Native American traditions – that of Deganawidah, the Peacemaker. This semi-mythical character, also known as the Man From The North, was born into the Wendot tribe, later known as the Huron, who lived along the northern shore of present day Lake Ontario. According to traditions, Deganawidah was born of a virgin who, when she confessed to her mother that she was pregnant but had never known a man, was revealed to have been visited by a messenger of the Great Spirit Tarenyawagon, who was

sending a messenger to bring lasting peace to humankind. At first there was much doubt among the tribes-people, and it is even told that Deganawidah's grandmother tried three times to kill the child after prophecies that he would bring no good to the tribe. Yet Deganawidah survived, and grew imbued with wisdom, intelligence, and kindness. He spoke with animals and birds, and began to teach a message of peace among his fellows. The warlike Huron found this distasteful and strange and tried to drive Deganawidah away. On reaching manhood he wandered in the wilderness for a time and then set forth in a white canoe said to have been made, astonishingly, of stone, to visit other tribes. In the years that followed he traveled among the tribes and eventually founded the great Iroquois Confederacy, a democratic union of five tribes from among the northeastern woodlands, the concept that influenced not only the founding of the United States constitution, but also that of the United Nations.

Deganawidah's death remains mysterious, and, like King Arthur, it is believed that he will return at the time of his country's need. Remembered still as the Peacemaker, he is seen as a harbinger of peace and as messenger of God. His life parallels that of Christ in many ways, especially in his birth and youthful deeds. He is a perfect example of the Children of Wonder, who come in the dark heart of Winter to bring light and a message of peace to the world.

ABOVE: *Deganawidah, the Peacemaker, was brought up with intelligence and kindness and, like Jesus, went on to spread a message of peace and democracy.*

The Boy Bishop

Christ is now born, on this very night, God's holy Child, at Fort Bethlehem

THE HELIAND
TRANS. G.R. MURPHY

The long-standing association of Midwinter and Christmas with St. Nicholas (in whatever guise he appeared) leads to another tradition that looks back to the earliest period of Christianity, and which celebrates the mystery of the Child of Wonder.

During the Middle Ages there came into being the tradition of celebrating St. Nicholas's Day (December 6th) by electing a choirboy as bishop. He ruled until St. Stephen's Day (also Holy Innocent's Day) on December 28th, wearing full vestments, mitre, and carrying a crook. The ceremony of investiture was a curious mix of sacred and profane, but the Boy Bishop was afterwards permitted to perform all of the normal duties of an adult holder of the post – with the exception of the celebration of Mass. In some places the actual bishop had to serve his substitute, while the rest of the choirboys appointed their superiors to menial positions. If the Boy Bishop had the misfortune to die while in office he was extended the full honors of an Episcopal burial. Salisbury Cathedral in Wiltshire still preserves a plaque believed to commemorate a boy who died under these circumstances.

The origins of giving this exalted position to a child are a combination of the traditions surrounding Holy Innocent's

ABOVE: The real figure behind Santa Claus was the Bishop of Myra, later canonized to become St. Nicholas.

Day in the Christian Calendar, episodes from the life of St. Nicholas himself, and the Midwinter celebration known as the Feast of Fools (*see Chapter 5*). On Holy Innocent's Day, the children killed at the behest of King Herod in an unsuccesful attempt to destroy the future Jewish Messiah were remembered. At the Feast of Fools, once celebrated widely throughout medieval Europe, a low-born person was chosen to become "king" for a day.

St. Nicholas and the Angels

The true origin of the Boy Bishop probably derives from an episode from the life of St. Nicholas of Myra, who later became better known as Santa Claus (*see Chapter 4*). From birth his life was touched by miracles. Around the year A.D. 300, Nicholas, then in his teens, persuaded his uncle and guardian to allow him to go on a pilgrimage to the Holy Land. At the time this was no easy journey, but Nicholas took ship and arrived in Jerusalem without incident. There he stayed with a small Christian community. Several months later he set out for home, but while the voyage out had been easy, this time the ship on which Nicholas sailed was beset by violent storms. When it seemed that all on board might perish, Nicholas prayed aloud, and at once the storm began to abate. Blown off course, they found themselves off the coast of Lycia, near Myra, and here they put in to make repairs and take in fresh provisions. Nicholas at once sought out the nearest church to give thanks for his safe delivery. Unknown to him the old Bishop

*ABOVE: St. Nicholas's Day (December 6th)
is still celebrated across the world with
processions and festivities.*

of Myra had decided to retire, and a convocation was then in progress to decide his successor. On the day previous to this, one of their number had received a vision in which an angel had told him that the next Bishop of Myra would be coming to the church the next morning and that his name would be Nicholas.

When the young man arrived he was greeted by the bishops who, when they learned his name and heard something of his life, decided to make him Bishop of Myra despite his young age.

Constantine's Miracle

That is not the end of the story. Three years after Nicholas's installation as bishop, the Emperor Diocletian decided to enforce the worship of the gods, and ordered all Christians to be imprisoned. Nicholas, along with his flock, was thrown into prison. Three years later he was released by the new Emperor Constantine, who, though he was himself a follower of Mithras, became converted to Christianity after experiencing a remarkable vision.

In A.D. 312 Constantine was about to lay siege to Rome. Beset by enemies on every side, he, having heard of the followers of Christ, prayed for a revelation. As he waited at the head of his army, he saw a cross of light appear in the heavens above the midday sun. On it were the words, "By this sign you shall conquer." Recognizing this as related to the symbolism of the Unconquered Sun, and to the Mithraic traditions he had followed all his life, Constantine vowed that if he was victorious he would become a Christian and make Christianity the official religion of the Empire. His triumph was absolute, and he kept his word, becoming the first Christian Emperor of Rome and changing the face of Western history for all time.

Released from prison, Nicholas continued as Bishop of Myra until his death in A.D. 342. In time his miraculous deeds were recognized and he became canonized. It is as St. Nicholas, the original Santa Claus, that we remember him today.

The remarkably youthful age at which Nicholas became bishop was undoubtedly a contributing factor to the tradition of the Boy Bishop festival in England during the Middle Ages. This custom continued right through until the reign of King Henry VIII, who finally suppressed it. It was then revived for a short time during Mary's reign, but died out again during the time of Elizabeth I. In parts of the country it enjoyed a further revival during the nineteenth century, and in the village of Berden in Wessex it was still being enacted as late as the 1930s.

CELEBRATION

There are many ways to celebrate the birth of the Wondrous Children, perhaps the most important of which is the honoring of our own children – or of our own childhood. You might write a brief account of your own childhood memories, or compose a poem or song on this theme. You might also feel called upon to create a shrine, similar to that outlined in Chapter 1, but which focuses upon any or all of the deities discussed above. It is important to recognize that when we celebrate the nativity of Christ we are also remembering the birthdays of older gods. If you are a Christian and feel unable to acknowledge any other deity than Jesus, then you might wish to create a more formal shrine to the Babe of Bethlehem.

ABOVE: Your shrine can include any animals of which you are especially fond.

THE BIRTHDAY OF WINTER: MAKING A SHRINE

At one time the making of the Christmas crib was as important a part of every household activity as that of the church where we still see the annual preparations and blessing of the crib. Traditionally, it was St. Francis of Assisi who created the first crib, in honor not only of the infant savior but also of the animals who had come to worship in the stable. Why not create your own nativity scene, using wood, sawdust, straw and any other natural element that comes to hand? If you happen to be good with your hands, you might even wish to carve your own nativity figures. Otherwise there are, of course, an immense range of good quality figurines to be had in every store during the Christmas period. Remember to give special place to the animals, perhaps importing more than the traditional ox and ass.

If you feel even more adventurous, why not include images or symbols of the older deities. A golden sun disk for Mithras, a pine cone for Dionysus, or some rose petals for Attis. Put plenty of green boughs of holly and ivy wreaths around the centerpiece, and to complete the shrine, place a long-burning candle in front (something in a red or green container would be ideal), to maintain the element of fire and light.

You may wish to create a shrine to all who are waiting to be born, both within yourself and the world about you. Within every child all the potentialities of life are all gathered. The innocence and truth of the child brings a new focus into every family, enabling us to see the world through the eyes of a child, rather than through the jaundiced gaze of an adult. Placing something emblematic of the birth that is waiting to be born at Solstice time helps us honor the spark of light that is manifesting within us. If you don't want to be exclusive to one spiritual tradition, a lighted candle can represent the Light of Life itself on your shrine.

A CAKE FOR THE MAGI

In France a cake (actually a kind of tart) is made for the Feast of Epiphany (Twelfth Night), traditionally the time when the Magi gave their gifts to the Christ Child. A golden ring, or a bean, are hidden inside the cake, and a gold crown laced around or on top of it. Whoever finds the hidden object was crowned "king" of the feast and became Lord of Misrule. Here is a recipe for such a cake:

ABOVE: Honor the importance of animals to the Solstice tide with a simple display.

MAKING A CAKE FOR THE MAGI

1. Sift 1½ cups/6oz/175g flour with a teaspoon of baking powder and a pinch of salt into a bowl; rub in 6tbsp/3oz/75g of butter until the mixture is like small crumbs. Gradually add approximately ¾ cup of water until the dough is light and non-sticky. Knead gently, then cover and leave for about 20 minutes in the refrigerator.

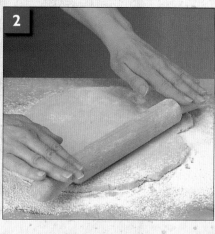

2. Roll out the pastry on a floured board until it is about a quarter of an inch thick. Fold it like a napkin, then cover and place in the refrigerator for a further 20 minutes.

3. Divide the pastry in half. Make a ball out of each piece and then roll out into a circle about 9in/20cm in diameter. Place one piece onto a greased cookie sheet.

4. Now make the filling. Cream 6tbsp/3oz/75g butter and 1 cup/6oz/175g sugar together until light and fluffy. Beat in 2 egg yolks, add 4 or 5 drops of almond essence, ½ cup/2oz/50g of freshly ground almonds, and 3 tbsp of kirsch or other liqueur. Mix to a smooth paste and spoon the paste onto the center of the round base only, leaving a small margin all round.

5. Hide the object you have chosen to include in the paste; insure that anything you include will tolerate high temperatures. Beat an egg with a drop of water and use it to brush the margin of the lower circle of pastry. Stick the second circle of pastry on the top. Place the cake covered in the refrigerator for a further 45 minutes.

6. Preheat the oven to 190°C/375°F/Gas Mark 5. Gather up the trimmings from the pastry, roll them out, and with a sharp knife cut into thin strips. Use this to fashion a star-shape for the top of the cake. Attach the strips to the top circle of pastry with beaten egg. Then brush the top with beaten egg yolk and bake for 30 to 40 minutes. Remove when the top is crisp and dust with powdered sugar to look like snow. Cut out a crown from gold foil and place on top or around the sides.

FOLLOWING PAGES: Bring offerings to the shrine of the Wonder Child in the spirit of the season.

ABOVE: The person who finds the token in their piece of cake is crowned Monarch of the Solstice.

Chapter 3

THE GREEN BOUGH

When rosemary and bays, the poet's crown,
Are bawled in frequent cries throughout the town,
Then judge the festival of Christmas near –
Christmas the joyous period of the year.
Now with bright holly all the temples strow,
With laurel green and sacred mistletoe.

JOHN GAY: TRIVIA 1713

very year we take a tree (usually one from the fir family), bring it into our homes, and decorate it with colored lights and sparkling ornaments. For a few brief days it becomes the center of the house: gifts are laid beneath it, family and friends are drawn to sit around it or beneath its boughs. Yet few remember, or even care to know, the symbolism that gave rise to its place in our lives, and which in some instances predates the celebration of Christmas by hundreds of years.

LEFT: The decorated tree at Christmas echoes many ancient beliefs, including the essential symbolism of light and life.

Solstice Evergreen

We can be certain that from the time of our earliest ancestors the existence of plants that were "evergreen," which did not wither and die with the onset of the long dark days of Winter, were perceived as a metaphor for the undying gods of the natural world. Just as the Midwinter fires celebrated the longed for return of the sun, so did the evergreen tree signify the continuing presence of burgeoning life in the midst of Winter's sleep of death.

ABOVE: The Holy Thorn, said to have grown from the staff of Joseph of Arimathea, flowers every Christmas.

Yet no one can say with any real certainty when the first such tree was decorated and made the focal point of the Midwinter celebrations. There may well be a connection with the celebrations of the god Attis, whose festival included the decoration of a pine tree (*see Chapter 2*), but the origins of the custom are generally seen as emerging from a combination of two traditions which were originally quite separate – the Roman custom of decorating their houses with greenery at the Kalends of January, and the popular belief that on every Christmas Eve, certain trees, the apple most especially, would either blossom or bear fruit unseasonably.

The latter notion derives in the main from a long-established belief that on the eve of Christ's birth, to signal the cosmic importance of the event, rivers ran with wine rather than water, while trees and flowers blossomed and fruited in the midst of the ice and snow.

The Holy Thorn

In Britain there is a particular story that illustrates this. In and around the Somerset town of Glastonbury the story is told that Joseph of Arimathea, the "uncle" of Jesus, came there bearing the Holy Grail. He planted his staff on Wearyall Hill, overlooking the town, and it at once put forth leaves, continuing to flower every Christmas thereafter. This story has a foundation in actuality: a thorn tree, which is said to be a scion of Joseph's staff, still grows there (though it has now been transplanted to the grounds of Glastonbury Abbey). It is of a species found more commonly in Palestine and does indeed flower every Christmas. A sprig of it is placed on the breakfast table of Her

Majesty the Queen every Christmas Day, a custom that has been followed since the 1950s.

Such was the strength of belief in this miraculous flowering that in Britain in 1752, when the new-style calendar was substituted for the old, causing Christmas Day to fall twelve days earlier, two thousand people went to the little town of Quainton in Buckinghamshire on the new-style Christmas Eve to view a blackthorn that had always blossomed at that time. When no sign of buds or blossom was forthcoming, they declined to accept the new dates! Similarly, in Glastonbury at the same time nothing occurred on December 24th, but, on January 5th (the correct date by the old style of calculation), the thorn blossomed on time! Such is the power of myth.

At Wormsley in Herefordshire, there used to be a holy thorn that blossomed at exactly twelve o'clock on Twelfth Night. The blossoms would open at midnight and would drop an hour later. A piece of the thorn gathered at this time brought luck if kept for the remainder of the year. As recently as 1908, forty people bore witness to this occurrence.

The Magical Cherry Tree

In other parts of the world cherry trees or hawthorns are placed in water or in indoor containers to encourage them to bud at Midwinter. In Italy in the nineteenth century the tradition was for young girls to stick a branch of cherry tree into wet sand – if it flowered their dreams of finding a good husband would be sure to come true.

The particular significance of the cherry tree in Christian tradition is remembered in "The Cherry Tree Carol," which recalls an apocryphal story concerning one the many miracles that attended the birth of Christ:

Joseph was an old man,
And an old man was he,
When he wedded Mary
In the land of Galilee.

Joseph and Mary
Walked through an orchard green
Where were cherries and berries
As red as any blood.

O then bespoke Mary,
with words so meek and mild,
"Pluck me one cherry, Joseph,
For I am with child."

O then bespoke Joseph
With answer most unkind,
"Let him pluck thee a cherry
That got thee now with child."

O then bespoke the baby
Within hid mother's womb -
"Bow down then the tallest tree
For my mother to have some."

Then bowed down the highest tree
Unto his mother's hand.
Then she cried "See, Joseph,
I have cherries at command."

O then bespoke Joseph –
"I have done Mary wrong;
But now cheer up, my dearest,
And do not be cast down.

O eat your cherries, Mary,
O eat your cherries now,
O eat your cherries, Mary,
That grow upon the bough."

Then Mary plucked a cherry,
As red as any blood;
Then Mary she went homewards
All with her heavy load.

ABOVE: Festoons of Christmas greenery reflect the ancient Roman practice of decorating houses with branches at the Kalends of January

Saturnalia

Earlier than any of these traditions, the Roman practice of decorating trees and houses at the Kalends of January is recorded by several classical authors. At this time green garlands were hung up and worn through the streets in celebration of the New Year. The newly powerful Christian Church, of course, condemned such pagan demonstrations of affection for the green world. As Tertulian, a Christianized Roman, grouchily affirmed:

> *Let them (the Heathens) kindle lamps,*
> *for whom fire is close at hand...*

But as folklorist Christina Hole puts it:

> *time, and the innate conservatism of ordinary people, gradually softened these harsh views, and eventually not only the houses of Christians, but their churches also, burst into a permitted splendour of greenery at Christmas...*

DICTIONARY OF BRITISH FOLK CUSTOMS

The First Christmas Tree

The first historically recorded mention of Christmas trees actually comes from an anonymous German citizen (indeed, most of the records we posses of early Christmas customs come from this country). Writing in 1605 he comments: "At Christmas they set up fir trees in the parlours of Strasbourg and hang thereon roses cut out of many coloured paper, apples, wafers, gold-foil, sweets, etc..." (A. Tille, *Yule and Christmas,* London, 1899). A few years later, we find a disgruntled Strasbourg theologian commenting on "people who set up the Christmas or fir-tree [which they] hang with dolls and sweets; and afterwards shake and deflower...Whence comes this custom I know not; it is child's play... Far better were it to point children to the spiritual cedar tree, Jesus Christ" (Tille, *Yule and Christmas*). This last comment is, as we shall see later on, very interesting, as it points to the continuing significance of the evergreen tree and its burden in several different traditions.

Despite these occasional reproofs from the pulpit, the idea of the Christmas tree began to catch on. In 1737, Karl Gottfried Kissling, a professor at the University of Wittenburg, tells how a country lady of his acquaintance set up a little tree for each of her sons and daughters, lit candles on or around them, laid out presents beneath and called her children one by one into the room to take both the tree and the gifts intended for them.

In England there are brief references in 1789 to the use and decoration of evergreen trees during the Christmas holiday, but it was not until 1840 when Queen Victoria and Prince Albert brought a Christmas tree to Balmoral, that the popular trend was finally set. The growth of the tradition is, in fact, clearly traceable; one can follow its progress throughout Europe in the nineteenth century, starting in Finland in 1800, through Norway and Denmark in 1830, to Sweden by 1862, Bohemia in 1863, and spreading through Russia, the United States, Spain, Italy, and Holland in the years that followed. By the beginning of the twentieth century the traditional Christmas tree was so firmly entrenched that its origins had been wholly forgotten except in the writings of a few obscure antiquarians.

ABOVE: The traditional Christmas tree as we know it today really began to catch on in Europe and the United States during the nineteenth century.

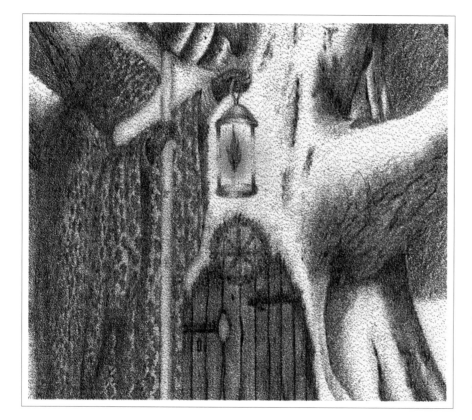

The villagers would then sit around the tree throughout the night, singing and telling stories, after which it was taken to a permanent site, where it remained for the rest of the year.

The "pyramid" was a popular alternative to the fir tree during the eighteenth century in Germany and England. This cone-shaped construction was made of wood, and was decorated with flowers, ribbons, and leaves woven together with evergreen branches, and filled up with fruit and nuts. The pyramids were paraded around the house and ceremonially introduced to every room, ending up in the main room where gifts were distributed on Christmas Day.

Decorating the Great Tree

A number of other traditions dealing with the decoration of trees are recorded throughout Europe from the seventeenth century onward. On the Greek island of Chios, for example, tenant farmers used to bring their landlords on Christmas morning a *rhamna*, a pole decorated with wreaths of myrtle, olive, and orange leaves, bound around with geraniums, anemones, strips of golden and colored paper, lemons, and anything else that was to hand. While in Circassia, in a festival that took place just before Midwinter, a young pear tree, heavily decorated with candles and with a cheese fastened to the top, was carried into every house in the village, accompanied by loud shouts and songs and a plenitude of wine.

The Trees of Paradise

We saw before, in the quotation from the eighteenth-century theologian of Strasbourg, the analogy of Christ to the cedar tree. Another contributory factor in the origin and traditions relating to the Christmas tree undoubtedly derives from the fact that in early Christian calendar December 24th was Adam and Eve's Day. Medieval legend stated that when the primal parents left Eden they took with them a slip from the Tree of Life, which in later times grew into the tree from which the wood of Christ's Cross came. The symbolism surrounding this is elegant and powerful. The scion of the Tree of Paradise was depicted, in medieval iconography, as growing from Adam's grave; Christ, also depicted as hanging on an actual tree, plucked the fruit of redemption from it. The Messiah is also often represented as the True Vine, the grape from which the wine of the New Covenant was pressed. Beliefs of this kind, along with the idea of Christ as the symbol of the Tree of Life and the Light of the World, are brought together in the symbolism of the candle-lit evergreen tree, and this in turn reflects back to the older beliefs concerning the sacredness of the evergreen and the vital symbolism of fire and light.

Christmas in the Old West

Even in the far off wilderness of the American frontier during the 1800s, the Christmas tree became a center of celebration. The cowboys' Christmas Ball was held throughout Texas, Montana, and New Mexico, where there was dancing to music played by ecstatic fiddlers that would not have seemed out of place in the Old World (indeed perhaps the very distance between one and another made the celebration all the more poignant).

In those parts of the country where good relations existed between pioneers and the Native American peoples, the Christmas period was referred to as "The Big Eating," while in areas where French trappers lived, it was called "Kissing Day," after their habit of exchanging a kiss with their Christmas gifts. Often Native American children were invited to see the Christmas tree, and extra food was shared out in a fine example of seasonal good spirit. On several occasions the Native American children were found dancing around the tree, remembering perhaps the similar celebrations that, for them, took place in the

Spring, when a mighty sacred tree was hung with gifts. In North Dakota, particularly, there was a very ancient tradition of planting a cedar tree every year near the big medicine lodge: the tree was then decorated with moccasins, shawls, pelts, and so forth to be shared out among the tribe. Called simply "Grandmother," this tree was honored throughout the Summer months and into the Fall, when it was uprooted and set adrift on the Missouri River to make its journey into the Otherworld of the Great Beyond.

Tree of Symbol

These elements, linking ancient and new traditions and beliefs in a pattern of unfolding imagery, invest the display of the evergreen tree at the turn of the Midwinter Solstice with a wonderful veracity that is every bit as powerful today as it was in ages gone by. In our own time the presence of huge and elaborately decorated Christmas trees in

RIGHT: When viewed in the light of its fascinating history, the humble Christmas tree can be a powerful and poignant addition to our Solstice celebrations.

places such as Trafalgar Square in London, or Rockefeller Center in New York, have become an essential part of Christmas.

In Britain, before World War II, going out to select, cut down, and bring back a tree was always done with ceremony. Today this has passed into American tradition, with images of tall fir trees tied to the back of horse-drawn sleighs, described and celebrated in story and song. Indeed, in many parts of the United States the disposal of the Christmas trees put out at the end of the holiday has itself become something of a tradition. In Rochester, Vermont, the local sanitation department collects all the dead and dying trees on Twelfth Night, and creates a vast bonfire that can be seen for miles. This is considered as much a part of the general holiday celebrations as the putting up of trees themselves before Christmas.

ABOVE: The custom of erecting Christmas trees originated in Germany in the seventeenth century.

The Mistletoe Bough

It is not very long since the custom of setting up garlands in churches hath been left off with us: and in some places setting up of holly, ivy, rosemary, bays, yew etc. in churches at Christmas is still in use.

W. COLES: THE ART OF SIMPLING, 1656

Especially important at this time of year were three plants that naturally bore fruit at the Solstice – the mistletoe with its spectral white berries, the holly with its scarlet fruit, and the ivy with its striking green and white leaves. Traditions about each of these abound, none more so than the mistletoe.

This plant, which is actually a parasite that attaches itself to certain trees, was held sacred by the Druids. The Roman author Pliny gives a striking account of the ceremony by which mistletoe was gathered:

The Druids ... held nothing more sacred than the mistletoe and the tree that bears it, always supposing that tree to be the oak. But they choose groves formed of oaks for the sake of the tree alone, and they never perform any of their rites except in the presence of a branch of it... In fact they think that everything that grows on it has been sent from heaven and is a proof that the tree was chosen by the god himself. The mistletoe, however, is found but rarely upon the oak; and when found, is gathered with due religious ceremony, if possible on the sixth day of the moon... They choose this day because the moon, though not yet in the middle of her course, has already considerable influence. They call the mistletoe by a name meaning, in their own language, the all-healing. Having made preparation for sacrifice and a banquet beneath the trees, they bring thither two white bulls, whose horns are bound then for the first time. Clad in a white robe, the priest ascends the tree and cuts the mistletoe with a golden sickle, and it is received by others in a white cloak. Then they kill the victims [i.e. the cattle], praying that God will render this gift of his propitious to those to whom he has granted it. They believe that the mistletoe, taken in drink, imparts fecundity to barren animals, and that it is an antidote for all poisons.

HISTORIA NATURALIS BOOK XVI, 249.
TRANS. A.J.CHURCH AND T.D. BROADRIB

ABOVE: The Druids, according to tradition, would use a golden sickle to cut mistletoe from the tree on which is was growing.

*ABOVE: Ancient Druids cherished mistletoe
for its reputed magical and medicinal properties.*

The Golden Bough

Pliny does not give very precise reasons why the Druids prized mistletoe so highly, other than its supposed healing properties. The name by which it is called here, "all-healing," is reflected in several variations on this. In Wales it is called "sap of the oak," or *druidh his*, "Druids' Weed," while in Brittany it is known as *dour dero*, "pith" or "vigor of the mistletoe." It was widely believed to be a specific medicine against various complaints, and although it is in fact extremely poisonous, it has been prescribed, in greatly and expertly diluted states, for many serious illnesses. When kept for a time, the leaves and berries turn yellow, and for this reason it is also called "Golden Bough," making it symbolic of both moon and sun. Other writers hint more strongly of its importance as a bringer of good luck and fertility, which probably derives from the resemblance of the berries when crushed to human seed. This almost certainly contributed to the custom we know today of claiming a kiss from someone standing beneath a sprig of mistletoe.

The connection between mistletoe and oak trees (sacred to the Druids) is further born out by two references that appear over widely distant periods of time. The antiquary William Stukley, writing in the seventeenth century, tells that mistletoe was carried to the high altar of York Minster on Christmas Eve, and that from that time onward a "universal liberty" pardon was extended to inferior and even wicked people (i.e. thieves and prostitutes) at the gates of the city. In ancient Rome, a similar amnesty was extended to criminals during the festival of Saturnalia, which was held on the Capitoline Hill, in a temple sacred to Jupiter, god of the oak, thunder and lightning. In Sweden the mistletoe is still known as the "thunder-broom." Placed over doorways and hung from the walls of houses, it protected the occupants from storms.

Loki's Spear

A central part of the mythology of mistletoe is the story of the Norse god Baldur, who one day began to dream of his own death. Learning of this, the elder gods extracted a promise from all of nature that it would never be the cause of harm to Baldur, who was thereafter invulnerable. But one of the plants, the mistletoe, was too young to swear, and when the evil and mischievous Loki became jealous of Baldur (who was a god of light just as Loki was a god of darkness), he looked for a means of destroying him. Eventually he persuaded the blind god Haldur to enter into a spear-throwing contest, and gave him a bough of mistletoe. The branch turned into a spear in mid-air and Baldur fell

dead. This was the cause of great sorrow among the gods and the mistletoe ever after had an evil reputation.

The Silver Branch

Among the Celts mistletoe had a very different function. As well as being sacred to the Druids, the mistletoe bough may also have been seen as a type of "Silver Branch." Frequently referred to in Celtic literature, the branch was generally cut from an apple tree (apples being especially sacred to the Celts) and served both as a means of announcing the presence of a bard in the halls of the Celtic lords, and as a token that offered admittance to the Otherworld. When a tumulus dating from the Bronze Age was investigated in Ireland in 1834, an oak coffin was found containing a skeleton that had been wreathed in mistletoe. This supplies more support for the theory that the plant was seen by the Celts both as a protection for the spirit and as a means of crossing into the Otherworld.

Today mistletoe is often seen among the greenery in churches, though it was proscribed far longer than any other evergreen decoration. Most households include at least a few sprigs in their decorations at Christmas, but for those seeking to celebrate the Solstice in all its powerful symbolic array, it is most appropriate to keep at least some of the bough throughout the year until shortly before the next gathering. At this time the old bough, which has been hanging in the house throughout the year, should be ceremonially burned – perhaps on a Midwinter bonfire, or at Halloween or on Guy Fawkes' Night. After this, the new bough is brought in and solemnly hung up as a token of the continuance of the seasonal round and the joy of human procreation.

The Kissing Bunch

The "kissing bunch" derives much of its potency from the presence of mistletoe, and despite its later Christianization (as in the following anonymous account from nineteenth-century Derbyshire, England) it once had a far more ancient purpose:

> The "kissing bunch" is always an elaborate affair. The size depends upon the couple of hoops – one thrust through the other – which form its skeleton.
>
> Each of the ribs is garlanded with holly, ivy, sprigs of other greens, with bits of coloured ribbons and paper roses, rosy-cheeked apples, specially reserved for this occasion, and oranges.
>
> Three small dolls are also prepared, often with much taste, and these represent our Saviour, the mother of Jesus, and Joseph.
>
> These dolls generally hang within the kissing bunch by strings from the top, and are surrounded by apples, oranges tied to strings, and various brightly coloured ornaments. Occasionally, however, the dolls are arranged in the kissing bunch to represent a manger-scene...
>
> Mistletoe is not very plentiful in Derbyshire; but, generally, a bit is obtainable, and is carefully tied to the bottom of the kissing-bunch, which is then hung in the middle of the house-place, the center of attention during Christmastide.

NOTES & QUERIES. 5TH SERIES. VOL VIII.

RIGHT: Mistletoe forms its own wild decoration every Solstice.

At one time the "dolls" hung amid the greenery would have been very different, representing male and female figures, bound together with colored thread. In parts of Sussex (England) this was still done as recently as the 1950s, and the sight of such a garland, hung from tree branch in the woods rather than in a house, served as an indication that seasonal fertility rites might be taking place.

The antiquity of such practices is born out by a custom that still takes place at the New Year in Austria. Here, a masked figure named Sylvester (from the Latin *sylvan*, meaning "of the woods") hides in the darkest corner of inns around the country. If either a youth or a maiden passes by, the figure leaps out and plants a rough kiss on cheek or lips. Significantly, the figure wears a wreath of mistletoe, which is also hung from roof-tree and window of these hostelries. When midnight comes the Sylvester is driven out to the

accompaniment of raucous shouts and songs, as a representative of the old year. This custom, which is clearly an aspect of the traditions of "guising" (*see Chapter 5*) has a very ancient ring to it. One imagines that at one time the dark figure with hair and beard woven with mistletoe may have done more than offer a kiss, and that he may well have served as a sacrifice for the propitiation of the New Year.

In Australia to this day the Aboriginal people believe that spirit children live in the mistletoe that grows on certain trees and that these are awaiting birth, a further indication of the connection that must have existed over a huge length of time between mistletoe and fertility. In parts of the United States country-folk still go out to "shoot down" the mistletoe, firing rifles into the air as though to somehow alert the spirits of the plant that they are about to take some away.

In parts of Britain up until at least the fifteenth century, the practice was to pluck one of the berries from the kissing bunch each time a kiss was given (or taken!) until there were no more berries left, at which point the practice ceased and the bough was considered spent and barren.

Certainly the long-standing association of mistletoe with fertility has remained in our consciousness, and is echoed in the continuing tradition of kissing under the mistletoe. In recognition of this ancient Solstice tradition you might wish to create your own kissing bunch, woven from strands of ivy, mistletoe, and holly, and hung with figures of your own

ABOVE: Numerous traditions connect the three Solstice plants, holly, ivy, and mistletoe.

devising, or even with corn dolls, which have their own detailed symbolism and can represent both male and female. (Incidentally "ivy girls" are known to have been made at the Solstice in certain parts of the country, a custom well worth reviving.) Hung in the center of the room rather than over the door as is presently more customary, this can become a striking centerpiece of your Winter Solstice celebration.

Holly and Ivy

Deck the Halls with boughs of Holly
Tra la la la la, la la la la!
Tis the Season to be jolly
Tra la la la la, la la la la!

TRADITIONAL CHRISTMAS CAROL

The two other plants that are most often found in our homes at the Solstice time have a less striking history, but a curious rivalry is personified in the well-known traditional Christmas carol, "The Holly and the Ivy" and elsewhere:

The Holly and the Ivy,
When they are both full grown,
Of all that trees that are in the wood
The Holly bears the crown.

The Holly bears a blossom
As white as the lily flower
And Mary bore sweet Jesus Christ
To be our sweet saviour.

The Holly bears a berry,
As red as any blood
And Mary bore sweet Jesus Christ
To do poor sinners good.

The Holly bears a prickle
As sharp as any thorn
And Mary bore sweet Jesus Christ
On Christmas day in the morn.

The Holly bears a bark
As bitter as any gall
And Mary bore sweet Jesus Christ
For to redeem us all.

Here the symbolism borrows clearly enough from Christian tradition, with the holly representing the spiked crown of the Crucifixion, and ivy the pale innocence of the Virgin. The word "holly," in medieval times, was spelt "holi" and the plant was often known by the name "holen," and derived from the Saxon words for "holy." The words wove around each other like the plant itself and doubtless added to the connection. But the tradition goes back much further than this, into the very beginnings of myth and belief in the powers of the elements.

The Holly King and the Ivy Queen

Holly was seen as a male plant, with its bright red berries and sharp prickly leaves, while ivy, clinging and gentler, was perceived as female. Greek myth supplies a reason for this in the story of the girl who danced before the god Dionysus with all the ardor of a flame – only to fall dead at his feet. The god, moved by her passion, placed her spirit into the plant that ever after bore her name, and which clung and embraced everything to which it came close. To this day it is believed to have the power to prevent drunkenness, which is best explained by its association with Dionysus, as god of wine, who was himself torn to pieces and consumed in a Bacchanalian festival that took place at Midwinter.

Traces still remain of a ritual drama in which the Holly King and the Ivy Queen fought or were fought for by two champions. A fifteenth-century carol, with its recurrent refrain, suggests how this may have developed. Here the ranks are drawn up all too clearly, with ivy described as having black berries, and as being cold, weepy, and accompanied by the owl, the bird of ill-omen. Holly is described as being red-nosed and cheerful, with merry men who dance and sing, and is accompanied by the nightingale and the lark.

ABOVE: *The personification of holly as "king" and ivy as "queen" derives from ancient times.*

Holly stands in the hall, fair to behold;
Ivy stands without the door,
  she is full sore a-cold.
Nay, ivy, nay, it shall not be I wis;
Let holly have the mastery,
  as the manner is.

Holly and his merry men,
  they dance and they sing,
Ivy and her maidens,
  they weep and they wring.
Nay, ivy, nay, it shall not be I wis;
Let holly have the mastery,
  as the manner is.

Ivy hath chapped fingers,
  she caught them from the cold,
So might they all have, aye,
  that with ivy hold.
Nay, ivy, nay, it shall not be I wis;
Let holly have the mastery,
  as the manner is.

Holly hath berries as red as any rose,
The forester, the hunter,
  keep them from the does.
Nay, ivy, nay, it shall not be I wis;
Let holly have the mastery,
  as the manner is.

Ivy hath berries, as black as any sloe;
There comes the owl and
  eats them as she go.
Nay, ivy, nay, it shall not be I wis;
Let holly have the mastery,
  as the manner is.

Holly hath birds a fair full flock,
The nightingale, the popinjay,
  the gentle laverock.
Nay, ivy, nay, it shall not be I wis;
Let holly have the mastery,
  as the manner is.

Good ivy what birds hast thou?
None but the owlet, that cries how, how.
Nay, ivy, nay, it shall not be I wis;
Let holly have the mastery,
  as the manner is.

Winter King

Behind this extends an even older group of traditions, surrounding the Green King of Winter and his yearly battle for the hand of the Spring Maiden. This theme extends throughout the literature of the Middle Ages in many forms, with the Green King appearing in the myths of King Arthur and the ballads and songs of Robin Hood. Even the legendary rivalry between the robin and the wren, celebrated in the familiar nursery rhyme "Who Killed Cock Robin?" may refer back to this, since in several traditional rhymes they are identified with the holly (robin) and ivy (wren).

A wonderful modern variation on this theme, written by Mark Vyvyan-Jones, who is himself a member of the Rag Morris team, brings all this to the fore:

The Four Noble Trees

O, the holly bears a berry as white as pure silk,
And the Lady bore the Green Man
*   when the ewes give their milk.*
And the Lady bore the Green Man
*   our first hope for to be,*
And the first Prince of the springtime
It was the birch tree,
Birch tree, birch tree.
And the first Prince of the springtime
It was the birch tree.

O, the birch he bears a leaf-o
*   as green as the moss,*
And the Lady bore the Green Man
*   to dance in the grass,*
And the Lady bore the Green Man
*   that merry we might be.*

And the Princess of the Maytime
Is the young hawthorn tree,
Hawthorn tree, hawthorn tree.
And the Princess of the Maytime
Is the young hawthorn tree.

O, the hawthorn bears a prickle
*   as keen as the sun,*
And the Lady bore the Green Man
*   to die in the corn,*
And the Lady bore the Green Man
*   our harvest for to be,*
And the first Queen of the autumn
Is the old apple tree,
Apple-tree, apple-tree.
And the first Queen of the autumn
Is the old apple tree.

O, the apple bears a fruit-o, as blood it is red,
And the Lady bore the Green Man
*   our last hope for to be,*
And the first King of the winter
He was the holly,
Holly-holly.
And the first King of the winter
He was the holly.

ABOVE: The significance of Winter trees to the Solstice is well-documented.

ABOVE: The prickly leaves and scarlet berries of traditional holly remind us of the crown of thorns worn by Christ at the Crucifixion.

Green King

I ride the white horse of Uffington,
The Green Knight rides at my elbow.
His axe is thirsty for the beheading game.

BILL LEWIS: HILL FIGURES

The Green Man, old as time itself, is another who brings gifts at Midwinter. This figure has undergone an extraordinary transformation over the centuries. Once he was the virtual embodiment of the life force that ran rampant through every green and growing thing. He is celebrated in extraordinary carvings found within medieval churches and abbeys all over Europe. Hidden amid the ridge poles and beams of these stone forests, the Green Man looks down on the congregations below with sly and sardonic humor. His presence within the hallowed precincts of these buildings is a testimony to his eternal continuity, which links the distant past with the present in a way that no one who has ever taken a walk in the country can fail to observe.

Today, indeed, the Green Man is recognized as a kind of patron of the ecological movement, a representative of the ancient rhythms of the natural world when humans and animals alike lived in harmony with the rest of creation. The dislocation that exists today between the species began in the Middle Ages, and it is perhaps no surprise to find the spirit of Winter represented in a fourteenth-century poem as offering to play a terrible Midwinter game with all who would oppose the power of the ancient Solstice. The scenario is set in Camelot, King Arthur's marvelous court, where the king would not dine until he had seen a wonder. The wonder that turned up was perhaps more than he bargained for, however.

This King Arthur was at Camelot at Christmas with many a lovely lord, and they were all princely brethren of the Round Table, and they made rich revel and mirth and were free from care. And betimes these gentle knights held many a tournament, and jousted in jolly fashion, and then returned they to the court to sing the Christmas carols...Scarcely had... the first course been served in the court, when there came in at the door an ugly fellow and the tallest of all men on earth. From his neck to his loins so square set was he, and so long and stalwart of limb, that I trow he was half a giant. And yet he was a man, and the merriest that might ride...

Great wonder of the knight,
Folk had in hall, I ween,
Full fierce he was to sight,
And over all bright green...

Thus gaily was this man dressed out in green, and the hair of his horse's head was green, and his fair, flowing locks clung about his shoulders, and a great beard like a bush hung over his breast, and with his hair was cut evenly all round above his elbows ... And he had no helmet nor hauberk, nor was he armour-plated, nor had he shield or spear with which to smite; but in one hand he held a holly branch, that is most green when the groves are all bare, and in the other he held an axe, huge and uncanny, and a sharp weapon was it to describe whoso might wish...

SIR GAWAIN AND THE GREEN KNIGHT.
ANON. 14TH CENTURY.

This character does more than usher in the cold breath of Winter to the halls of Camelot; he brings a challenge to all who would deny the power of the ancient Solstice rites. In the ritual contest that follows, an exchange of blows takes place, between the Green Knight and Arthur's nephew Gawain. But, when Gawain strikes a blow that severs the stranger's head, the Green Knight is able to retrieve the grisly object and to remind Gawain of the return blow still to come!

Again, the theme here is one of dismemberment followed by restoration, the death of the old year and the birth of the new, and the Green Knight carries a bough of holly as a token of his true nature.

LEFT: The spirit of the Green Man is symbolic of the emergence from the death of Winter to the birth of new life in Spring.

ABOVE: The opposing forces of Winter and Summer are represented in the struggle between Robin Hood and the Sheriff of Nottingham for the hand of the Spring Maiden, Maid Marion.

Robin in the Green

This story's origins derive from the even older, Irish tale called "Bricriu's Feast," where three heroes of Ulster are challenged by the fearsome giant Cu Roi mac Daire, to a similar beheading game. Only the great solar hero Cu Culaine has the courage to accept the proffered blow, proving that he was the bravest of the three and suggesting that at one time he too featured in a struggle between the champions of Summer and Winter.

In the Robin Hood ballads we find the same scenario worked out as Robin, the Green King of Sherwood, struggles against a polar opposite, personified by the Sheriff of Nottingham, or Guy of Guisborne, for the hand of the Spring Maiden, Marion. This was played out every year in various parts of the country. In South Wales there is a long standing tradition of a ceremony that is vividly described in this nineteenth-century account:

Two companies of men and youths were formed. One had for its captain a man dressed in a long coat much trimmed with fur, and on his head a rough fur cap. He carried a stout stick of holly and a kind of shield, on which were studded tufts of wool to represent snow. His companions wore caps and waistcoats of fur decorated with balls of white wool. These men were very bold, and in songs and verse proclaimed the virtues of Winter, who was their captain. The other company had for its leader a captain representing Summer. This man was dressed in a kind of white smock decorated with garlands of flowers and gay ribbons. On his head he wore a broad brimmed hat trimmed with flowers and ribbons. In his hand he carried a willow wand wreathed with spring flowers

and tied with ribbons. All these men marched in procession, with their captain on horseback heading them, to an appropriate place. This would be on some stretch of common or wasteland. There a mock encounter took place, the Winter company flinging straw and dry underwood at their opponents, who used as their weapons birch branches, willow-wands, and young ferns. A good deal of horse-play went on, but finally Summer gained the mastery over Winter.

MARIE TREVELYAN:
FOLK-LORE AND FOLK-STORIES OF WALES

The symbolism is clear enough here, the age-old struggle between the opposing forces of Summer and Winter, between Dark and Light, continue to ensure the restoration of the New Year. A ceremony, based on this tradition, combined with elements from the Robin Hood myths, will be found at the end of this book. It is intended to be performed over the Solstice by a small group, who thus enact the age-old myth of the dying and rising god.

ABOVE: Robin in the Green, or Robin Hood, may be a further reworking of the mythical Green Man figure.

Bringing in the Yule

A central part of the interplay between darkness and light, the natural and the human worlds, which is so central to the celebration of Midwinter, is the burning of the Yule Log. The origins of this ceremony are vague, though they probably spring from the Norse celebration of Midwinter which, like the Roman Saturnalia, lasted for around two weeks. The actual season was reckoned to last from mid-November to the end of January, more in keeping with the Celtic Wintertide, which extended from Samhain on November 1st to Imbolc on February 1st. Similarly until Vatican II, in the Christian calendar the liturgical Christmas season ended at Candlemas, on February 2nd, showing how consistently the period of the Winter Solstice was celebrated.

The word *yule* has been variously interpreted as deriving from the Saxon word *hweol*, wheel, referring in this context both to the circling of the year and the circular motion of the sun. A more distinctive meaning here may be to the wheels of the Norse god Odin's chariot, in which he sped through the air in search of the souls of recently dead heroes. One of the many names born by Odin was Jolnir, which is etymologically associated with Yule, and there is no lack of evidence to suggest that the Midwinter festival among the peoples of the North (and later in England) included some kind of sacrifice to the god. At one time this festival may have included human sacrifice, but in the records that have survived it seems to have been a time when cattle were slaughtered in large numbers. The early Christian historian, the Venerable Bede, referred to November as *Blotmonath* (Blood Month) because of this.

The word *yule* can also mean "a loud shout," which may be linked to the custom,

ABOVE: In the depths of Winter, the symbolic burning of the Yule Log reminds of the importance of fire and light.

still practiced in Yorkshire until the middle of the seventeenth century, of shouting "Yole" in church at the end of the Christmas Day service. This was perhaps less in celebration of "Yule" than as a warding off of the god and as part of a distant memory of the ancient Teutonic Solstitial festivals once celebrated in Britain and gradually absorbed into the more general Christmas celebrations.

The Yule Log itself is above all a reminder of the importance of fire in the depth of the cold and darkness of Midwinter. Throughout Europe and the United States the tradition continued until recent times (indeed it is by no means dead today). Accounts of the traditions surrounding the cutting, bringing in, and kindling of the log are plentiful, as in the following account by the Provençal poet Frederic Mistral, who describes how, on

Christmas Eve during his childhood (toward the end of the eighteenth century), his whole family went forth to fetch the log, which had to be cut from a fruit tree in token of the fertility of the next year in the land:

Walking in line we bore it home, headed by the oldest at one end and I, the last born, bringing up the rear. Three times we made the tour of the kitchen, then, arrived at the flagstones of the hearth, my father solemnly poured over the log a glass of wine, with the dedicatory words:

Joy! Joy! May God shower joy upon us, my dear children. Christmas brings us all good things. God give us grace to see the New Year, and if we do not increase in numbers may we at all events not decrease.

In chorus we responded: "Joy, joy, joy!" and lifted the log on the fire dogs. Then as the first flame leapt up my father would cross himself, saying, "Burn the log, O fire," and with that we all sat down at the table.

MEMOIRS OF MISTRAL,
TRANS. C.E. MAUD, LONDON, 1907

ABOVE: The word Yule *may be derived from the alternative name for the Norse god Odin: Jolnir.*

The Christmas Brand

C. S. Burne, writing in *Shropshire Folklore* (1883), records how the "Christmas Brand" was drawn by horses to the farmhouse door and placed at the back of the wide open hearth, where the flame was made up in front of it.

The embers... were raked up every night,
and it was carefully tended that it might not
go out during the whole season, during
which time no light might either
be struck, given, or borrowed.

Here, as in all the great Solstice festivals, the celebration was of the turning wheel of the year, and the log must not be allowed to burn through, but a fragment preserved that would then be used to kindle the next year's fire, thus bridging the gap between the old and the New Year. The importance of keeping the fire alight, and of passing its flame from one year to the next is a very ancient one, dating back to a time when to keep one's fire burning might meant the difference between life and death. Small wonder if the ancient peoples of Europe and the northern lands placed such importance on this action, which was both symbolic of the eternal nature of fire and the sun, and a reminder that life itself depended on its continuance.

Thus the great medieval English poet Robert Herrick remembers in a famous poem:

Kindle the Christmas brand, and then
Till sunne-set let it burn;
Which quencht, then lay it up agen
Till Christmas next returne.

Part must be kept wherewith to tend
The Christmas log next year;
And where 'tis safely kept, the Fiend
Can do no mischief there.

It is interesting to see that in many parts of Scandinavia St. Nicholas or his helpers carry the ashes of the Yule Log, seen as a source of fertility in many parts of the world. Again it would seem to reflect the shamanistic nature of the Christmas gift-bringer, as well as emphasizing the continuity of the Solstice.

ABOVE: The ritual bringing-in of a Yule Log may well represent the hopes of fertility for the coming year.

ABOVE: The figure of the Winter King appears in a great number of medieval myths and stories.

ABOVE: St. Lucy's Day in Sweden coincides with Little Yule Day, and represents the start of the Midwinter festival.

The Freedom of the Yule

In the United States in the 1800s the Yule Log attained its own particular importance in the Old South, where it was tied in with the laws relating to slaves. Contracts between master and slave often specified a period of seven days' rest around the time of Christmas, and in some areas this was extended to the time it took for the log to burn – for which reason the slaves would soak the log in water to ensure that it kept burning for longer! Any water-logged tree trunk was known as "having as much water as a Christmas Log." This was a time for celebration and dancing, despite, or even because of, the privations that obtained throughout the rest of the year.

William Sunson, in his *A Book of Christmas*, describes the traditional Southern Christmas as "a scene of familiar amplitude and splendor, of old green sheen and brown-basted

foods, of wild turkeys and sweet potatoes and sucking pigs and hams and all the gracious delights of a near aristocratic table, in country of hickory and pine and holly, magnolia and mistletoe." Throughout Virginia the log received libations of wine rather than water and dry holly was thrown onto it, which burned with a crackle, carrying off the troubles of the old year in preparation for the blessings to come.

Little Yule

In Sweden the Midwinter festival begins on December 13th, which is referred to as "Little Yule." This also happened to be St. Lucia's Day, and since at least the twelfth century this day has been celebrated by the choosing of a "Queen Lucy" from among the young women of the villages throughout Sweden. Dressed in white and with a crown of lighted candles on her head, the Lucia sets forth through the dark led by a mounted man and a group of maidens and "star-boys," who are said to represent the demons and trolls conquered by the newly risen sun. Queen Lucy visits houses to bring blessings and prosperity for the New Year. In some more isolated dwellings the youngest daughter of the house will assume the role of Lucia for her family and circulate through the house wearing her candle crown, accompanied by carols and songs. This is followed by a breakfast celebrated in a room illuminated by dozens of candles – yet another indication of the eternal importance of light at this time.

In the northern lands in particular a great "Yule Candle" resembling the Pascal flame of the Christian Easter is lit on the morning of Christmas by the oldest member of the household and allowed to burn throughout the day. Sometimes the same candle will be rekindled every day of the festival (usually until Twelfth

Night). An ancient stone candle sconce, traditionally used to hold the Yule candle during the late Middle Ages, can still be seen in St. John's College, Oxford, though it is no longer used. In the eighteenth century, chandlers in Ripon, Yorkshire, sent their customers large candles, and the coopers sent logs of wood. The antiquary R. T. Hampson, writing in 1841, says:

> In some places candles are made of
> a particular kind, because the candle lighted
> on Christmas Day must be
> so large as to burn from the time
> of its ignition to the close of the
> day, otherwise it will portend evil
> to the family for the ensuing year.
>
> The poor were wont to present
> the rich with wax tapers, and
> Yule candles are still in the
> North of Scotland given by
> merchants to their customers.
>
> At one time children in the village
> schools in Lancashire
> were required to bring
> each a mould candle before...
> the Christmas holidays.

MEDII AEVI KALENDARIUM,
LONDON, 1841

In our own time, as recently as 1926, houses in Campden Hill Square in London renewed the ancient custom of placing lighted candles in every window in the house on Christmas Eve as a memorial to the magical significance of the season. By placing candles in our own windows (even if they are electric!), we not only remember the older practice but show that we welcome the Midwinter spirits of the season – be they the Christ Child, Mithras, or the Green Man.

It is from this practice that the idea of putting lighted candles on a Christmas fir tree probably derives. However, there is a legend that tells of the spiritual revolutionary Martin Luther who, after walking out one Christmas Eve beneath the stars, returned home with a young fir tree, which he set up and decorated with candles to remind his children how Christ had so gloriously brightened the Winter sky on this night of nights.

ABOVE: The Christmas tree transports the energy of the green, natural world into the house and brings with it good fortune.

CELEBRATION

As a means of celebrating the ancient tradition of Yule, a large candle can still be made or purchased and lit with ceremony either on Christmas Eve or on the day itself. This may then be circulated throughout the house before being ensconced either on the dinner table or in the hearth. It might also be found meaningful to observe the hours of the candle's burning throughout the day, pausing in your activities for a brief meditation or invocation to the spirits of Midwinter. If it is centrally set near the hearth, then it may act as a reminder of the sacred dimension of the Solstice. Even this simple act can bring the whole season into focus in a direct way and enable us to connect with the ancestral celebrations of earlier times.

THE YULE LOG

The kindling of the Yule Log remains one of the longest lasting of the ancient traditions of the Solstice and acts as a counterbalance to the Midwinter bonfires that are still lit in most parts of the world. The fact that it has begun to die out in cities and towns is the result of a comparative lack of fireplaces. If you are lucky enough to be blessed with one of these, the Yule Log remains a powerful means of celebrating the ancient Midwinter feast. There follows a ceremony which is designed to include many of the Yule customs but in a contemporary setting that nonetheless looks back to more ancient times.

A YULE LOG CEREMONY

The brief ceremony that follows incorporates many of the most ancient traditions that have centered around the Yule Log. It is assumed that you possess an open fireplace that is still in daily use, but even if you have one that is no longer used, you can still do most of the following ceremony, omitting only the actual burning of the log, and replacing this by setting a circle of candles around it in token of the sacred fire. In the former Yugoslavia, as recently as the first half of this century, ceremonies similar to those described here still took place to celebrate the Midwinter fire and invoke a positive future for the household.

RIGHT: Burn your Yule Log in an open fireplace; if you don't have one, candles can be lit as a token of the Yule fire.

PREPARING A YULE LOG

1. First select the log you are going to burn. This can be anything from a small branch, cut to a suitable length, to a larger piece of trunk.

2. Generally this should be sufficient to fit safely within the hearth, and large enough to burn for perhaps an hour every day from Christmas Eve to Twelfth Night.

3. When selecting your Yule Log remember that you should refrain from cutting down a living tree, but instead take what you need from a fallen trunk or branch, enough for your needs and no more.

4. If you are managing your trees in October or November (a good time to lop or prune them), you may be able to set aside a log of suitable size ready for your Yule Log.

5. I always make a point of thanking the spirit of the tree before I begin chopping or sawing — this brief memorial serves to insure that the log will burn brightly and bring the energy of the green world to the house.

6. In some instances a specific tree is selected during the course of the year, rather as a fir tree may be selected to adorn the house. In this instance the tree may well be blessed and thanked several times leading up to the day on which it is to be cut. It may also be decorated.

In Celtic literature there is a whole lore of sacred trees. This is wonderfully celebrated in the following text, which advises against burning certain trees and encourages the burning of others:

The pliant woodbine if thou burn, wailings for
misfortune will abound...
burn not the precious apple tree
of spreading and low-sweeping boughs...
the surley blackthorn is a wanderer,
a wood the artificer burns not...

The noble willow burn not,
a tree sacred to poems...

The graceful tree with the berries,
the wizard's tree, the rowan, burn;
but spare the limber tree,
burn not the slender hazel...

Fiercest heat-giver of
all timber is green oak...
holly, burn it green holly, burn it dry;
of all trees whatsoever the best is holly.

FROM THE DEATH OF FERGUS MAC LEIDE
TRANS. T.P. CROSS AND C.H. SLOVER

Whichever tree you decide to use, once you have selected it, gather together with friends and family to dress the tree ceremonially with red ribbons, ivy strands, and seasonal blossoms. Then, as twilight falls on the Eve of Christmas, solemnly bring the log into the house. As you cross the threshold have someone scatter some grain or a few drops of wine or water onto the log, and welcome it to the house as though it were a friend:

Welcome Log, welcome,
Bring your blessings to this house
And all who dwell herein.
Welcome log, welcome!

Carry the log three times around the room in which it is to be lit, and have the oldest member of the family place it in the hearth, kindling it with some appropriate words, such as:

I kindle this Midwinter fire
In the name of the Ancestors,
And of the Holy Ones
Who guard the world;
May its flame warm us all
And may its light remind us
Of the ever-returning sun.

To which everyone adds:

Burn the Log, O fire!

You may wish to burn aromatic herbs or resinous leaves, such as fir, juniper, or sage. Then, as you sit down to dinner, set the Yule Candle alight (see page 104) and place it at the center of the table. The Yule Log should be kept burning throughout the night and the following day (Christmas Day), after which it should be burned again for a short time (about an hour, depending on the size of the log) every day until Twelfth Night. At the end of this time remember to keep a small piece of the log so that it may be used as kindling next year.

Traditionally this fragment of the Yule Log is a very lucky object and should be kept safely somewhere where it will not be burned accidentally, and from where it can radiate luck outward to the home and family who live there. If you happen to move in the ensuing year, be sure to take the remains of the log with you and set it first in the hearth of your new house, or if you no longer have a fireplace, then preserve the fragment of the Yule Log and place a circle of candles around it on Christmas Eve and every night thereafter until Twelfth Night ends.

ABOVE: Christmas trees should be honored and respected and thanks given for the protection and energy which they give us.

THE WISHING TREE

1. If you cannot go outside, have no garden, or live in an apartment, you can still bring in the green bough to your home. Find an evergreen tree in the countryside and carefully take one of the smaller branches. Cut it with a small saw, cleanly. Don't just break it off and leave the tree open to infection.

2. Now bring your branch home and set in a pot of soil or, if it is a very small one, you can set it in a florist's block – a kind of light green polystyrene brick into which stalks can be put for floral decorations. You could partially spray-paint it with a frosting of silver or gold paint if you wish.

3. Now you need to create some labels. If you have a family, your children could make some leaf-shapes from green sugar paper.

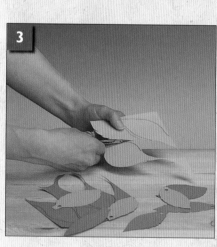

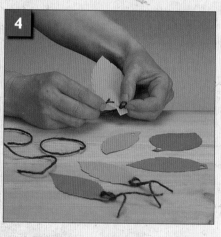

4. Punch a hole in each of the leaf-labels and attach a tie of thin green string.

5. When you have guests, invite each of them to write their wishes on a label. These might be something that has been their heart's desire for some time, or else their wishes for the world.

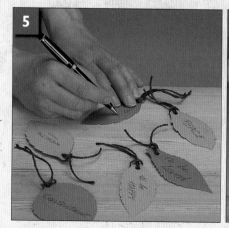

6. Attach the labels to the tree, invoking the power of the evergreen to realize your wishes.

HONORING THE EVERGREEN

All of these customs hark back to a time when the evergreen was clearly recognized as representing the promise of renewed fertility, just as the fires that accompanied them, either as bonfires, candles, or the burning of the Yule Log, promised the return of the sun. Remember these things when you decorate your own evergreen fir tree or its equivalent, and set candles all about it. Do these things with intent and find words to invoke and celebrate the symbolism of the tree, as protector, as messenger of the flowering of the New Year, and as a bringer of good fortune to the house and all who dwell therein.

Perhaps you might seek out a thorn or other plant not normally given to flowering at Midwinter and set this in a pot of soil or wet sand, encouraging it to bud or flower on or near the time of the Solstice. Above all, dedicate your home by decorating it with as much greenery as possible, bringing the essence of the natural world inside, celebrating the long darkness of Midwinter and its eventual yielding to the longer and warmer days of Spring.

Gather around the tree to sing songs and tell stories and their seasonal riddles. Make your home a temple to greenness and growing things (always remembering to take these things only with permission from indwelling spirits and to give thanks even if your greenery is bought from a store). To sit in a room, lit only with fire and candlelight, to see the flames reflected in the glossy surfaces of the leaves of holly, ivy or laurel, is to be in a magical place, where the dreams of our ancestors, and the magical reality of the Solstice, come alive in ways we can scarcely imagine if we do no more than erect a dead tinsel tree hung with lifeless baubles and electric lights. The natural way may take a little more effort, but the rewards are far greater!

ON TWELFTH NIGHT

Finally, tradition speaks of the importance of taking down all decorations by the end of the Solstice period – usually by Twelfth Night. This seems self-explanatory: the season is the season, and ends when it ends and not before. The mounds of dead and dying evergreens left out in gardens and on garbage dumps as early as December 27th demonstrate how little this is still observed. Yet if the season is to be properly celebrated, it seems wrong to dispose of the greenery that has brought its good energy into the house so perfunctorily. Therefore, when you have finished the cycle of celebration outlined in this book, make your final action a ceremony of taking down and disposing of the greenery in a thoughtful manner.

In most places arrangements can be made to recycle old Christmas trees, or you can even plant them in the yard, along with some other leftover evergreens. I have personally derived great pleasure from watching a seemingly spent fir tree put out fresh greenery throughout the Spring months, and return, as bright as ever it was, to the house at the next Winter tide. As each branch or garland comes down, place them with reverence in their boxes, even saying aloud: "Thank you for adding your luster to my home in this magical season." Such small ceremonies insure that we really do appreciate the magical quality of the Solstice tide.

RIGHT: Leftover evergreens can be planted outside in the yard to return at the next Solstice tide.

FOLLOWING PAGES: The evergreen holds the promise of renewal in the depths of Winter.

Chapter 4

OLD SIR CHRISTMAS

England was Merry England, when
Old Christmas brought his sports again.
'Twas Christmas broach'd the mightiest ale
'Twas Christmas told the merriest tale;
A Christmas gambol oft could cheer
The poor man's heart through half the year.

SIR WALTER SCOTT: MARMION

We all know him of course – the "jolly old elf" of Clement C. Moore's poem, "The Night Before Christmas," the man in the red suit with the white beard who drives a sleigh pulled by flying reindeer, and who comes down our chimneys on Christmas night to bring gifts to children who have been good. But, do we really know him? Do we really know his true origins, or his original purpose?

LEFT: The traditional figure of the
"jolly old man" has a fascinating, often
complex history that few people know.

The Birth of Santa Claus

His story is a complex one. Many will know that *Santa* means saint, and is of modern usage. Others will tell us that the nearest point of origin for Santa Claus – in time, anyway – is St. Nicholas of Patara, a third-century Bishop of Myra, near the present-day village of Demre in Asia Minor. Born in Turkey to a wealthy family around A.D. 270 he became well known for his anonymous gifts to the poor. Tradition has it that he left these offerings in the houses of selected recipients, sneaking in during the night to leave money or food in the shoes or stockings of children – though it is doubtful whether they would have worn either in that hot land, assuming they could afford such luxuries anyway. However, such is the tradition, and it is from this that we derive the custom of hanging stockings by the fireplace, while in various countries such as Austria, Germany, Switzerland, Belgium, and Holland, December 6th, St. Nicholas's official day, is also Children's Day, and is considered just as important as Christmas Day itself. In fact, it is only in comparatively recent times that we have conflated the two dates – the 6th and the 25th – making the latter a general festival for the exchanging of gifts.

Good Old Saint Nick

If we go back to the Middle Ages, about 1,200 years after St. Nicholas actually lived, we can see how this might have begun. In the words of Naogeorgus, the author of the Latin *Vita Sant Nicolai (Life of St. Nicholas)*:

The mothers all their children
on the eve do cause to fast,
And when they every one
at night in sense sleep are cast,
Both apples, nuts,
and prayers they bring,
and other things beside,
As caps, and shoes, and petticoats.
with kirtles they hide,
And in the morning found,
they say: "St. Nicholas
this brought."

ABOVE: *The figure that we know today as Santa Claus has undergone many transformations through the ages to reach his present incarnation.*

This has most of the ideas that we associate with the figure of Santa Claus, but there is another, stranger story told of St. Nicholas, which actually points the way to his true origin far more clearly:

An Asiatic gentleman, sending his two sons to Athens for education, ordered them to wait on the bishop for his benediction. On arriving at Myra with their baggage, they took up their lodgings at an inn, proposing to defer their visit till the morrow; but, in the meantime, the innkeeper, to secure their effects to himself, killed the young gentlemen, cut them into pieces, salted them, and intended to sell them for pickled pork. St. Nicholas, being favoured with a sight of their proceedings in a vision, went to the inn, and reproached the landlord with the crime, who, immediately confessing it, entreated the saint to pray to heaven for his pardon. The bishop, moved by his confession and contrition, besought forgiveness for him, and supplicated restoration of life to the children. Scarcely had he finished, when the pieces reunited, and the resuscitated youths threw themselves from the brine tub at the feet of the bishop; he raised them up, blessed them, and sent them to Athens, with great joy to prosecute their studies.

A.T. HAMPSON: POPULAR CUSTOMS AND SUPERSTITIONS OF THE MIDDLE AGES.

On one level this story may be regarded as nothing more than a pious anecdote illustrating the sanctity and goodness of the saint. But there is more to it than that. The notion of a person being dismembered and put back together, as portrayed in this tale, again derives from a far older time, and when it is placed in conjunction with certain other factors, a surprising new image begins to appear that has all the characteristics of the traditional Santa without any of its later overtones of bishops and Christianity.

ABOVE: The restoration of the dismembered youths by St. Nicholas carries an echo of more ancient traditions.

The Gift Givers

In comes I, Old Father Christmas.
Welcome – or welcome not,
I hope Old Father Christmas
Will never be forgot.

THE LONGPARISH MUMMERS' PLAY

Santa Claus is really only the latest of many figures which have come to be associated with bringing gifts on the night of December 25th. In France presents are given on New Year's Day and called *entrennes*, a name that can be traced back to the *strenae*, green branches, exchanged between people at the Roman feast of the goddess Strenia. In Sicily it is an old woman named Strina who brings gifts at Christmas, continuing a tradition that began in the days of the Roman Empire.

The figure who stands behind the jolly old man of Christmas is older even than this, however. In fact, his story takes us back to the beginning of recorded history, when some other characters climbed up trees of a different kind, and returned with gifts for everyone. These were not toys or perfume or watches, but messages concerning the year to come, or the turning of the seasons, or the fate of the world. These people were the shamans, who performed the functions of priest, historian and record keeper, scientist, and magician. Of course there were shamans all over the world, and in most cases they performed the same or similar functions, but, for obvious reasons, it is those who originated in the far North – anywhere from Lapland to Siberia – that interest us most in this context. It is these people who often wore bells on their ritual costumes, who shinned up the central poles of their skin tents, and who returned with the gifts of prophecy and wonder from the Otherworlds. It is to these

LEFT: *Putting one finger to the side of your nose is an ancient Celtic signal of shamanic "knowledge."*

people that we have to look for the first appearance of the figure who, thousands of years later, evolved into the jolly old man of Christmas himself, Santa Claus.

If we look for a moment at some of those similarities we can catch a glimpse of the evolution of one into the other. If we dip our hands into Santa's sack – so like the shaman's bag of tricks – the first thing we find are the bells that jingle on the harness of the eight magical reindeer. Contemporary accounts of northern shamans, including those of the Altaic and Buryat regions of Siberia and those of the Finns and Laplanders, again and again emphasize the importance of bells in their traditional costumes. These form a double function; as noise-makers to announce the presence of the shaman as he enters the spirit world, and to frighten off any unfriendly spirits who might be lying in wait for him. In addition, iron disks representing the sun or curved in the shape of the moon represent the importance of solar and lunar rites among these Northern people – an important point in our consideration of the Solstice itself.

Red Robes and Firelight

Reaching into the sack again we find a red robe or cloak, trimmed with white. Many authorities on shamanic tradition have commented on the importance of the color red in the shaman's costume. This is, on one level, significant of the sacred blood that links all human beings and that is also perceived as a link between humans and animals, and between the shaman and the earth. It is also, of course, a symbol of fire, that most powerful of magical weapons, as well as the gift of warmth and life to all, especially significant in such cold lands as those we are considering here.

Next in the sack we find a burning brand that signifies the eternal light and the warmth without which all life would perish. The shamans possessed this gift of fire, which initially perhaps they alone had the power to kindle (the number of flint fire-lighters found among shamans' bundles alone is enough to suggest this) and which was a gift they brought to the tribal people they served. It was believed that these gifts were entrusted to them for the people by the gods and spirits of the land. Here, the symbolism of red fire in the white desert of Winter is a vital image. Is it stretching the point too far to see an echo of this in the red and white costume and white beard of a certain other figure? Certainly the importance of these colors throughout the northern world is beyond question.

Dipping into the sack again we find reindeer with bells on their harnesses, who can fly through the sky and cover vast distances in no time at all. This is yet another echo of the shaman's journey into and through the heavens, in search of the gifts of fire and prophecy. In addition, there is the obvious importance of reindeer to the people of

ABOVE: The shaman's drum and bells are recalled by Santa's jangling reindeer harness.

Lapland and Siberia is obvious. To these people the reindeer not only provided a source of food but also skins for clothing and tents, sinews for thread, bones for needles, and, when rendered down, fat for rush lights and glue to mend pots and fix spearheads in place.

So Santa is an old man dressed in red who comes out of the dark forest of the North on a sleigh pulled by reindeer. It is significant then that the shamans hunted the reindeer, ran with them in spirit form, drew their shapes on rocks with red ochre as a means of capturing them, even saw them as a symbol of the newly born sun of Midwinter. A wonderful modern poem speaks of the hunting of spirit deer, who, impervious to the hunter's arrows, were a symbolic reference point for hunting the real creatures:

> *A red deer comes over the hill,*
> *Shoot your arrows as you will,*
> *The deer will stand there still!*

ALISON MCLEAY: SOLSTICE

The Shaman in the Tree

Consider the image of the shaman climbing down through the smoke hole of a skin tent with bells jingling, bearing in his hands a red painted wooden reindeer. The shamans saw to it that the sun returned from that point when, at the very edge of the horizon, it dipped and, for a moment, was gone. Then, summoned by the ancient language of the elements, it returned. Sun images were hung on a tree, that also formed the central pole of the tent and represented the axis of the world, the connection which leads to the heavens the final destination of the shaman who was, indeed, the midwife of the sun.

Imagine some of the questions asked of the shaman. As Alison Mcleay put it in her wonderful evocation of the Solstice in a radio broadcast she made in 1985:

Shaman, will the sun be reborn? Will we have a good harvest? Will we catch enough fish, will there be enough meat to eat, will the reindeer drop enough offspring to keep us through another year?

What will the new year bring for us, for me? Tell us, shaman, make your journey and bring us the gifts of your seeing!

You are the bringer of gifts, the protector, the magician, the future is yours to see, the sack on your back carries the gifts of the future and the past – tell, us shaman, tell us.

Sacrifices were hung on the living tree: animals, birds, perhaps once even humans, such as Odin hanging on the windy tree of Yggdrasil to bring back the gifts of the runes. Odin's eight-legged horse Sleipnyr may also be linked with Santa's sleigh and its eight reindeer. And that song – next out of the sack:

O the rising of the sun, and the running of the deer, The playing of the merry organ, sweet singing in the choir

THE HOLLY AND THE IVY

BELOW: Shamans were believed to be able to call back the disappeared sun.

These are old images, stolen by a later time, and reflect two aspects married under the Solstice tree: the running deer who were the totem creatures of many different Northern tribal groups, and the singing of carols in the stone forests of the Christian world. The old ways were not wholly forgotten, not even after the coming of the Christ child, who brought the gifts of light and eternal life to the world, and who received gifts from the wandering wise men – the Magi of biblical and pre-biblical tradition. They too contribute to the image of Santa the gift bringer, and, as we have seen, there is more to them than meets the eye.

ABOVE: Santa's reindeer take him on an archetypal shamanic journey to the heavens.

Solstice Evergreen

As we saw in Chapter 3, the other eternal icon, the Solstice evergreen, is itself a reminder of the life that never dies, and continues even when the sun is at its lowest ebb. It is this tree that the shaman climbs to get through the smoke hole into the bright heavens, where the spirits wait to take him on a journey to find the gifts of the subtle realms – the gift of fire, the gift of life, and the gift of the newborn sun itself. The Christmas tree is a cosmic tree, an axial pole connecting heaven and earth. As that marvelous chronicler of the heavenly mythologies, E.C. Krupp, put it:

> *If a cosmic tree points the way to heaven for us every Christmas, Santa Claus undertakes the magical flight of the shaman. He is sometimes said to be responsible for erecting the Christmas tree sky pole himself. Descending vertically down the chimney Santa returns by the same route back to the roof. Our chimneys, like the cosmic axis, carry him from on realm to the other...*

KRUPP: BEYOND THE BLUE HORIZON

Gift Giving

Even the giving of gifts can be a ceremony all of its own. In Sweden and Germany a tradition still retained until recently was the *Julknapp*, a gift wrapped in layers of paper or cloth. The person bringing the gift would knock at the door and, when it was opened, fling the package into the house before running off. This was sometimes used as a means of making a marriage proposal, or declaration of love, in which case a golden heart or a letter was hidden within. One can imagine the shaman doling out gifts in this way, packages containing surprises both pleasant and unpleasant according to the nature of their vision.

In the United States, the Native American peoples of the Northwest have their own tradition of gift giving – the *Potlatch* or "Give-Away" in which people bring gifts to a ceremonial gathering and vie with each other in friendly rivalry as to who can give away the most precious things. This custom caught on among the European settlers of the 1800s and is still widely practiced today, the word "potlatch" having entered everyday vocabulary.

The Sooty Boys

Christmas comes but once year,
When it comes it brings good cheer;
With a pocket full of money
And a cellar full of beer.

THE LONGPARISH MUMMERS' PLAY

From the time when Bishop Nicholas began to be seen as a gift giver and miracle worker, things moved on fairly briskly. The figure of the gray-bearded, robed and mitred figure of "Sinta Klass" became established in Germany first, and his own feast day was soon subsumed by the larger festival of Christmas itself. But some rather curious figures accompanied this aspect of St. Nicholas on his journey through the towns and villages of Germany. Who, for example, are Perchta and Berchta, who follow in his train wearing hideous masks and distributing fruit and nuts to the good children, and scaring the bad with cries and screeches? Or who are the straw clad "ghosts of the field" who go before the saint carrying whips and flails to clear the way? We don't have to look too far to see echoes here of older, pagan beings, gods and goddesses or spirits of the forest such as those once sought by the shamans of the North.

In fact the saint's party is made up of all kinds of strange figures depending on where you are. In Germany there is the Klaubauf, a frightening being with fiery eyes and a long red tongue who carries clanking chains not unlike those carried by the ghost of Jacob Marley in Dickens' *A Christmas Carol*. In Lower Austria there is the Krampus, who also carries a chain; in Styria he is called the Bartel; in Swabia the accomplice is female and named the Budelfrau; while in Augsburg she is called Buzebergt.

But by far the most interesting figure is the German Knecht Ruprecht. Roughly dressed in skins and straw, he is considered a *ru-klas* or "Rough Nicholas," riding or capering before the saint, who is usually mounted on a white horse called the Schimmel. He is very much like the old shaman figures we looked at, carrying a bag of ashes from the Yule Log and hung around with bells and chains. As with many of these attendant figures, he has a dark and a light side, doling out both gifts and blows depending on how he perceives your track record for the past year!

Another of Santa's helpers is the German Pelznickel or "Fur Nicholas" who, despite his name, is actually the saint's servant. He wears old fur clothes, has a white beard and distributes toys – perhaps an attempt from long ago to separate the figures of the saint and the more secular Father Christmas. Like many of the others mentioned here, he also carries a rod to punish evil-doers, and the cry "Look out, he'll get you!" can often be heard preceding his coming.

In Britain, the figure of Father Christmas makes an appearance in the ancient Mummers' plays that date back at least as far as medieval times. There are suggestions here of an older and more heavyweight role, perhaps as a defender of Christmas against the darker characters such as Beelzebub or The Turkish Knight – a hang-over from the Crusades when Turks were the bugbears of the western, militantly Christian nations. *(See also Chapter 5.)*

ABOVE: This Russian image of St. Nicholas
recalls more ancient figures.

In Holland this aspect – Santa as challenger – is upheld by the tradition that has the saint visiting houses and holding a riddling exchange with the people within, somewhat like the more primitive and terrifying Mari Llwyd of Wales, in which a horse skull is born around the town and an age-old exchange of riddles must be made before the strange creature can be admitted.

There is something wonderfully ancient and primeval about this, and we shall meet this character again in Chapter 5. The challenger comes to the door and asks to be admitted, but only when the right questions have been asked and answered, in an ancient ritual pattern, can the Mari gain entrance – and this is usually to the accompaniment of much ribaldry and horseplay and followed by good-natured singing, eating, and drinking.

In Holland the exchanges are more benign and generally have to do with the gifts to be given. A rhyme (generally improvised) must give a clue as to the gift and something about the person for which it is intended, as in the following rhyme for a paint-box:

ABOVE: *By the turn of the century many aspects of the modern Santa Claus were in place.*

THE SPHERE
CHRISTMAS
1903

*I saw through the window
Said St. Peter to the Saint,
That Gerrit loves nothing
So much as to paint.*

*This box of paints will bring
Delight to Gerrit's artistic heart.*

Rhymes and songs are also made up about the saint, as in this example from a recent Dutch Christmas festival:

*Hear the wind o'er the
roof-tops humming
Through the chimney
hear it blow.
Will St. Nich'las
still be coming
Through the storm and through
the snow?
Yes, he comes
though storms be beating,
On his horse so strong and fast.*

*Could he hear our
hearts a-beating
Surely he would not ride past,
Surely he would not ride past.*

*Hear who knocks there children,
Hear who raps there children,
Hear who taps against the window-pane?*

*It's a stranger surely,
Who is lost here, surely,
Let us ask him what be his name...*

*Saint Nicholas, Saint Nicholas,
Pay us a call tonight, please do.
We'll put hay and carrots
In each and every shoe.*

Here Nicholas is helped by Black Peter, who is probably left over from Moorish slaves, or perhaps he is this color because he has been grubbing in the ashes of the Yule Log! Here, perhaps, it is worth noting that the smith, who also handled iron and fire as well as ashes, has always been important, both in shamanic traditions, and among the native peoples of this land, where "sooty" characters are beings of considerable magic power.

ABOVE: Knecht Ruprecht is just one of
Santa Claus's many European counterparts.

The Solstice Smith

In Celtic tradition it is more often than not the smith who is a figure of power and importance, as in the story of "Niall of the Nine Hostages," which dates from fourth-century Ireland. Here the smith Sitchenn is asked to judge among the five sons of King Mongfind, of whom Niall is one, as to who should inherit the throne of Ireland. Sitchenn sets fire to his forge and sends the five youths into it to save whatever they can. One brought out the bellows, another the hammers, one the weapons that were being crafted, but only Niall remembered to bring out the most important object, the anvil, without which no smithying could take place. He alone recognized the importance of the almost mystical nature of fire and smithying.

Elsewhere in Irish tradition we find mention of the Feast of Goibniu, the Celtic smith-god, at which the kings and heroes who had passed to the Otherworld celebrated by eating the sacred pigs of the sea-god Mannannan, which could be killed at this time, but which later returned to life to supply yet further feasts.

The Great Sleigh Ride

At Chrissemas, at Chrissemass
Long time ago,
Brave St. George he singed aloud
All in the snow.

SOMERSET CAROL

RIGHT: In Celtic tradition the figure of a smith god is central to Solstitial celebrations.

124

LEFT: *Dickens' "Spirit of Christmas Present" reflects an earlier, more primitive image of Santa Claus.*

To bring the story of the jolly old man up to date we need to look back to the seventeenth century. Suppressed, along with the rest of the more secular Christmas celebrations in 1664 by the Puritans, Santa Claus reappeared amid much jollification in 1660 as "The Spirit of Christmas Rejoicing," a role he was to adhere to brilliantly for the next three hundred years, gradually transforming into the figure that we recognize today. Queen Victoria's German husband, Prince Albert, played a large part in this transformation, bringing a Teutonic element into the mix. At this point Santa began to ride on a sleigh, to descend chimneys, and to fill stockings, just as he had in Germany in the Prince's own childhood.

Charles Dickens took up the reins in this period and in his immortal *Christmas Carol* captured an image of Santa that was a blend of both old and new. Although he is ostensibly describing the "Spirit of Christmas Present" there is enough here in which to recognize almost every aspect of Santa:

*He was clothed in one single green
robe or mantle, bordered with white fur.
The garment hung so loosely on the figure,
that its capacious breast was bare, as if
disdaining to be warded or concealed by any
artifice. Its feet, observable beneath the
angle folds of the garment, were also bare,
and on its head it wore no other covering
than a holly wreath, set here
and there with shining circles.*

CHARLES DICKENS: A CHRISTMAS CAROL

Santa in America

It was in the United States that the twenti-ethth-century image of Santa evolved. Indeed many of the associations we hold current today were quite consciously reinvented during the nineteenth century, by merchandisers and city fathers throughout the United States. This was done in part from a desire to redress the balance between the often violent and drunken behavior of people reacting against the earlier prohibition against Christmas by the Puritans, and in part to steer the holiday season toward consumerism. Thus, the public's attention was focused upon hearth and home, children and gift giving, and while this gave us much of the modern-day holiday, it also successfully edited out much of the passion, vigor, and life of the older celebration.

Thus, many of the traditions surrounding the holiday season and the character of Santa Claus stem from this period and have become established so deeply in our consciousness that we seldom think to question them or their point of origin. (This process of acceptance has been charted in great detail by Stephen Nissenbaum in his 1996 book, *The Battle For Christmas*.)

On St. Nicholas Day in 1809 the great American humorist Washington Irving published a book called *Father Knickerbocker's History of New York* in which he described Santa riding over the rooftops in his sleigh, putting his finger to the side of his nose, and bringing gifts to good children. In fact the book was intended as a satire of life in New York at the turn of the century, but in the end it went a long way toward the "reinvention" of St. Nicholas as Santa Claus. It became the basis of many of the modern myths, and can be clearly seen as an influence on Clement C. Moore's famous poem.

A few years after this, in 1821, an anonymous work appeared called *The Children's Friend: A New Year's Present, to Little Ones from Five to Twelve*. It is overwhelmingly sentimental by today's standards, but it added details to the new and old traditions of Santa, establishing his red costume and bulging sack of toys, as well as his ability to cover vast distances in a night.

BELOW: The modern emphasis on children and gift giving has removed much of the ancient drama and mystery of the Solstice festival.

The Jolly Old Elf

Then, on Christmas Eve 1822, a journalist named Clement C. Moore put pen to paper and gave us the "jolly old elf," the eight Teutonic reindeer, and all those details that everyone knows and loves.

He was dressed all in fur,
from his head to his foot,
And his clothes were all covered
in ashes and soot;

A bundle of toys he had
flung on his back,
And he looked like a peddler
just opening his pack.

His eyes how they twinkled!
His dimples how merry!
His cheeks were like roses,
his nose like a cherry!

His droll little mouth
was drawn up like a bow,
And the beard on his chin
was as white as the snow.

The stump of a pipe
he held tight in his teeth,
And the smoke it encircled
his head like a wreath.

He had a broad face
and a little round belly
That shook, when he laughed,
like a bowl full of jelly.

He was chubby and plump,
a right jolly old elf,
And I laughed when I saw him,
in spite of myself.

THE NIGHT BEFORE CHRISTMAS

With this single stroke the character of Santa became fixed in place for our time. Yet Moore drew quite consciously on Irving and other writers in his circle (who referred to themselves as the Knickerbockers) and hoped that his composition would have a powerful effect on his readership. Just how well he judged this may be seen not only from the continued popularity of the work (there are at least five different editions in print as I write) but also the fact that so much of the essence of his poem has entered into the imagery and substance of Santa Claus throughout the West.

An even more fantastic element entered the story when L. Frank Baum, the creator of the Oz books, wrote a biography of Santa called *The Life and Adventures of Santa Claus*, in which the jolly old man quits the North Pole for the Forest of Burzee, on the southern border of Oz, and has a series of amazing adventures that have little or no connection with the older traditions except to borrow the emerging character of Santa from Moore and his fellows in the Knickerbocker club.

Then, between 1860 and 1881, the New York illustrator and cartoonist Thomas Nast produced a series of drawings of Santa that added a selection of significant details. Santa's "workshop" was sited at the North Pole, his costume assumed the color and style with which we are now most familiar, and he acquired a book in which he recorded the names, addresses, and deeds of the children he would soon be visiting. When the Coca Cola company adopted these images as a basis for a coast to coast advertising campaign, the iconography of Santa Claus changed forever.

RIGHT: Children's continuing belief in Santa Claus is indicative of the enduring romance and magic of this time of year.

Virginia's Big Question

Much of the contemporary feeling was summed up in a famous letter written to the *New York Sun* newspaper by Virginia O'Hanlon in 1897. The letter read:

Dear Editor, I am eight years old. Some of my friends say there is no Santa Claus. Papa says, if you see it in THE SUN it's so. Please tell me the truth, is there a Santa Claus?

This drew forth an impassioned response from a journalist named Francis P. Church, who wrote:

Virginia, your friends are wrong. They have been affected by the skepticism of a skeptical age. They think that nothing can be which is not comprehensible by their little minds... Yes, Virginia, there is a Santa Claus. He exists as certainly as love and generosity and devotion exist, and you know that they abound and give to your life its highest beauty and joy. Alas! how dreary would the world be if there were no Santa Claus!

It would be as dreary as if there were no Virginias. There would be no childlike faith then, no poetry, no romance to make tolerable this existence. We would have no enjoyment, except in sense and sight.... No Santa Claus! Thank God he lives and lives forever. A 1,000 years from now, Virginia, nay, 10,000 years from now, he will continue to make glad the heart of childhood.

These sentiments were later to be echoed in the movie *Miracle on 34th Street*, written for the screen in 1947 and directed by George Seaton from a story by Valentine Davies. This became a perennial favorite that is watched by many people every Christmas. The story revolves around a department store "Santa," hired by Macy's, the famous New York store. When he claims to be the real Kris Kringle, he causes such disruption that he is arrested, and in the trial that follows everyone's belief in Santa Claus is put to the test.

Just as in the story of Virginia O'Hanlon, it is a child who believes in the claims of the old man, and who teaches others to follow her lead. In the end, all are vindicated when thousands of letters pour into the court pledging their support and belief, and the judge rules in favor of the existence of Santa Claus. The movie was successfully remade in 1994 with Richard Attenborough donning the red suit in the role previously made famous by the actor Edmund Gwynn.

A Christmas Nightmare

The most significant contribution of our own time to the myths comes, not surprisingly, from Walt Disney. What is surprising is that it is neither sentimental nor trivialized. The animated film *Nightmare Before Christmas*, written and directed by Tim Burton, who is best known for his moody "Batman" movies and the modern fairy tale *Edward Scissorhands*, transforms the myth yet again. Here the two festivals, Halloween and Christmas, get mixed up, with bizarre and disastrous results. Santa is imagined to be a monster, a huge red creature called "Sandy Claws," by Jack, the Pumpkin King of Halloween Town. Jack tries to emulate the monster, analyzing the mystery of Christmas in a science lab! Finally Jack sends his gruesome followers to kidnap Santa, and then tries to fulfill the role himself! In Burton's own words, parodying Clement C. Moore:

'Twas the nightmare before Christmas,
and all through the house,
Not a creature was peaceful,
not even a mouse.

The stockings, all hung
by the chimney with care,
When opened that morning
would cause quite a scare!

The children, all nestled
so snug in their beds,
Would have nightmares
of monsters and skeleton heads.

TIM BURTON:
THE NIGHTMARE BEFORE CHRISTMAS

LEFT: Even today the Santa Claus figure is being explored and reinvented, as in the 1994 remake of the movie Miracle on 34th Street.

Thankfully, Santa is rescued in the nick of time, and the age-old pattern of Christmas is restored. In the end Santa brings Christmas to Halloween Land and all is well in both worlds.

Other Santas

What we might call the darker side of the jolly old man surfaces in a deliciously satirical story by the renowned horror writer Dean Koontz. In his "Santa's Twin" (1996) we find some very contemporary imagery applied to the old story, and in the process learn some new things about Santa, such as that he has a twin named Bob who is as wicked as his brother is good. In this story of a dysfunctional family Bob steals Santa's sleigh and stuffs his toy sack with mud, broccoli, and other even worse substances. In his very modern fairy tale Bob is described as "deeply troubled" and in the end is brought to book when his brother threatens to tell his mother about his behavior! After which, the brothers fly off in the sleigh together, to put right all the mischief done by Bob.

Much more in line with tradition there recently appeared *The Autobiography of Santa Claus* (1994) "ghosted" by Jeff Guinn. In this, the jolly old man is allowed to tell his own story, and crops up throughout history, assembling a fascinating gallery of helpers including King Arthur, Attila the Hun, Leonardo da Vinci, Christopher Columbus, and Theodore Roosevelt! It actually makes an enjoyable read, and includes many of the myths of Santa in an accessible form, as well as adding significantly to them. What is interesting about the book is the way in which it demonstrates that the spirit of Santa Claus cannot die. He lives on through time, not as a ghost but almost in a state of suspended animation, where time itself slows almost to a halt and Santa grows older so imperceptibly that thousands of years pass in what seem to him but brief moments.

The history of this single being not only lies at the heart of the Solstice but sums up much that we have already seen throughout our investigation into the history of the traditions surrounding Midwinter. Santa is a supreme example of the human ability to create enduring myths.

LEFT: *In folklore, the darker side of Santa Claus is often expressed in an accompanying character, such as the Swiss Schmutzli, who appears in order to punish bad children.*

E.C. Krupp, from whom we have already heard several times, sums up the true character and purpose of Santa:

Santa Claus... has his grip on the world axis. His yearly tour steadies us all. Remote, at the top of the world, in a land of eternal snow, he gathers the energy spent in the year's passing.

Then he sails like a shaman, off into the solsticial darkness, to re-allocate the power to the world's children.

It's a promise in Christmas presents that through children and through the seasonal renewal, the world is ever young.

E.C. KRUPP: BEYOND THE BLUE HORIZON.

ABOVE: Santa Claus is the ultimate embodiment of the human need and ability to invent myths.

CELEBRATION

Perhaps the central aspect of the Midwinter and Christmas celebrations is the giving of gifts. There are many ways to celebrate this, other than in giving each other presents. Giving to a charity that reflects the deeper concerns of the Solstice, such as animal shelters, or one of the many ecologically based organizations, is a good alternative. As our ancestors remembered the rest of the natural world of which they were only a part, so should we. Gifts of fire, light, and the multifarious powers of the creatures of the natural world were celebrated by our ancestors at Midwinter from the beginning. In our own time we can do so simply by lighting a fire outside or, if we have one, in our own fireplace (see "The Yule Log Ceremony" in Chapter 3). Or we can decorate our tree with representations of sacred animal and bird images made from wood or cardboard.

ABOVE: *The light and warmth of a cheary fire has brought comfort to humans since the dawn of time.*

THE GIFTS OF THE SOLSTICE

Now Christmas is come
Let us beat up the drum
And call all our neighbors together.
And when they appear,
Let us make them such cheer
As will keep out the wind
and the weather.

WASHINGTON IRVING

If you are able to create a fire, do it ceremonially. Start by laying the pieces of wood in a pleasing pattern and use dead wood that has fallen from trees. When you are ready to light it, do so with some words. These can be of your own devising, but here is a suggested formula:

I dedicate this fire to the eternal light of Midwinter. May its warmth remind me of the Summer, and may its brightness be a guiding star to all kindly spirits who bless this season and this place with their presence.

Think of the holy darkness of the Solstice and the returning light that will come back to bless and renew the land in Spring. Look into the flames or the glowing heart of the fire and see what dreams are there. In doing so you will be sharing an experience as old as time.

As always, it is worth looking out for local events in the calendar of folklore celebrations. To find yourself in the presence of a traditional personage who echoes the ancient origins of the figure, you could do no better than seek out one of the many ancient Mummer plays that still take place annually around Britain, and which have begun to be re-enacted at country fairs in the United States in the last few years. (See also Chapter 5 and Resources p. 242.) When "Old Father Christmas" comes in, give him a rousing cheer and remember that he represents all of the ancient gift givers down through the ages.

ABOVE: *Santa Claus is a modern incarnation of all the ancient gift givers that have appeared throughout the history of the world.*

MAKING A SHRINE

1. *Make a shrine to the shaman Santa just as our ancestors did long since. Decorate it with evergreen boughs and small stones chosen with care and attention for their beauty.*

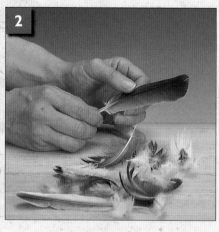

2. *If you live somewhere where you are likely to find feathers or bones from dead animals or birds you may choose to use these. Clean them to create something beautiful that both honors the life of the animal who gave you its remains, and as an offering at your hearth or fireplace.*

3. *You can add to your winter shrine, creating a tepee of birch-bark or a lodge of green branches for the shaman, the master of the animals to inhabit. Install a figure of Santa Claus with due ceremony, acknowledging the immanence of the mighty gift-giver.*

4. *When you do any of these things remember the ancestors who celebrated the Solstice in ways similar to this thousands of years ago. When you retire to bed on Christmas Eve, leave a saucer of milk and a piece of bread or cold meat out – not only for Santa but for those same ancestors who knew of him long years ago.*

5. *Find a figure of the Saint in the green robes of the Winter King, or look for realistic images of reindeer. (On my own Midwinter altar, for example, I always place a bag made from reindeer hide, found on a trip to Finland.)*

6. *A candle placed on the table, surrounded by green boughs and small images of wooden animals (readily obtained from nature stores or Natural History museum shops) is in keeping with the ancient celebration of Midwinter.*

FOLLOWING PAGES:
Welcome the gift
giver to your hearth
and home.

ABOVE: *Invoke the power of the ancient shamanic tradition by creating
a shrine to the spirit of the Solstice.*

Chapter 5

THE SOLSTICE ANIMALS

Animals all, as it befell,
In the stable where they did dwell!
Joy shall be theirs in the morning!

KENNETH GRAHAME: THE WIND IN THE WILLOWS

Out of the smoke of the Midwinter fires come strange figures, faces masked in wild and fearsome shapes, bodies clad in animal skins, with the skulls of horses and birds mounted on beribboned poles. These are the "guisers," men and women disguised as creatures, whose presence takes us back to the earliest hunting rituals and ceremonies which were supposed to appease the spirits of beasts killed for food. For, as an Iglulik Inuit speaking to the anthropologist and explorer Knud Rasmussen explained earlier this century: "All the creatures we have to kill and eat, all those we have to strike down and destroy to make clothes for ourselves, have souls, as we have."

LEFT: The theme of wildness that underlies the celebration of Midwinter is evidenced by the ancient ritual of guising with animal masks.

The many animals that throng the Winter months are particularly present during the Twelve Days of Christmas, those days in which guising is performed, when we walk between the worlds, masking and veiling our features so that animal spirits can move through us and among us, bringing their gifts and challenges. These customs embrace us all, for we are all still animals and are all part of the pattern of ancient "wildness" that threads through the celebration of Midwinter.

This is itself a reflection of a once-powerful but now neglected sense of oneness between human beings and the natural world that was our environment before we began to build cities and gather together in amorphous groups. That this ancient wildness is still there, only a little bit below the veneer of our civilized lifestyles, is apparent by the number of traditions still in practice that involve dressing as animals and performing ancient rituals. Thus, in Wales a beribboned horse skull called the Mari Llwyd (see page 156) is carried in a procession through towns and villages. In Ireland on St. Stephen's Day a very ancient and sacred ceremony still takes place that involves the ritual sacrifice of a bird.

Before we look at these extraordinary events of Midwinter tradition, we need to familiarize ourselves with some of the creatures that appear, especially in the folk songs that are sung around this time of year. These were often performed with appropriate ritual and mumming (*see Chapter 1*), and have done much to preserve the ceremonial dimension of the Solstice.

ABOVE: The wearing of animal masks was believed to encourage animal spirits to enter us and reconnect us to the wild essence of our being.

Here We Come A-Caroling

The custom of singing carols at Christmas is itself an old one. A carol is properly a song with a dance, and singing and dancing are never far apart at this time. If we look at some of the songs of Midwinter, particularly those that are to do with animals, or with animal disguises, we find something very much like a magical bestiary emerging.

In Shakespeare's *As You Like It*, there is a song concerning the wearing of stag's antlers, that goes:

> *What what shall he have*
> > *that killed the deer?*
> *His leather skin and horns to wear.*
> *Take you no scorn to wear a horn*
> *It was a crest ere thou wast born,*
> *Thy father's father bore*
> > *and thy father wore it too*
> *The horn, the horn, the lusty horn*
> *Is not a thing to laugh to scorn.*

Indeed not! For throughout northern Europe the wearing of antlers or horns is an ancient and important ritual act that dates back thousands of years. Throughout the North the Winter season begins with the rutting of deer in October. This is a time when normally quiet glens and deep forests ring with the roaring and bellowing of stags and the clash of their great branching antlers. Perhaps this yearly struggle may have played a part in the fact that deer have long been perceived as sacred animals. Certainly it is easy to see how they might have become associated with the age-old battle between the old year and the new.

Song of the Deer

The oldest known animal masks are of deer – they were unearthed in Britain at Star Carr near Scarborough, and dated to 7500 B.C. No fewer than twenty-five deer frontlets were found there, with antlers still attached to a plate of bone that had holes drilled through it, so that the whole thing could be attached to a helmet. A reconstruction of one of these masks can be seen in the British Museum in London. It suggests that over nine thousand years ago our ancestors were disguising themselves as deer, perhaps in order to hunt them. Likewise the oldest known masks found among the Native American tribes are of deer, and numerous deer-hunting songs have been preserved, such as this one, found in a wonderful collection called *Yaki Deer Songs*, collected and edited by Larry Evers and Feklipe S. Molina:

> *Although unseen in the wilderness*
> *I am just running,*
> *My antler crown with these three branches*
> *is showing, moving.*
>
> *Over there, I, in the center*
> *of the flower-covered grove,*
> *I am walking,*
> *my antler crown with these three branches*
> *is showing, moving.*

These songs provide an intimate portrayal of the hunt, just as they must once have done among the indigenous tribes of northern Europe.

LEFT: Deer masks and headdresses feature in many ancient rituals that date back thousands of years.

141

The Horn Dance

In Britain, in the area extending roughly between Burton-upon-Trent and Stafford, the sacred role of the deer has been preserved in a custom that dates back at least to the early Middle Ages. The "Abbot's Bromley Horn Dance," once danced at Christmas time but now on the Sunday after September 4th, consists of six dancers carrying huge racks of reindeer horns. These are immensely heavy and some have been carbon dated to A.D. 1000. They are accompanied by a hobby-horse, a boy with a bow and arrow, a She-Male (*see page 162*) with a pot and ladle, and a fiddler. The dancers move about the village to an ancient, haunting tune that still sends chills up the spine as it approaches through the dawn light.

The Old Buck

A similar custom is still celebrated in the United States in North Carolina, where the Old Buck, a steer's head held up by two men garbed in a white sheet, goes about frightening folk and demanding money with menaces. Around New Orleans the echo of an older French folk belief is to be seen every Christmas, when a huge beribboned ox, known as *le grand boeuf*, is paraded through the streets, bedecked with holly on its spreading horns.

The Cow and the Ox

While reindeer remain the main source of life for people just below the Arctic Circle, in Britain the cow is the major domestic animal, providing leather, milk, cheese, meat, and horn. In ancient times, cows were a great form of wealth, and the Celtic tribes of Britain and Ireland spent much of their time raiding each other's territory to steal cattle. Cows were sacred to the Celts as well, just as they are today in India. In Scotland and Ireland we catch a glimpse of this in a ceremony known as the *tarbh-feis* or "Bull-Sleep," which was part of the ancient king-making rites. In this ancient tradition a

ABOVE: The Abbot's Bromley Horn Dance is a European dance that has survived from a time before the Middle Ages.

white bull was ritually slain and a broth made from the flesh. This was then drunk by anyone wishing to have a particular vision. The seeker then wrapped himself in the flayed skin of the bull and lay down to sleep. Four Druids then stood over him and chanted a *firindi* or "true speech," which was meant to ensure that he received the vision. This was done on occasions to discover the identity of the truer kin when there was dispute over succession.

In the Medieval Welsh story "Rhonawby's Dream" the hero falls asleep on a yellow bull's hide and dreams of the warrior Arthur and his band of extraordinary heroes. To this may be added the practice of the Yakut shamans of northern Siberia, who wrap themselves in a mare's skin (*see also the Mari Llwyd on page 156*) before beginning their spirit-journey to the Otherworld.

Guising and rituals based upon the hunt were common among the Pueblo Indians. On one well-recorded occasion more than fifty men dressed as buffalo, bison, deer, mountain sheep, and antelope danced in procession to the nearby mission, and performed their ancient mimetic ritual in the church before then attending the Christian service.

An American surgeon, Ten Broeck, recorded a further incidence of the eternal cross-over points between Christian and native traditions, when, on visiting a church near Albuquerque in 1851, he saw Native American men and women asking the priest to bless the small objects that they were carrying. It turned out that these were small images of their domestic

animals – or those they hunted – made from mud or dough. The blessing of the new god was still believed to be efficacious enough to insure a fortunate and prosperous beginning to the dawning year.

Culling the Herds

The period around the Winter Solstice, from November to December, was traditionally the time when beasts were culled from the herds to be slaughtered and salted away for the long hard Winter that lay ahead. The Saxons referred to this time as *Blodmonath* ("Blood Month") and we derive the word "to bless" from the Saxon *bleodswean*, "to sanctify by blood." There were undoubted ritual connections here, with selected animals slain as offerings to the gods. The Advent bull-baiting that took place in Madron, Cornwall, and at other places throughout the country as recently as the eighteenth century may have been a memory of this, as it undoubtedly was in some way a recollection of the Mithraic bull-slaying (*see Chapter 2*).

Both the bull and the cow were considered sacred in classical Greece, and earlier still in Mesopotamia. The bull usually represented the sun and the cow the moon. Together they reigned over the heavens and insured the fertility of the earth.

There are very many archeological findings of ox burials throughout Britain and northern Europe and it is clear that the actual animal was sacrificed regularly in rituals, as a means of insuring the health and fertility of the land.

ABOVE: Seasonal stag hunting at this time of year may have helped develop the significance of the animal to Winter time rituals.

ABOVE: Animal sacrifices to appease the unseen forces of creation were central to the world-view of the ancients.

The Ooser and Others

Ritual cow disguise is found in Gloucestershire and the Cotswolds in Britain, and it occasionally appears elsewhere in Dorset and Wiltshire. One of the most famous instances is called "the Broad," a bull's head mounted on a pole, which went about wassailing through the local villages. Another, the famous Dorset Ooser or Wurser, is still preserved to this day. The headpiece is particularly grotesque. Made from wood, it is brightly painted, has bulbous eyes, large teeth, long flowing human-looking locks, and sports a pair of curving bullock horns that project from either side of the head. It is very clearly meant to represent a bull-man. The last traditional mask vanished mysteriously from its home in Melbury Osmond, in West Dorset toward the beginning of the century, but fortunately photographs of the mask survived and reconstructed Oosers are now to be seen again in Dorset.

Yet another bullmasked man is named Old Bronzon Face and he used to appear at the Black Godiva festival in Southam near Coventry. He is believed to have been associated with the Horned God of the Witches. Similarly, the Abingdon Morris team in Oxfordshire still have bull's horns attached to their staff.

"The Somerset Wassail Song," collected by
Cecil Sharp at the beginning of the century
from the Drayton wassailers in Somerset,
England, harks back to earlier times as it
invokes protection upon the householder and
remembers the cow who winters in the barn:

There was an old man,
  and he had an old cow,
And how for to keep her
  he didn't know how;
He built up a barn for
  to keep his cow warm.
And a drop or two of cider
  will do us no harm;
No harm, boys, harm;
  no harm, boys, harm;
And a drop or two of cider
  will do us no harm.

The girt dog of Langport
  he burnt his long tail,
And this is the night
  we go singing wassail.
O master and missus,
  now we must be gone;
God bless all in this house
  till we do come again;
For it's your wassail,
  and it's our wassail!
And it's joy be to you,
  and a jolly wassail!

This is echoed by a tradition that still held good
in Wales up until the nineteenth century.

On Christmas Eve a bowl of hot beer,
sweetened with sugar and flavoured with
spices, was prepared by the master of the
household, while the mistress brought
forward a basket containing a cake. The
bowl and the basket were decorated with
evergreens, holly, and ivy wreaths. A

*ABOVE: The cow and the ox have been ritually
slaughtered for thousands of years as a means of
ensuring the fertility of the land.*

procession was then formed and the bowl
and basket were carried in state to the stall
of the finest ox belonging to the family.
There the men of the household stood on one
side, and the women were arranged opposite
them. The mistress then placed the cake on
the horns of the ox, and the master stirred
the beer, drank a mouthful, and passed the
bowl on after the fashion of a loving
cup...While this was going on, one or two
persons in the assembly carefully noted the
behaviour of the ox. If the animal remained
quiet and peaceful, it was a token of good
luck for the ensuing year. If, on the
contrary, the animal became restless and
angry, bad luck was supposed to follow.

MARIE TREVELYAN:
FOLK-LORE AND FOLK STORIES OF WALES

145

*ABOVE: The ram, traditionally symbolic of male
virility, is significantly associated with many solar deities.*

The Sheep and the Rams

Sheep are normally only considered in a Mid-winter context in such carols as "While Shepherds Watched," but they have a more active role in Derbyshire folk tradition. Here a sheep's head is carried as part of a procession, usually as a hobby sheep, with cloth over the operator. This is known as "The Old Tup." A team of between four to six men and boys accompany it. This comprises the Butcher (who has a knife and leather apron); the Old Man and Old Woman; Beelzebub and Devil Doubt, and a boy to carry a bowl to catch the Tup's blood. As with the Mari Llwyd (*see page 156*), the Tup comes to the door with a song and a demand for money, and is sometimes accompanied by a Mummer's play. The ritualized exchange begins:

*Here comes me and my owd lass
Short of money, short of brass
Fill up your glass, give us a sup,
We'll come in and show you the Tup.*

This tradition is reflected in the following song, which was first recorded in the 1940s but probably goes back a few years beyond that.

As I went up to Derby,
upon a Derby Day,
I brought one of the finest rams, sir,
that ever was fed on hay.

And it's Aye me dingle Derby,
to me Derby dingle day
It was one of the finest rams, sir,
that ever was fed on hay.

This ram he had a horn, sir,
that reached up to the sky
The birds went there to build their nests,
you could hear the young ones cry.

This ram he had another horn,
that reached up to the moon
The birds went up in February
and didn't come back till June.

This ram was fat behind, sir,
this ram was fat before
And every time his hoof went down,
it covered an acre or more.

This ram he had four legs, sir,
that stood incredible wide
A coach and four could drive right through,
with room to spare each side.

This ram he had a tail, sir,
that reached right down to hell
And this was hung in the belfry
to ring the old church bell.

This ram he had a belly, sir,
and so I heard 'em say
And every time he ate a meal,
he swallowed a Rick of hay.

This ram he had a tooth, sir,
in the shape of a huntsman's horn
And when they opened it up, sir,
they found a bushel of corn.

And when this ram was killed, sir,
there was a terrible flood
Took four and twenty butcher boys
to wash away the blood.

The blood became a river, sir,
that flowed down Derby Moor
It turned the biggest mill wheel
that ever was turned before.

The wool that came from his back, sir,
it was both thick and thin
Took all the women of Derby
the rest of their lives to spin.

Then all the boys in Derby, sir,
came running for his eyes
To make a pair of footballs for
they were football size.

All the girls of Derby, sir,
came running for his ears
To make them purses and
aprons to last the rest of their years.

Took all the dogs in Derby, sir,
to cart away his bones
And all the horses in Derby
to roll away his stones.

THE DERBY RAM

BELOW: The function of the sheep
as witnesses of Christ's birth is
just one of their mythical roles.

In Scotland, a strip of skin was taken from the breast of a sheep killed at Christmas or New Year and the Hogmanay custom was that the company walk clockwise round the fire and pass the burning skin from hand to hand, making the sign of the cross upon themselves with it and waving the strip three times over their heads.

A Krampus at the Gate

King Arthur is shown riding on a ram in a famous mosaic at Modena Cathedral in Italy, although this is arguably a badly drawn goat, the Zodiacal Capricornus of this Midwinter time. Goats themselves have always had a strange mythology – their yellow eyes and cloven feet being seen as insignia of the devil. In Austria on St. Nicholas Eve (December 5th) a creature known as the Krampus sometimes accompanies St. Nicholas or goes about on his own. He wears a goat-horned mask, a shaggy coat, has a long tail and brandishes a bundle of birch twigs to purify children who have misbehaved during the year. In Sweden, the *Julbok* or "Yule goat" is dressed in buckskin or sheepskin with horns and a beard appears. An old custom used to see him killed and resurrected again, a sure sign that a more ancient time would have involved a sacrifice that the New Year might come again.

The Big-Bristled Pig

When you knuckle down to the depths of Winter, there's usually a pig in the story, and it's the same here. Pigs were especially sacred to the Celts, who believed that they were given as a gift from the Otherworld. The Welsh poet

The Midwinter Butcher

That the Tup was at one time the center of a ritual slaying and resurrection, a symbolic enactment of the death of the old year and its rebirth as the new, is echoed in these lines from the Morris play that sometimes accompanies the procession of the Tup:

BUTCHER:

Here comes I the Butcher good,
I stuck a fat heifer and never drew blood,
I hit him and pricked him
and left him for dead
When I come the next morning
he was stood on his head.

DOCTOR:

Here comes I the Doctor,
Here Jack, take a little out o' my bottle
And let it run down thy throttle,
If thou be not quite dead,
rise up and walk again.

WORKSOP MUMMERS PLAY

148

and seer Merlin left a poem behind in which he addresses his oracular sayings to a pig, while in the medieval Welsh story of the smith god, Gofannon's Feast, we hear of a pig that is eaten but never consumed and who comes to life again as long as the bones are not eaten (*see "Goibniu's Feast" in Chapter 4*). This is a common theme throughout the world and is sometimes ritually recreated. In eighteenth-century Lapland, Danish missionaries were told that the bones of sacrificed animals must be carefully gathered and arranged so that the god to whom they were offered could restore life to the animals, making them fatter than before. Such rituals were performed so that the deity might provide more animals of the same kind in due course.

Queen's College in Oxford still sings the traditional "Boar's Head Carol," to the accompaniment of which a finely stuffed pig's head is carried in procession through the dining hall. In Cleveland, Ohio, a similar tradition is found at Trinity Episcopal Cathedral. A procession winds through the streets and into the church, bearing a boar's head on a mighty platter and accompanied by five choirs, and over a hundred performers dressed as wise men, shepherds, woodsmen, beef-eaters, yule boys, knights, and heralds.

These customs celebrate the sacredness of the animal, but there is another song, in which other animals partake in a battle of the fields. It is a carol, from Bedfordshire, England, which links the season with the round of planting and harvesting.

There was a pig, went out to dig
Chris-i-mas Day, Chris-i-mas Day
There was a pig went out to dig
On Chris-i-mas Day in the morning.

There was a cow, went out to plow,
Chris-i-mas Day, Chris-i-mas Day
There was a cow, went out to plow
On Chris-i-mas Day in the morning.

There was a sparrow, went out to harrow,
Chris-i-mas Day, Chris-i-mas Day
There was a sparrow, went out to harrow
On Chris-i-mas Day in the morning.

There was a crow, went out to sow,
Chris-i-mas Day, Chris-i-mas Day
There was a crow, went out to mow
On Chris-i-mas Day in the morning.

There was a sheep, went out to reap
Chris-i-mas Day, Chris-i-mas Day
There was a sheep, went out to reap
On Chris-i-mas Day in the morning.

There was a drake went out to rake
Chris-i-mas Day, Chris-i-mas Day
There was a drake went out to rake
On Chris-i-mas Day in the morning.

There was a minnow, went out to winnow
Chris-i-mas Day, Chris-i-mas Day
There was a minnow, went out to winnow
On Chris-i-mas Day in the morning.

ABOVE: The worship of the pig was widespread among the Celts.

The Midwinter Cock

We expect to find a well-roasted bird on our tables at Christmas, but while the turkey has been a latecomer to our tables, the chicken has been eaten for a long time. Of course the cock was one of the animals sacred to the British Celts according to Caesar, and its crowing may have been oracular. St. Columba averred that he "gave no reverence to the voice of birds, nor to the oracle of sneezing or any other charm, and that his druid was Christ."

The twelfth-century carol of "King Herod and the Cock" seems to bear this tradition out in a curious way:

There was a star in David's land,
In David's land appeared,
And in King Herod's chamber,
so bright it did shine there.

The Wise Men they soon spied it,
and told the King a-nigh
That a Princely Babe was born that night,
no King shall e'er destroy.

If this be truth, King Herod said,
That thou hast told to me,
The roasted cock that lies in the dish shall
crow full senses three.

O the cock soon thrustened and feathered
well by the work of God's own hand
And he did crow full senses three in the dish
where he did stand.

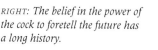

RIGHT: The belief in the power of the cock to foretell the future has a long history.

King Wren

The wren, the wren,
The king of all birds,
On St. Stephen's Day
Is caught in the furze.

TRADITIONAL SONG

One of the most remarkable and dramatic Solstice customs involving animals is the Hunting of the Wren, which traditionally takes place on Boxing Day or St. Stephen's Day. The custom lasted longest in Wales and the Isle of Man and still takes place today in Ireland. A description from 1840 describes it thus:

For some weeks preceding Christmas,
crowds of village boys may be seen peering
into hedges, in search of the tiny wren; and
when one is discovered the whole assemble
and give wager chase until they have slain
the little bird. In the hunt the utmost
excitement prevail; shouting, screeching,
and rushing, all sorts of missiles are flung
at the puny mark... From bush to bush,
from hedge to hedge, is the wren pursued
until bagged with as much pride and
pleasure as the cock of the woods by the
more ambitious sportsman... On the
anniversary of St. Stephen... the enigma is
explained. Attached to a huge holly-bush,
elevated on a pole, the bodies of several little
wrens are borne about... through the streets
in procession... and every now
and then stopping before some
popular house and there
singing the Wren song.

QUOTED IN K. DANAHER:
THE YEAR IN IRELAND.

150

Various versions of this song have survived. Here is a typical one:

The wren, the wren, the king of all birds,
On St. Stephen's Day was caught in the furze;
Though his body is small, his family is great,
So if it please your honor, give us a treat.
On Christmas Day I turned a spit;
I burned my finger, I feel it yet.
Up with the kettle, down with the pan,
Give us some money to bury the wren.

IBID

The antiquity of this rather barbaric custom is clear enough. At one time the Wren, the "king of all birds," must have represented the dying year-king and was sacrificed on his behalf for the good of the land. A story from Scotland suggests the reason for this rather plain little bird being addressed as King.

BELOW: This Roman mosaic shows a cockerel, the animal of light, confronting a tortoise, symbolic of darkness.

The Parliament of Birds

At a gathering of birds, it was decided to elect a king by seeing which could fly the highest, and nearest to the sun. The eagle's broad strong wings bore it higher than any other. It was about to acclaim its prowess, when it became aware of a "whirr-chuck" sound – the little wren had flown yet higher than the eagle, because it was cheekily perched on its back.

For many years during the eighteenth and nineteenth centuries, the Irish Wren Boys were accompanied by masked guisers, including the ubiquitous *láir bhán* or White Mare. Nowadays, due in part to a shortage of wrens and to a somewhat more bird-conscious awareness, they are seldom hunted. Although the Wren Boys still circulate in Ireland, they no longer kill a wren, but proceed from house to house with a decorated cage. Here is a different wren song sung by the guisers in Pembrokeshire, England, where the custom is no longer practiced, but the sacredness of the bird is remembered:

Joy, health, love and peace
be all here in this place
By your leave we will sing
concerning our king.

Our king is well dressed,
in silks of the best,
In ribbons so rare,
no king can compare.

We have traveled many miles,
over hedges and stiles,
In search of our king,
until you we bring.

Old Christmas is past,
Twelfth Night is the last,
And we bid you adieu,
great joy to the new.

It is not of the newborn king of Winter, the Wondrous Child, they are speaking, but King Wren, who is remembered in a curious song from Oxfordshire, that manages to encapsulate the more ancient significance of the custom:

The Cutty Wren

Oh where are you going?
says Milder to Malder.
– We may not tell you, says Festle to Fose.
We're off to the wild wood,
says John the Red Nose.
We're off to the wild wood,
says John the Red Nose.

And what will you do there?
says Milder to Malder.
We may not tell you,
says Festle to Fose.
We'll hunt the Cutty Wren,
says John the Red Nose.
We'll hunt the Cutty Wren,
says John the Red Nose.

How will you shoot her?
says Milder to Malder.
We may not tell you,
says Festle to Fose.
With bows and with arrows,
says John the Red Nose.
Bows and with arrows,
says John the Red Nose.

That will not do,
says Milder to Malder.
What will do then?
says Festle to Fose.
Big guns and big cannons,
says John the Red Nose.
Big guns and big cannons,
says John the Red Nose.

How will you bring her home?
says Milder to Malder.
We may not tell you
says Festle to Fose.
On four strong men's shoulders,
says John the Red Nose.
On four strong men's shoulders,
says John the Red Nose.

That will not do,
says Milder to Malder.
What will do then?
says Festle to Fose.
With carts and big wagons,
says John the Red Nose.
With carts and big wagons,
says John the Red Nose.

How will you cut her up?
says Milder to Malder.
We may not tell you,
says Festle to Fose.
With knives and with forks,
says John the Red Nose.
With knives and with forks,
says John the Red Nose.

That will not do,
says Milder to Malder.
What will do then?
says Festle to Fose.
Big hatchets and cleavers,
says John the Red Nose.
Big hatchets and cleavers,
says John the Red Nose.

How will you cook her?
says Milder to Malder.
We may not tell you,
says Festle to Fose.
In pots and in pans,
says John the Red Nose.
In pots and in pans,
says John the Red Nose.

That will not do,
says Milder to Malder.
What will use then?
says Festle to Fose.
A bloody great brass cauldron,
says John the Red Nose.
Oh a bloody great brass cauldron,
says John the Red Nose.

Who'll get the spare ribs?
says Milder to Malder.
We may not tell you,
says Festle to Fose.
We'll give it all to the poor,
says John the Red Nose.
We'll give it all to the poor,
says John the Red Nose.

RIGHT: *The wren, also known in legend as the King of the Birds, often features in ceremony and song.*

153

*ABOVE: In Native American myth the
Raven steals away the sun.*

Raven Steals the Sun

A bird that has never had a good press is the
raven. Considered unlucky by most cultures
because of its scavenging habits, there is the
suggestion of a more ancient animosity against
the bird that tried to steal the sun itself. Among
the Haifa people of the North America, there is
a tale called "How Raven Stole the Light,"
which supports this.

At the beginning of the world, there was
no light at all, and the reason for this was that
an old man, who lived by a river with his
daughter, had it all shut up in a tiny box,
which was inside another box, and so on for
dozens and dozens of boxes. Now at this time,
Raven, who had existed since before the

beginning, happened to overhear the old man
singing to himself, singing about the boxes
and what was inside them. Raven at once
desired to have this light for himself, so that
he could see what he was hunting. He gave
much thought to how he might steal it, and
eventually, after many failed attempts, he
turned himself into a pine needle, and when
the old man's daughter came to the river to
get water, she swallowed the needle. Nine
months later she gave birth to a strange boy
with a long beak-like face and feathers down
his back. He soon started talking and walking
and began to beg his grandfather for the
largest box. At first the old man denied him,
but in time he gave in, just as he was to do
with all the other boxes, until finally there
was only one left – the smallest, from which
leaked a strange glow. The boy begged and
pleaded with his grandfather to open the box,
and, at last, he did so. Out came the brightest
ball of light imaginable, and at once Raven
turned himself back into his true form and,
seizing the light in his beak, flew off out of
the smoke hole and into the sky. At once the
light dawned and for the first time the sparkle
of the river and the glory of the sky and the
earth could be seen.

Raven was so happy as he flew about that
he did not see where Eagle rose from his rock
into the sky. Only at the last moment did
Raven notice him, and in terror he bit off a
piece of the light, which fell and bounded
onto the earth. Small bits broke off of it, and
flew up into the sky along with the bigger
piece. They are still there to this day – we call
them the moon and the stars. Raven flew as
hard as he could to the edge of the world and
there he was forced to let the biggest piece of
light go. It drifted up to the outer rim of the
universe and there it stayed and remains to
this day – we call it the sun.

*ABOVE: The prehistoric Europeans celebrated the horse as sacred
in cave paintings such as those found in the caves at Lascaux, France.*

Riding the Mari

*Mari Llwyd, Horse of Frost, Star-Horse, and
White Horse of the Sea is come to us.*

VERNON WATKINS,
THE BALLAD OF THE MARI LLWYD

The horse has been considered sacred in Britain since very ancient times (witness the White Horse carved out of the chalk on the Ridgeway at Uffington in Oxfordshire) and horse customs abound throughout the country. In both western and central Britain, as well as areas of the North, the custom of hoodening is well known. The Hooden Horse was a man disguised as a horse, often decked out in a costume that had been handed down for generations. Along with a team of supporters, numbering between four and eight, the Hooden Horse traversed villages and towns collecting money from every house in return for songs, dances, and general fun and games. The horse was generally made from a wooden carved head on a pole (not unlike the Hobby Horse that derives from it) with a hinged jaw that clacked in time to the singing. The "hoodener" who carried the horse was covered with a sheet, and was accompanied by a groom, a jockey, a man dressed as a woman named the Molly, and two or three musicians. During the passage through the houses, coins were placed in the horse's mouth, and in return the Hooden offered blessings and wise sayings – hence the term "from the horse's mouth."

155

The Hooden Horse

Several suggestions have been put forward as to the origin of the term *hoodening*. According to some it means "Wooden Horse," while others suggest "Woden Horse" (after the Norse god). Others are in favor of "Robin Hood's Horse," or (the most likely of these theories) the "Hooded Horse." All of these may indeed be correct as the custom is probably very ancient and thus may have acquired various properties at different times.

The Woden association is certainly right for this time of the year, when, as we saw in Chapter 4, the god is perceived as descending on his white horse at time of the Solstice. The connection with Robin Hood (or Robin in the Hood) is equally interesting as it suggests that the hooding ceremony may have been part of the cult surrounding the Green Man (*see also Chapter 3*). Robin is undoubtedly a late Saxon interpretation of this ancient representative of the natural world, and as such belongs very much in the season of the Winter King, despite his more usual association with May Day.

Irrespective of the origins of this ceremony, there is a good deal of evidence that suggests that the celebration of the sacred horse was widespread and that the ceremony was firmly attached to the Winter Solstice celebrations.

RIGHT: Many pre-Christian artifacts testify to the importance the horse.

The White and Gray Mares

In Ireland we hear of the *láir bhán* or "White Mare," which went round with the Wren Boys. A framed-hoop covered with white cloth, it was a frightening presence. But by far the most dramatic of these hooded horses is the Welsh *Mari Llwyd* or "Gray Mare." This resembled the Hooden Horse in most respects, except that the head was made from an actual mare's skull. Decorated with ribbons it was also called the *Aderyn Bee y Llwyd* or "Gray Magpie." A description dating from 1819 shows that this was actually a derivative of the older horse custom:

The Adryn Bee y Llwyd ... is formed from the skeleton bones of a horse's head, furnished with artificial eyes and ears, and highly decorated with ribbons and coloured paper; it is borne by a man whose person is concealed beneath a long cloth; his art is to imitate the amblings, curvetings, startings and kicking of the horse; he is attended by a groom, whose business it is to soothe his affected angers and fears, and keep him within proper bounds; three or four partners in the profits of the expedition, who are by turns horse, groom or attendants, accompany him from house to house, and after a due exhibition of the horse's various antics, a hat is put into his mouth, and a collection levied upon the spectators.

QUOTED IN CAWTE,
RITUAL ANIMAL DISGUISE

Other accounts suggest a more elaborate ritual in which a kind of riddling exchange was carried on between the Mari Llwyd's and people within the houses. The first few verses were standard, but after this they became extempore, with each side vying to keep the song going, fitting elaborate and increasingly surreal lyrics to the traditional tune. An example from the Rhondda Valley in Wales began as follows:

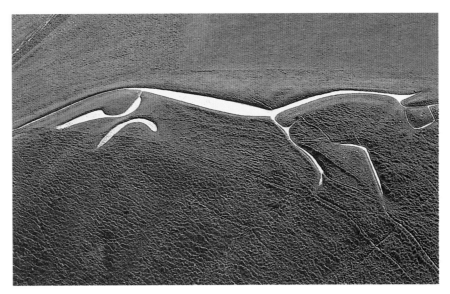

ABOVE: The Uffington White Horse etched into a hillside is probably the oldest image of the sacred horse to be found in Britain.

Well here we come,
Innocent friends,
To ask leave, to ask leave
To ask leave to sing.

To this the inhabitants of each house had to answer, in verse, and keeping to the tune. As the contest progressed, the Mari would become increasingly difficult to understand, as in the following examples:

Mari Llwyd the cheerful,
A frisker would enter,
And to sing is her object,
I trow.

You need not push
And raise the latch tonight,
I'm an unbeatable poet
And that I will prove.

There will also be Punch and Judy,
Both with the same instinct,
Two villains of the color of the Devil,
Or of the chimney place itself.

In the end, if the singer representing the Mari felt unable to continue (often he was thoroughly drunk by now) he might sing:

Now I finish my singing,
Open the door to us,
It's cold outside for the gray mare,
Its heels are almost frozen.

The Mari having been admitted, the exchange finished with blessings:

We wish you joy,
To sustain a new year,
While the bell is rung,
May you prosper every day.

In Gower, also in Wales, the horse's head was buried and dug up again every year, suggesting the even older tradition of a preservation of a sacred skull. It is evident that what we are seeing here is the last vestige of a truly ancient ceremony in which a mare's skull was ritually circulated and some kind of combat, or mock combat, entered into.

The Feast of the Dead

Behind this ritual lies a very ancient ceremony that has to do with the passing of the dead and our own continued connection to them. The Celtic festival of Samhain, celebrated from November to December, was essentially a feast of the dead, celebrating those who had passed into the Otherworld, but who were still welcome at the table. It was a time of mystery and darkness, just like the Solstice itself, and the mystery is carried over into the memory of those ancient ceremonies, such as that of the Mari Llwyd and the Hooden Horse.

At one time these may well have been associated with a horse sacrifice, or even as a means of selecting a human victim whose death would ensure the rebirth of the New Year. Even as recently as the last century the horse visitors retained something of this fearsome aspect. Reports from nineteenth-century Kent and Pembrokeshire speak of the horse frightening women to death; yet at Lower Hardres in 1857, a German woman in an invalid chair was galvanized out of it into good health again. The hobby horse is very interested in women, while the Padstow 'Oss is reputed to make women pregnant. There is a typical ribald nature to all of these beings which hearkens back to an earlier society where fertility was a funda-mental matter of the future survival of the community. When the Mari, with its eyes gleaming in its parched white skull, came to the door it was better to open up at once or be prepared to defend oneself with poetic skill.

LEFT: Dances with a Hooden Horse are still widely performed in Britain today.

Soul Cakes and the Wild Horse

All Saints' and All Souls' Days, which fall on the first two days in November, are now recognized as Christian holidays, though they are of much older origin, celebrating the period when the ancestors were close at hand. At one time "soul cakes" were baked and set out for ghosts to eat. In later times, during the Middle Ages and the Reformation, this became part of a ritual exchange – a cake was given in payment for prayers uttered for the dead. By Victorian times it was the "souling gifts," usually beer or money given in exchange for the cakes, that were all important. A song, still sung by children in and around Cheshire, England, goes:

> *A soul, a soul, for a souling cake*
> *I pray, good missus, a souling cake*
> *Apple or pear, plum or cherry*
> *Anything good to make us merry.*

In the same area a "Souling" or "Soul Cakers" play is also performed. This consists of a team of men and boys who parade around the local villages in much the same way as with the Mari Llwyd or the Hooden Horse (*see page 156*). But at the end, almost as an appendix to the play, the Wild Horse and his Driver come in, and the horse proceeds to mock and jest with the audience while the driver tries to pacify him. This is finally done by speaking a kind of calming, praising formula, which quiets the beast and makes him receptive to the giving of coins and cakes. The following words were recorded at Antrobus in Cheshire:

> *Now ladies and gentlemen just look around*
> *and see if you saw a better class beast*
> *out of England's ground.*
>
> *He has a h'eye like a hawk, a neck like a*
> *swan, a pair of ears made from an old*
> *lady's pocket book, so read it if you can!*
>
> *Every time he opens his mouth his head's*
> *half off. Tell you what, if you can look down*
> *his mouth you can see*
> *the holes in his socks!*
> *Whoa! Stand still Dick!*
>
> *He's a very fine horse, he's very fine bred!*
> *On Antrobus oats this horse has been fed.*
> *He's won the Derby, and the Oaks,*
> *and finished up pulling an old milk float!*
> *So stand still, Dick, and show yourself!*
> *Whoa now, stand still, stand still!*

Such fierce rivalry existed between the various villages in the area that it was not unusual for one to steal from another. The Antrobus men stole the Comberback horse in 1953, but afterwards returned it, while a team from Warburton stole the Lynn horse in 1960. At one time there may well have been a ritual battle to decide the disposition of the Wild Horse, possession of which would have brought good luck as well as high regard to those who kept it through the year.

ABOVE: The symbol of the horse is ancient and may be connected to fertility – this could explain the bawdiness of many modern horse rituals.

The Year Horse

That the horse itself, in all its many guises, was once identified with the old year, is evidenced by a song collected in Derbyshire:

> He once was a young horse,
> And in his youthful prime,
> My master used to ride on him,
> And thought him very fine.
>
> And now that he's grown old,
> And nature doth decay,
> My master frowns upon him,
> And these wor's I've heard him say:
>
> It is a poor old horse,
> And he's knocking at your door,
> And if you please to let him in,
> He'll please you all I'm sure,
> Poor old horse, poor old horse...

Throughout most of these customs we are seeing the last vestiges of a once extensive cosmic drama, enacted across the northern lands at the time of the Solstice to determine that the old year's passing gave way properly to the birth of the new.

The Great Bear

In Europe the season of Winter closes with the emergence of the bear at Candlemas, or St. Blaise's Day, called "The Bear's Fart." The Armenian St. Blaise is said to have hidden in a cave while under persecution; he is the keeper of the winds, and, like the bear who doesn't eat, excrete, or urinate during hibernation, but on arising issues a long farting blast to announce the coming of Spring. The bear is thus a prophet of the seasons, and since it is popularly believed to hibernate for six weeks, if it does indeed come forth on Candlemas, this makes its sleep date from Midwinter itself. As one who seems to turn the wheel of the seasons miraculously in its annual renewal, the bear is one of the chief animals of winter.

The importance of the bear was acknowledged in a number of ceremonies throughout Europe. At Arles-sur-Tech in southern France during the Middle Ages, on the Sunday following Candlemas, a cave was constructed in the middle of the town square, and a man dressed in a bearskin ran about wildly chasing a "victim," chosen from among the people, who was subsequently caught and dragged into the "cave." Then, at a table set with cakes and wine, the "victim" was married to the bear. We are not told whether the victim was male or female, but in the hunting customs of the Finns, we find remnants of a similar ritual marriage where, setting out for the bear's den, hunters would be said to "go and wed the forest virgin." In Andorra, a bear guiser goes about with a trainer at Christmas time. He is primed with a gallon of wine, chases people, catches a girl and takes her to an improvised cave where he is given a pretend shave, shot, and then resurrected.

Since we have exterminated most of our bears in urban Europe, the bear's myth and qualities have been transferred to the badger. However, memories linger on in Poland, Hungary, and Austria, where Bear's Day is still celebrated at the same time as Ground Hog Day in the United States.

The Straw Bear

The cult of the Bear Mother is a part of European culture that stretches from Artemis in Greece to Artio in Celtic Switzerland. In Britain this ancient reverence is focused on the ceremonial procession of the Straw Bear, in which a man, wrapped from head to foot in twisted straw bands, dances through the

*ABOVE: The bear's yearly hibernation cycle has made
it an important symbol of annual renewal.*

streets of Whittlesey, near Peterborough, Cambridgeshire. This now takes place on the Sunday before Plough [Plow] Monday (usually the first Monday after Twelfth Night, when the plow and the plowman receive blessings from the church), but before 1909, when the custom was temporarily suppressed as a form of begging, the Straw Bear was to be found throughout the fenlands of eastern Britain between Peterborough and Huntingdon. At this time he was accompanied by the "Plough Monday Witches," and took part in a Mummer play or mock combat in which the bear was slain and resurrected. Before this he went around by night instead of in daylight, knocking on the doors of houses and demanding money in a more menacing fashion reminiscent of the Mari Llwyd or the Hooden Horse.

The tradition is probably very ancient, given the importance of the bear cult in Britain right up until the Middle Ages. Similar practices were also once common in Germany and Andorra, and probably the custom in its present form was brought into Britain by the Saxons during the sixth century.

The Mothers

And what of the merry band that make their tour of a locality with a sacred animal disguise, the band of dancers, singers, taunters, and good fellows? Are they the disruptive companions, the *genii cucullati*, the small hooded spirits who in Celtic tradition accompany the great female principles known simply as the Mothers?

In Britain, the She-Male – Mollie with her broom in Kent, Judy with her broom in Wales, or the nameless dual-sexed character in Cheshire and Dorset – frequently accompanies the Midwinter Beasts on their passage through the villages. We may recall the She-Male who carries a stick and ladle in the Abbot's Bromley Horn Dance (*see page 142*), and who rattles the stick in the ladle in a suggestive manner. Do we see here earlier figures, like the Celtic goddess or Regain with her churn, or the Russian Baba Yaga with her pestle and mortar? All are stirrers of creation, such as the Indian goddess Durgha whose festival involves nine days and nights of dancing.

Behind all of these figures stands an even more ancient goddess, known variously as the Gyre Carlin, Nicneven, the Cailleach Beare (Old Woman of Beare or the Cailleach Bheur), the Blue-Faced Hag, or Black Annis. She is the old mountain mother in whose care the elements are stirred up, and the goddess with the hammer who strikes the ground at the festival of Samhain in November to make the ice, and from

ABOVE: Putting on the skin of a bear brought strength to its wearer.

whose apron the snows are thrown down. She is the Scandinavian Mother Hulda or the American Mother Carey who plucks her goose to make it snow. Hulda (or Holde) has her own wild hunt for unbaptized babies and children. She is associated with the Sleeping King myth of Barbarossa. Their procession makes the fields give forth double, for she is a mistress of fertility. The broom, so often carried by the She-Male, is a symbol of female sexuality, and in rural areas a broom outside a door was a sign that a man was welcome, especially if the woman were a widow.

The place of the mother in the pattern of the Solstice was celebrated on *Modranect* or "Mothers' Night," as noted by the seventh-century chronicler the Venerable Bede, who says that the Angles began their year on December 24-25th with this celebration. Indeed the cult of the Mothers was widespread in northern Europe, and the festival did not belong to the Mother of God – or to her Son – but to the plurality of the Mothers who gave birth to the Midwinter sun.

The Twelve Beasts of Winter

The Twelve Nights of Christmas are remembered through a whole variety of reckoning songs. We are all familiar with "On the First Day of Christmas," but there is another – discovered by Cecil Sharp in Bridgewater, Somerset – which, though less well known, adds an interesting dimension to the listing of creatures that can be associated with the season.

Jolly Old Hawk

Jolly old hawk and his wings were gray
Now let us sing:
Who's going to win the girl but me?

Jolly old hawk and his wings were gray
Sent to my love on the firstmost day:
A jolly old hawk and his wings were gray.

Sent to my love on the secondmost day:
Two little birds and a
Jolly old hawk and his wings were gray.

Sent to my love on the thirdmost day:
A three-thrustled cock,
Two little birds and a
Jolly old hawk and his wings were gray.

Sent to my love on the fourthmost day:
A four-legged pig...
Jolly old hawk and his wings were gray.

Sent to my love on the fifthmost day:
Five for a fifth and a faring...
Jolly old hawk and his wings were gray.

Sent to my love on the sixthmost day:
Six old cows as they was a-bawling...
Jolly old hawk and his wings were gray.

Sent to my love on the seventhmost day:
Seven young calves as they run before them...
Jolly old hawk and his wings were gray.

Sent to my love on the eighthmost day:
Eight old bulls as they was a-blaring...
Jolly old hawk and his wings were gray.

Sent to my love on the ninthmost day:
Nine old hens as they was a-quarreling...
Jolly old hawk and his wings were gray.

Sent to my love on the tenthmost day:
Ten old cocks crow loud in the morning...
Jolly old hawk and his wings were gray.

ABOVE: The ox and the cow were traditionally believed to be present on Christmas Night, but folklore across Europe suggests the importance of other beasts at this celebratory time.

Sent to my love on the eleventhmost day:
Eleven old mares as they were a-brawling...
Jolly old hawk and his wings were gray

Now let us sing...

Sent to my love on the twelfthmost day:
Twelve old bears as they was a-roaring,
Eleven old mares as they were a-brawling,
Ten old cocks crow loud in the morning,
Nine old hens as they was a-quarrelling,
Eight old bulls as they was a-blaring,
Seven young calves as they run before them,
Six old cows as they was a-bawling,
Five for a fifth and a faring,
A four legged pig,
A three-thrustled cock,
Two little birds
And a jolly old hawk.

A Seasonal Sacrifice

Ring out wild bells to the wild sky
The flying cloud, the frosty light;
The Year is dying in the night
Ring out wild bells and let him die.

TENNYSON, RING OUT WILD BELLS

Among indigenous peoples whose very life is dependent upon the livestock of the land, the necessity of eating wild or domestic animals brings them to a relationship with their food sources that even we are now recognizing in our lives. The Native American Cheyenne have a saying, "Let us all be meat, to nourish one another, that we all may grow."

The idea is as ancient as the human species. The need to identify with, to become symbolically related to the animals you kill and eat, inevitably gives an idea of the special relationship of humans to their gods. "The first religion is to kill God and eat him or her," says the anthropologist, Weston LaBarre. "The second is to give yourself away, to surrender yourself to something other, to become one with the universe as it is represented by bird or beast, fish or flesh." This is arrived at by putting on the skins of animals, or the feathers of birds, and of moving into a sort of trance that gives one the sense of being the creature whose form one somehow inhabits. Ritual animal disguise has been known over most of the world, and its association with the Winter months is consistent.

Death of Beasts

In pastoral societies not dependent on the hunting or trapping of wild animals, the major slaughter of livestock traditionally took place at the heart of Winter (in the rural calendar of Britain at Martinmas on November 11th) since the over-wintering of great numbers of beasts was not practical from the point of view of fresh fodder and shelter. It is at this time that the greatest number of rituals involving animal disguises take place.

There is no doubt that killing vast numbers of animals at special ceremonies and at ritual sites was usual in pre-Christian times. These sacrifices weren't about creating lots of barbecue meat, but about offerings to the spirits of Midwinter. The persistence of this tradition has been acknowledged throughout history. As long ago as A.D. 601, Pope Gregory the Great instructed Abbot Mellitus on his departure for Britain on ways that he might deal with this tendency:

Since they have the custom of sacrificing
many oxen to demons, let some other
solemnity be substituted in its place,
such as a day of Dedication...

They are no longer to sacrifice beasts to
the Devil, but they may kill them for food to
the praise of God, and give thanks to the
Giver of all gifts for the plenty they enjoy.

But slaughtering animals in sacrifice was not the only problem rife in pagan Europe – there was the small matter of people doing bestial things. The seventh-century Archbishop of Canterbury, Theodore, wrote in his penitential:

Whoso goeth about at the Kalends of
January attired as a young stag or as a calf
or changes himself into the likeness of wild
beasts by dressing himself up in animal-
skins and masking himself with their heads:
to any who disguise themselves in this way,
let them take three year's penance, for such
acts are devilish.

Three hundred years earlier, in a homily delivered by Caesarius of Arles in about A.D. 400 we find the following:

Behold the days come, behold the kalends come, and the whole devilish public procession goes forth. The new year is consecrated with old blasphemies. Whatever deformities are lacking in nature, which creation does not know, art labours to fashion. Besides, people are dressed as cattle, and men are turned into women. They laugh at honor, they offend justice, they laugh at public disapproval, they mock at the example of our age, and say that they are doing this as a joke. These are no jokes, these are crimes. A man is changed into an idol, and if it is a fault to go to an idol, what can it mean to be one?

This is a good question, and it brings us back to the idea of our being intimately connected with the natural world. This mode of consciousness is recognized nowadays as a central part of the activity of the shaman, who once had the care of the spiritual selves of people across most of the inhabited world. The putting on of a disguise or mask has a direct effect upon the wearer, who partakes of and adopts the spiritual identity of the mask. The communion of the actor with the mask's spirit is a very profound one, and ritual theater of many kinds – whether it be spirit dancers in Nepal or Greek actors in a drama – acknowledges the respect that is due to the mask. When a guiser puts on animal disguise, he or she enters into communion with that animal's spirit. And when that happens, behavior changes radically. This is

why "persones wyth Vysours... disgysed or apparelde as Mommers" were suppressed by a law of 1511, and remained so until 1829. But Mummers and guisers continued to celebrate the old ways by blackening their faces and hands and drawing patterns on them, rather than in masking – keeping the old rituals alive for hundreds of years after they had ceased to be fully understood either by performers or spectators.

Animal Disguise

The ritual procession of animal disguises shows us dance as both a service and a duty, a necessary reciprocation between ourselves and the spirits of animals who are eaten at this season, and the animals who have ritual relationship with the Winter time. The opening of the underworld entrance performed during the games of Ops and Consus, and the classical idea of the gates of the Solstices (*see Chapter 1*) is echoed in the presence of the She-Male, who sweeps the way for the hobby horse serving as an opener of the gates between the worlds. Holda's underworld realm is reached through a deep well: perhaps by concentration upon the thread that falls from her drop-spindle do we access the lower world. Perhaps we also may find our way into the place where the old year dies and witness the miracle of its rebirth.

RIGHT: Guising is a way of entering into communion with the natural world and the spirit of the animals we rely on.

CELEBRATION

Hallowmas, Halloween, Samhain, whatever name we call it, the night between October 31st and November 1st is traditionally associated with a feast in honor of the Ancestors. It comes a little before the actual Solstice tide, but acts as a satisfying introduction to the coming celebrations. Many ceremonies cluster around this time, and if we simplify these we arrive at certain key incidents that can still be celebrated with meaning.

A SOULING RITUAL FOR HALLOWMAS

On the night of Halloween set the dinner table with an extra place and put a glass and a plate with some food on it. Make an offering to the Ancestors – who may be specific members of your own family, or more generally the ancestors of your own race or culture. If you are of Celtic stock, no matter where you live, you may wish to make your invocation to the ancient lineage of that people. (The same applies whatever the country of your family's origin.) You may wish to make a formal invocation of the Old Ones, using your own words, but here is a suggested formula that may be freely adapted to your needs.

On this holiest night
I call out to the Ancestors
Of my family, my tribe, and my race.
And I ask them to be present for this time,
and I welcome them with kindness
and this offering of food and drink,
that they may bring a blessing
into this house and all who dwell herein.

Make sure there are plenty of candles around the room and especially in the windows (covered lanterns will do as well if there is a safety factor). These serve as a sign to the spirits of the departed that they are welcome in your house.

ABOVE: Candles will not only give atmosphere, but will also welcome the spirits of the Ancestors into your home.

SOUL CAKES

The making of Soul Cakes is a tradition that stretches back to the time of the Ancestors. Shared out at the time of Samhain or Halloween they can become once again a part of this ancient celebration. While on a visit to friends in the United States a few years ago, I introduced the idea of Soul Cakes to the family with whom I was staying. This caught on and, much to my delight, was enacted again on the following year. It is in this way that ancient traditions are preserved and reinstated, sometimes long after they had been forgotten.

MAKING SOUL CAKES

1. *Cream ½ cup/4oz/100g of butter and ½ cup/4oz/100g of fine white sugar in a bowl. Beat in three egg yolks.*

2. *Sift together 2 cups/8oz/225g of unbleached white flour and 1tsp of mixed spice, and add to the mixture.*

3. *Stir in ¼ cup/1½oz/40g of raisins and add a little milk to make a soft dough.*

4. *Shape the dough into flat round cakes and place them on a greased cookie tray.*

5. *Mark each cake with a spiral using a knife.*

6. *Bake the cakes in a oven preheated to 180°C/350°F/Gas Mark 4 for 10-15 minutes until brown.*

INVITING IN THE CREATURES OF THE SOLSTICE

Nowadays we tend to live with our animals as pets, allowing them different levels of closeness according to our personal habits. At one time when we all lived closer to the natural world, as part of a farming community, or as hunters or trappers, we had a far greater sense of oneness with all creatures. Because the Solstice is, as we have seen, a time of special importance to the animals, you may wish to make a feast for them, inviting them to share the bounty of the old year and the promise of the new. But whether or not you are close to any one creature or creatures, you can still celebrate the importance of animals by making a special kind of cake.

The idea for this came out of a celebration for the shamanic power animals and spirit helpers of an individual working in the shamanic tradition of Europe. It is simple and requires only the baking of a cake of any kind. Once the cake has cooled it can be decorated with appropriately colored icing, then a number of animal figurines are placed upon it. A circle of animals is the traditional pattern. These are easily obtained from hobby or toy stores, most of which have these kind of figures readily available. The cake can then be finished off with a frill made from straw or cornstalks, and a few candles if required. This makes a dramatic and powerful centerpiece to the Midwinter table and becomes a very real celebration of the importance of the Solstice animals. Finally, you may wish to make an invocation of the animal powers over the cake:

Creatures of the wild world,
We honor your strength
We honor your power,
We honor your joy!

May you bring us:
The Gift of your presence,
The Blessing of your truth,
The Light of your being,
Now and through the year to come.

A PLACE FOR ALL

The best way to welcome in the animals of the Solstice is by making a place for them in your own world. If you have a yard you can erect and decorate a special tree on which birds may come and perch — after all why should we be the only ones who enjoy a Christmas tree? You can make a rocky area the special preserve of frogs and toads, birdhouses, a pool for small fish or tadpoles, and if you are really in the wilds, a welcome shelter for wintering animals. Offering the hospitality of your yard in this way is something that can be planned earlier in the year. Plant flowers to attract pollinating insects, leave some ground untended to offer shelter for creatures, plant native species of plants to encourage local wildlife. Once again, at a time when we feed ourselves to a full sufficiency with Christmas fare, it is well worthwhile remembering the other species at this time, putting out food for them wherever we can.

Those who live in country areas may find that the natural scavengers and local wildlife do not need encouragement to come closer to human dwellings — they already come down from woods and mountains, drawn by the waste and plenty that we offer. As a practical commitment to helping wild animals preserve their natural habitat, become involved with local and national groups who are doing their best to restore or maintain animal habitats.

GUISING TODAY

The tradition of guising has retained a hold on our imagination through the tradition of Trick or Treating on Halloween. If you live in or near a rural area of Britain and can visit any number of places where the old mumming or guising events still take place, and you can very easily get caught up in the power of the Midwinter celebration in this way. In the United States, the Revels movement performs Mummer plays and many other ancient Solstice celebrations (see Resources p.247).

However, if you live in a country or part of the land where these old customs have been forgotten, why not revive them? You can begin in a small, community way, with a group of friends. Find out about the local traditions of animal disguising, about stories of animals that are strongly associated with the Solstice tide. (There are probably more of these than you realize.) If you decide to have a guising around Solstice, people will need to prepare masks and costumes. Some guisers wear old warm clothing upon which strips of different colored, tattered rags have been sewn in layers to create a shaggy effect. To the viewer, even though the animal head may be quite naturalistic, the effect of a human body from the shoulders downward is always surprising, and brings an atavistic shiver to the spine. The intention of guisers is to represent the spiritual aspect of the animals who are the sacred guardians of Winter.

Beneath the many customs of guising in Britain, there is an ancient tradition of honoring the animal that represents Winter's most prehistoric remembrance. The Wittlesey Straw Bear parade, during which a man dressed as a straw bear walks the streets to music, takes place in East Anglia in early January, and is a distant echo of the ancient bear-rites enacted in caves. Among indigenous peoples who still maintain customs of guising, we can still perceive how deeply sacred these ceremonies are. They are an archaic bridge to the beginnings of our human existence, in which we may rediscover a proper humility and thankfulness for the gifts of animals to our own kind.

It is comparatively easy to construct an animal mask or even a more elaborate "hobby" horse. You could then proceed around the neighborhood with a few friends singing the old songs (of which there are several examples in this book) and offering these in exchange for cakes and ale or candies. You could even collect corn or other seeds that can be planted later in an appropriate fashion and with the right words of blessing.

FOLLOWING PAGES: Dressing in animal costume is a powerful way of acknowledging our connection with the animal world.

RIGHT: Guising is a traditional Solstice practice that is very easy to take up.

*ABOVE: The Twelve Days of Christmas stand outside of
"ordinary time," and celebrations focus on the return of the
sun and a continuation of the eternal cycle of life.*

Chapter 6

THE TWELVE DAYS OF CHRISTMAS

Here at the Gateway of the year,
Let us strive upward toward the heights.

LA FÊTE DE L'ANE

The days from Christmas Eve on December 24th to Epiphany on the 6th of January (actually fourteen days as the first two are not included in the twelve) really exist outside of linear time. They are, in a sense, the fruit of the past year, one day for each month that has passed. No matter which calendrical system one follows there are certain extra days – called intercalary – such as the 29th day added to February in a Leap Year, which make up the necessary fluctuations in the earth's orbit around the sun.

ABOVE: In the West the importance of the Twelve Days to the Christian calendar is well known, but it is also an extraordinary time in many other ways.

In 1582 Pope Gregory reformed the calendar originated by the Roman Emperor Julian to correct the imbalance. He noted that the Julian calendar, which extended to 365$\frac{1}{4}$ days, meant that by the sixteenth century ten days had been "lost," and set about the correction of this. It was not until 1751 that the new calendar was accepted in Britain. By then the number of "lost" days had grown to eleven, and when an act of Parliament made the new calendar law, rioters stampeded through the streets of London demanding the return of the days the government had "stolen" from them!

In both ancient Egypt and the Classical world, the intercalary days were regarded as special, and were given over to the honoring of the gods – a custom that continues in the Christian calendar in the giving of certain days to the honoring of the saints. Although the twelve days are not really intercalary days, in A.D. 560 the Council of Tours declared them part of the festival of Christmas, and for some time after this the tradition in parts of Europe was to light twelve bonfires in honor of the twelve apostles during the festival.

In both Christian and pagan traditions the twelve days have included a wide variety of customs and celebrations. In this chapter will be found a brief account of the associations appropriate to each day, followed by a meditation or activity to do with the feast. In this way, those who wish may celebrate the whole festival, and discover for themselves the shape and meaning of the Winter Solstice.

Of course the best way to appreciate the pattern of the Solstice is in the same way our ancestors used to do – in the open air. In order to experience the turning and returning of the sun, go out every day with a partner as near to midday as possible from two weeks before to two weeks after December 22nd. Stand at the same point and have your partner mark the length of your shadow with a stick. Make a note of the difference every day and at the end of the time you will have a pattern of the falling and rising arc of the sun. This will show you as well as anything could, that the Solstice is the festival of the returning sun.

DAY 0

CHRISTMAS DAY: BIRTHDAY OF JESUS, MITHRAS, ATTIS, AION, HORUS, DIONYSUS, AND THE UNCONQUERED SUN

Since Christmas Day itself is not counted as one of the Twelve Days, we shall call it 0, and for this day we begin with a meditation.

LEARNING TO MEDITATE

The best way of doing this is to ensure a measure of uninterrupted privacy (not always easy on Christmas Day) in a place where you feel comfortable and at ease. Read the meditation onto a tape. Then, seat yourself in an upright chair, press the "play" button, close your eyes, breathe deeply and regularly until you are completely relaxed, and follow the meditation where it leads you. You will get the best results from this if you try to be present with the action rather than watching it in your head like a story on a television screen. You may also wish to have pencil and paper close by to write down any realizations which come to you during the meditation.

The Sun at Midwinter: A Meditation

I invite you to come with me on a journey. Closing your eyes, and sinking deeply into meditation, allow the surroundings in which you are seated to fade slowly into the background.

You find yourself standing within a circle of twelve mighty trees, on each of which is carved a symbol connected to the changing seasons of the year. Turn to face one of these trees, and see carved upon it the sign of the holly, and above it the Unconquered Sun – the signs of Midwinter. Looking up into the tree, which towers impossibly far above you, see that the branches are evenly spaced as though in the rungs of a ladder. The tree whispers to you: "climb! climb...!" This you do, setting your hands upon the first branch and springing lightly upward; setting your feet on the next branch and reaching up for the one above that....

You climb swiftly and easily, but as far as you go there always seems another branch above you until, suddenly, you reach the top. You step out from the last branch and find yourself in a snowy landscape, lit by the glow of the glorious Midwinter sun, which lies low upon the horizon. Ahead and on all sides are gentle slopes, some crowned by trees, each branch and twig outlined in white. The snow is soft beneath your feet, and a sharp wind nips your face. The stillness wraps around you like a blanket.

Then you hear a sound, a distant, far-off drumming and jingling, which gradually become distinguishable as the thunder of hooves and the jingling of small bells. There comes toward you from the North a marvelous figure. Dressed all in skins, from head to toe, long hair streaming in the wind, a huge man – tall and powerful, riding astride a great reindeer whose antlers seem to sweep the sky. Bells are sewn all over his costume, and he carries in his hand a mighty bough of holly in full green leaf. Reaching out with his holly staff he touches you on the head and you are at once transformed into the likeness of bird or beast, your heart filled with the joy of the Midwinter sun.

Now the mighty figure on the reindeer's back wheels away and is off across the white world and you follow, flying and racing and bounding at his back. How long and how far you run there is no saying, but when at last the great figure slows to a halt you are no more tired than when you began. You feel as if you could run forever, and that to do so would be to honor the joyful life of the earth and the sun that warms your blood and pierces your heart with its burnished rays. Now the mighty figure leaps down from the reindeer's back, and beckons you to follow. You find yourself back in your own shape, standing among a ring of huge tumbled rocks, which rise like sharp fins above the ocean of snow. Here, in the center of a dip in the ground a great fire, as yet unlit, has been laid. You stand beside it in silent waiting, while the great one who has led us here strides to where a single tall tree stands alone.

Here the mighty figure raises to his lips an ancient horn and lets blow a blast that echoes again and again from the rocks. For a moment there is silence, then from all sides come animals and birds of every kind – slow-moving bears, fast-leaping hares, foxes, weasels, stoats, badgers, and all their kin. Robins fly down to perch on the horns of the deer, wrens,

ABOVE: Running hares and other woodland creatures can be part of your meditation on the wonders of nature.

plovers, partridges, and strutting cockerels with their harems of hens. All these and more, more than you can name, come flocking near, hunter and hunted standing side by side without fear.

There also come other beings: spirits of the unseen worlds – dryads and fairy folk and the people of the sidhe; strange and wondrous beings whose names you no longer recall, until the circle if filled and overflows beyond your sight. Then a silence falls over all, humans and spirits and creatures alike, and there is a sense of waiting, a quietude. Your eyes are drawn towards the West, where the great round red ball of the Midwinter sun hangs just above the horizon.

Now the figure of the mighty one comes forward, the bells on his costume chiming softly, and there at the foot of the solitary tree he bends and unwraps a bundle. Within are flint and tinder, ancient and dark. Crouching down, he strikes a spark, and at once a flower of light blossoms between his hands. The fire licks hungrily at the tree, and then in flash strikes upward, clothing the tree from root to tip in a vestment of light.

Yet, although the fire burns bright and hot, the tree is not consumed; through the leaping flames you can see the trunk and branches clearly. And, as though at a signal, the sun begins to descend and in moments is gone below the horizon's edge, leaving all there surrounded by the dark, eyes and hearts turning eagerly toward the burning tree.

The great one turns his bright and laughing face toward you, and you become aware that you are holding a torch in your hand, as yet unlit. With a wave of his hand the figure bids you come forward and take the light from the burning tree. This you do, and others follow suit, until you stand in a circle of light, your brand held high in your hand, torch light dancing on the creatures who surround you on every side.

Then in your mind you hear words, bidding you to light the central fire. You set your burning brand to the heaped up brushwood, which bursts into incandescent flame with a great whoosh! of energy and heat. Then again you hear words, the voice of the great one echoing in your ears, though his lips never seem to move:

Behold the Solstice fire!
Behold the wonder of
the sun at Midwinter!
Accept the blessing of the
old ones and take the
light back into your world in the
kindled fires of your heart!

As you hear these words a great warmth spreads through you, and wherever you look you see the light burning within and around those who stand with you. And, though it seems but a moment since it set, the sun rises in splendor and casts is light upon all. You stand in absolute silence for a moment, then you join with all those present in a great shout of acclamation, praising the newborn sun.

Then in good time the great being swings a huge sack from off his back, and with laughter and joy invites you to come forward and receive a gift, something for yourself alone, the gifts of the Midwinter god to his children.

ABOVE: Make the ancient sacred animals, such as the deer, a part of your Midwinter meditation

When all there have received a gift, again you hear the great voice speaking to your innermost self:

You have journeyed far to bear witness to the birth of the Unconquered Sun. Be sure that you take with you to your own world the glorious Solstice light. And I bid you never to forget the weight of the sack on your own back, the sack of tradition, born and yet unborn, which it is your bounden duty to reverence and respect. For remember, if the old ways are allowed to die, there may come a day when the sun will not arise on this day of days, and only darkness will remain. May that time never come, and may we meet again in the silent heart of the solstice this many a day!

With these words ringing in your ears, you take up your burning brand and turn away from the great tree and the mighty figure who stands beneath it, but not before you have glimpsed, somehow present within the form of the mighty one, other figures: ancient reindeer men with antlers upon their heads; gift-bringers from the dawn of time, light-bearers and lantern holders from the mystery of time. And, somehow among all these, you see the mighty figure of the spirit of Christmas: Sintaklass, Odin, Nicholas, Old Sir Christmas – by whatever name and whatever form he has been recognized since the beginning. To you he raises his hand and sends you back, through the veils between the worlds, back and down and inward, until you awake, slowly and gently, in our own place and time, conscious of the fire that has been ignited in your hearts, and ready for the joyful celebration of the Solstice Revels.

DAY 1

ST. STEPHEN'S DAY, BOXING DAY, DAY OF THE WREN

Then followeth St. Stephen's Day,
whereon doth every man
His horses jaunt, and course
abroad as quickly as he can,
Until they do extremely sweat,
and then they let them blood;

For this being done upon this day,
they say doth do them good,
And keep them from all maladies
and sickness through the year,
As if that Stephen any time took
charge of horses here.

NAOGEORGUS.
TRANS. BARNABE GEORGE

ABOVE: The horse is central to many of the stories surrounding St. Stephen, and can be a good focus for St. Stephen's Day celebrations.

St. Stephen's Day, or Boxing Day as it is known in Britain, from the custom of giving a Christmas Box to servants on this date, draws together a number of Solstice traditions. We have already learned of the ancient practice of hunting the wren, the King of all birds (*see Chapter 5*), and of displaying the tiny corpse around the villages throughout Britain and Ireland. The origins of this custom probably date back to the time when kings were slaughtered after a year in office – and in France up until the seventeenth century the first person to kill and display the body of the wren was chosen king for a day at the time of the Feast of Fools (*see Chapter 1*).

The association of the wren killing with St. Stephen's Day may well derive from a legend of the saint's visit to Scandinavia. In this story Stephen, having been captured by soldiers, was about to make his escape when the wren uttered its noisy song and awoke his guards – for which reason the wren is said to be unlucky

and it is, indeed, considered a misguided act to kill the bird on any other day of the year.

St. Stephen himself, according to legend, was once a servant of the biblical King Herod. When he saw the star of the nativity he sought to know more of the Child of Wonder born in the stable, and as a result changed his allegiance to a new king.

Not a great deal more is known of this saint, who is generally called the first Christian martyr, but a number of interesting legends have gathered about his name. In one of these he is said to have reached Sweden, and to have established a church there from which he rode forth to preach and teach the Christian message. To enable him to travel the great distances through often inhospitable country he had a string of five horses: two red, two white, and one dappled. Whenever one of these became tired Stephen would simply mount another. However, as he was traveling through a particularly deep stretch of forest, he was set upon by brigands, who killed him and tied his body to the back of an unbroken colt. This beast, bearing the saint's body, galloped all the way back to Stephen's home. His grave there subsequently became a place of pilgrimage, and perhaps because of the association with horses, sick beasts were brought there for healing. Stephen is still known as the patron saint of horses to this day.

The themes of Boxing Day, then, have to do with death and resurrection and animals. The former makes it particularly appropriate that it is on this day that the Mummer plays are most often performed.

BELOW: You can get inspiration for your celebrations from ancient sources, such as this "newspaper" rock found in Utah, in the United States.

CELEBRATING THE ANIMALS

Make any kind of favourite cake, ice it and decorate it with a circle of animal figures. These can be homemade of modeling clay, or bought from any toy store. Read the following invocation over the cake as you serve it.

Creatures of the wild world,
We honor your strength,
We honor your power,
We honor your joy!
May you bring us:
The Gift of your presence,
The Blessing of your truth
The Light of your being,
Now and through the year to come.

DAY 2

MOTHER NIGHT, ST. JOHN'S DAY

*Heaven distill your
balmy showers
For now is risen the
bright day star...*

*The clear sun,
whome no cloud devours
Surmounting Phoebus
in the east
Is come out of his
heavenly towers
And to us a son is born.*

WILLIAM DUNBAR:
THE NATIVITIE OF CHRIST

*ABOVE: The Twelve Days of Christmas were said to be a time when the
supernatural realm was close, and when the Wild Hunt rode through the night.*

In the Christian calendar the second day of Christmas is given over to St. John, the beloved disciple. Throughout Germany and Austria, it is still customary to have the priest bless the wine on this day. The resulting "St. John's wine" is considered very lucky and is believed to have healing properties. It is preserved throughout the year, and even ordinary bottles placed next to it are said to taste better!

From the earliest times the twelve days have been regarded as a time when supernatural events can easily happen, when the dead are close at hand and might often be seen. One reads of the Wild Hunt, or the Fairy Host riding across the lands of Britain and Germany in particular, led by characters such as King Arthur, Woden, and Arawn, the Celtic god of the Underworld. In Ireland these supernatural hunters are known as the Yule Host, and in common with all of these bands they are believed to gather up wandering souls and carry them away to the Otherworld.

Another older figure was known throughout Germany as Frau Holle, (Holda, Hulda), but a better name for her might be Mother Christmas. Deriving from the ancient figure of the Mother Goddess, the feminine principle of deity, she was regarded as a bringer of fertility, abundance, and justice. Usually depicted as a tall and beautiful woman dressed in white and with a golden girdle, she rode though the land during the twelve days dispensing gifts from a sleigh pulled by dogs. In Germany she is known as Frau Gode and if she passes a house with an open door she sends one of her dogs in to take up residence. If this gift is turned away, or harmed, ill luck will follow. In the United States in more recent times, she has become associated with Mother Carey, a folk figure who combines many of the aspects of Frau Holle.

It was probably this figure, or a variant of her, to whom the Saxons in Britain devoted a day at this time of year, calling it *Modranicht* or

Mother Night. The Church tried to replace the real object of worship for this day with the Virgin Mary, and turned Holda from a gentle goddess whose special care was for children, into a horrible witch who stole the unbaptized souls of children and carried them off with her. Yet her name, *Holda*, literally means "kindly one" and she often rewarded people who were kind, or helped her, with gold or other gifts. In the Tyrol the following story is told. At midnight on the Eve of Epiphany a peasant was walking home when he heard behind him the sound of many voices. Berchtl, as she is called here, swept past him in her long white robes, with her train of children running and laughing at her heels. The last, and smallest, was a boy, who kept tripping over his long shirt, and in kindness the peasant gave him his belt to tuck it into. When she saw this, Berchtl turned back and promised him that for his kindness his own children should never want for anything.

Perhaps the most famous story about Mother Holle is the folk tale collected by the Brothers Grimm. In this a woman has two daughters, one fair and hard working, the other ugly and lazy. One day the hardworking girl was sitting spinning beside the well and accidentally pricked her finger so that some blood got onto her spindle. She leaned over the well to wash it and the spindle fell into the water and sank out of sight. Desperately, the girl leaned down to get it back and fell in after it. At the bottom of the well she found herself in a beautiful country, and set out to explore. Along the way she found herself passing an oven full of bread and the bread was crying out: "Take us out, take us out, we are done!" So the kind girl took out the bread. Then she walked on until she came to an apple orchard, and there she heard all the apples calling out, "Shake the

tree, shake the tree, we are ripe!" And she did as she was asked. Then she walked on until she came to a cottage where an old woman was sitting outside. She had very big teeth and the girl was frightened, but the old woman spoke kindly to her and asked if she would work for her. "If you do you'll be rewarded" she said, "for I am Mother Holle." So the girl went to work for Mother Holle and she swept and cleaned and shook out the bedding – and when she did so it snowed on earth, for it is well known that snow is really the feathers from Mother Holle's covers.

Time passed and the girl grew homesick. "I really like being here," she said, "but I want to go home." "You have worked well for me," said Mother Holle, "so you shall go home and I will take you there myself." She led the girl to a gate and opened it. As the girl passed through, golden pieces fell out of the air and covered her, sticking to her until she seemed made of gold. Then Mother Holle gave her back the spindle and sent her home.

When the girl's lazy sister heard what had happened she rushed to the well and made her fingers bleed on a thorn bush, then she threw her spindle into the well and jumped in after it. She soon found herself in the lovely land and walked along until she saw the bread oven. Again the bread called out to be taken out of the oven, but the girl was far too lazy and went on. Nor could she be bothered to shake the apple trees, but hurried on until she came to Mother Holle's cottage. There she asked for work and for the first day or two worked really hard. Gradually she fell back to her old lazy ways until finally Mother Holle told her to go home. But at the doorway from one world into the other it was pitch, not gold, that fell on the girl. And when she got home she could not wash it off and had to go about with the sticky black stuff all over her!

LEFT: In the midst of the numerous male deities and characters associated with the Solstice, try to make room for the remembrance of female ones too.

HONORING THE MOTHERS

There are so many male figures associated with the Solstice we should give room to at least one female character, and who better than Mother Christmas? On this day, include a figure of Holda upon your Winter shrine.

Here is a modern invocation for Holda (Holla) by Diana Paxson:

Holy Holla, in the heavens,
A snowy featherbed you're shaking –
Bless the earth with your white blanket,
Moist the mantle you are making.

Holla high above come riding,
Your Wagon rolls through winter weather;
Turn away your face of terror,
Bless us as we bide together.

Holy Holla, here we gather,
Send us skill in all our spinning,
Huldrefolk [Gnomes] to help in housework,
Wealth and health with your aid winning.

A WINTER SHRINE TO HOLDA

Cut a handful of 10in/25cm lengths of white yarn; fold these together in half and tie them with a contrasting color to create a ring. Into the hollow of the fold, at the head end, you can insert a specially prepared face that you've drawn or else place a sparkling crystal bead. Give your figure arms, if you wish, by pushing a twig wrapped with the same yarn through her belt at the back. She can also have a staff to represent her spindle – the traditional emblem of life's delicate thread. As you place her in your shrine, feel how this figure relates to the other ones that you have placed upon it. Experience her as the one who oversees the household of the Earth, giving all creatures what they need – food and nurture, but also the mercy of death's release when pain and suffering grow too great. Be aware of her as the receiver of all souls who leave this life at Solstice time. But be aware of her also as the one who can bless the household and keep everything running smoothly over the holiday.

DAY 3

HOLY INNOCENT'S DAY, CHILDREMASS

Unto us, a child is given!

GEORGE FRIEDRICH HANDEL: MESSIAH

This day has always, in one way or another, been associated with children. In more recent times the connection is specifically with the children slaughtered at the orders of Herod, who feared the prophecy of the Magi that a new King of the Jews had been born in Judea. On this day the Boy Bishops were installed and led their masters a merry dance (*see Chapter 2*). Throughout the Middle Ages this day was considered particularly unlucky and it was believed that no task begun on December 28th would prosper. Both the French King Louis XI and the English King Edward IV refused to do any business on this date, and the latter postponed his coronation when it was originally planned for this inauspicious date. In Northamptonshire it was known as Dyzmas Day and a local saying was: "What is begun on Dyzmas Day will never be finished." A more barbaric practice that continued well into the eighteenth century was to beat children on this day. This seems to have been a curious mixture of ideas – that if the children were made to suffer on this day they would be spared the rest of the year, and, moreover, that such beatings would drive out any evil spirits who might have taken up residence in the child. These beatings rarely involved real cruelty. Indeed, the underlying theme of the day was of a kind of equality. Thus wives and husbands exchanged token blows, and in parts of Germany and Sweden children were permitted to beat their parents (the custom

also extends to St. Stephen's Day, suggesting that the idea originally had nothing to do with any one of the saints). Freshly gathered evergreen branches were used for this task, with birch and rosemary being particularly popular. A chant preserved from this time goes:

Fresh green! Long life!
Give me a coin!

while in other places servants beat their masters crying:

Fresh, green, fair and fine,
Gingerbread and brandy-wine!

The whole idea seems to have been to show that by expressing individuality and exchanging gentle blows, true anger and aggression might thus be waived for the coming year – an enlightened notion from which we might well learn today!

ABOVE: *Honor children and the innocence of childhood on Holy Innocent's Day.*

HONORING THE CHILDREN

On this day especially we should reflect on the nature of children, about our own childhood and that of our own offspring. Consider the things that you best love about them, as well as their foibles, and your own. Honor your childhood and remember the happy days as well as the sad. What we are as adults comes from what we were as children, so it is worthwhile to reflect on this as well.

ABOVE: Childhood is so often undervalued that it is worth setting time aside to meditate on its wonders.

CELEBRATE CHILDHOOD

• Make a list of the five qualities which best describe your own childhood, and if you have children of your own, ask them what things are most important to them right now. Compare the two, and be prepared for some surprises!
• Now compare your life before they came along, and after.
• Most importantly, praise your children on this day, and honor the qualities of youth that never truly leave us – they are still buried somewhere inside you, even if you are sixty plus!

DAY 4

THE FEAST OF FOOLS

Whoever you are, whatever you sing,
And whatever the thing you're known for,
Come whenever you wish, take what you see,
And once come, stay as long as you like.

DAFYDD BACH AP MADAWG WLADAIDD:
A CHRISTMAS REVEL

TRANS. JOSEPH P.CLANCY

The Feast of Fools, when the normal order of things was ceremonially reversed, has been neglected now for a long while – unfortunately, as it could well serve in our own times as a safe way of letting off steam. Essentially, it allowed people who were restricted from even the most casual of pleasures by the Church, to act in an abandoned way. It was also a time of festivity that was both part of, and sometimes even superseded, Christmas. The following description, from a late medieval chronicler, Edward Hall, describes some of the festivities that took place at the court of King Henry VIII in 1512:

In the hall [was made] a castle, gates, towers and dungeons, garnished with artillery and weapons, after the most warlike fashion: and on the front of the castle was written Le Fortress Dangereux, and within the castle were six ladies clothed in russet satin, laid over with leaves of gold, and every one knit with laces of blue silk and gold. On their heads, coifs and caps all of gold. After the castle had been carried about the hall, and the queen had beheld it, in came the king with five others, apparelled in coats, the one all of russet satin, the other half of rich cloth of gold; on their heads caps of russet satin embroidered with works of fine gold bullion.

These six assaulted the castle. The ladies seeing them so lusty and courageous, were content to solace with them, and upon further communication to yield the castle, and so they came down and danced a long space. And after, the ladies led the knights into the castle, and then the castle suddenly vanished out of their sights. On the day of Epiphany at night, the king, with 11 others, were disguised, after the manner of Italy, called a masque, a thing not seen before in England [sic]; they were apparelled in garments long and broad, wrought all with gold, with visors and caps of gold. And, after the banquet [was] done, these masseurs came in, with six gentlemen disguised in silk, bearing ...torches, and desired the ladies to dance; some were content and some refused. And after they had danced, and communed together, as the fashion of the masque is, they took their leave and departed, and so did the queen and all the ladies.

ABOVE: Perceval, the "Perfect Fool," is a model of what can be achieved by "letting go" at the Feast of Fools.

DOING SOMETHING FOOLISH

Why not celebrate the Feast of Fools by having your own party where things get reversed, where your guests are invited to act as foolishly as they can? Or, if you are alone, and the idea of a party does not tempt you, just spend a short time considering what prevents you from letting go. What constraints are placed on you and by whom – yourself or others? Does the idea of being perceived as foolish trouble you? Think about the foolish knight who achieved the quest of the Holy Grail – Perceval, sometimes called "the Perfect Fool" whose innocence took him where few dared to go, and made him appear foolish.

Meditate on all these things, and then read the accounts of the Feast of Fools again and see if your perception of the celebration has changed. Nowadays it is far easier to act the fool than it once was, and it might be worth while asking why this is. Above all let this be a day of joyful fun and blissful games – even if you do no more than make faces at yourself in the bathroom mirror!

A PARTY OF FOOLS

Invite the guests to put on some silly or inconsequent clothes, paint their faces or fingernails blue (men as well as women!) and organize a food fight or a pie throwing contest. Ask your guests to each write down a forfeit – an action that involves something very silly such as shaving with real cream, singing the words of one song to the tune of another, juggling with oranges – whatever they like. Then each guest should pull out a forfeit from the hat and do their best to obey the instruction.

LEFT: Recreate the old Feast of Fools tradition with role reversal, masks, and general mayhem.

DAY 5

BRINGING IN THE BOAR

Then the grim boar's head
frowned on high,
Crested with bay and rosemary

SIR WALTER SCOTT: MARMION

Two traditions honor the importance of the boar at Solstice tide. In Scandinavia, Frey, the god of sunshine, rode across the sky on his golden-bristled boar, Gulli-burstin, who was seen as a solar image, his spikes representing the rays of the sun. In actuality, the hog, which was sacred to the Celts, provided the meat for the Christmas table, but it seems as though the recurrent references to the boar identify it as a totemistic memory of something older. At any rate the boar seems to have been virtually extinct in Britain before the time of Henry II, who died in 1185. Despite this, the boar continued to exercise a curious fascination, and the ancient University of Oxford boasts not one but two customs that continued until recently. The first of these, at St. John Baptist's College, is described in the following verse dating from 1607:

The Boar is dead,
Lo, here is his head,
What man could have done more
Than his head off to strike,
Meleager like,
And bring it as I do before.

His living spoiled,
Where good men toiled,
Which makes kind Ceres sorry;
But now, dead and drawn,
He is very good brawn,
And we have brought it for ye.

Then set down the swineherd,
The foe of the vineyard,
Let Baccus crown his fall;
Let this boar's head and mustard,
Stand for pig, goose and custard,
And so ye are welcome all!

This is something very reminiscent of an ancient sacrificial event, perhaps not unconnected with the decoration of carcasses hanging in butcher's shops, which only ceased in the last fifty years or so. In Queen's College, Oxford, the ceremonial parading of the boar's head still takes place, to the accompaniment of the famous carol:

The Boar's head in hand bear I
Bedecked with bays and rosemary;
And I pray you, my masters, be merry
Quot estis in convivo.
[So many as are in
the feast]

The Boar's head, as I understand,
Is the rarest dish in all the land
When thus bedecked with a gay garland
Let us servire cantico.
[Let us serve with a song]

Caput apri defero,
Reddens laudes Domino
[The Boar's head I Bring,
Giving praises to God].

Our steward hath provided this
In honor of the King of bliss,
Which on this day to be served is,
In Reginensi atrio.
[In the Queen's Hall]
Caput apri defero
Reddens laudes Domino.

It is not hard to believe that an older ceremony lies behind this, and that when we sing this old song we should remember the great boars of the Solstice and maybe even make some small offering to their memory, such as an apple or orange placed at the back door, should the bristled one pass by.

ABOVE: The passing of the sacrificial boar
is a tradition that has survived in
Britain, despite the animal's extinction by
the beginning of the twelfth century.

MAKING A BOAR'S HEAD

• You can make your own boar's head without loss of bristle to any creature, by using a well-stuck pineapple or other fruit.

• Twist a 6in/15cm piece of string around a pencil and secure with tape and put this in the freezer.

• Cut off the pineapple's leaves and cut it down the middle, taking out the hard core with a sharp knife and leaving on the rind. Put the two halves back together again.

• At the end, which you cut cleanly to reveal the golden fruit, set two cocktail cherries on sticks as eyes. Cut a generous apple-slice mouth and secure with cocktail sticks beneath it.

• Cover the boar-pineapple's back with cocktail sticks and place your desired snacks on its spines – cubes of cheese, chocolates, etc.

• Now retrieve your frozen pencil and slip off the string to make a curly tail.

• Place upon a presentation platter and convey, with suitable flourishes, candles, and accompanying songs, into your dining room. When you've eaten all the snacks off the "bristles," cut up the pineapple as dessert.

ABOVE: *Revive the boar's head tradition without harming any creature.*

DAY 6

NEW YEAR'S EVE, HOGMANAY

Ding, Ding! Bells o' the Barony!
Ding! Ding! Hogmanay harmony,
Naebody greets for the year that's awa'

W. D. COCKER: THE AULD YEAR

In Scotland the New Year celebrations overshadow those of Christmas, and there is a greater hearkening to the idea of the old year's end and the new beginning. The name given to the feast is Hogmanay, a word of obscure origin which may derive from a French term for New Year. Another, more intriguing suggestion is that it is a corruption of *au gui menez*, which means, literally, "lead to the mistletoe." This suggests a Druidic origin for Hogmanay, and it is said that the ancient priests of Britain used to cut the sacred plant on what was to them, the equivalent of New Year's Day (i.e. the Solstice). Children in parts of France today still run through the streets crying "Au guy l'an neuf, au guy Gaulois" (To the mistletoe the New Year, to the French mistletoe). With these thoughts in mind it may well be that we are indeed seeing a memorial of a far older time, when the Druids convened to cut the sacred plant and to pass it out among the people (*see also Chapter 3*). Dr. Henderson, one of the earliest scholars of Celtic myth and lore, suggested that an old song that began *oge midne* (new morning) might have been the origin of the word, while another source quotes the chant that rang out in the streets of Edinburgh in 1598, of "Hogmanay Trololay, give us your white bread and none of your gray." Whatever it originally meant, it has come to be linked to the New Year's Eve celebration. That this night has been celebrated with similar enthusiasm for a good period of time may be seen in the following description, which dates from 1893:

Toward evening the throughafairs become thronged with the youth of the city... As the midnight approaches, drinking of healths becomes more frequent, and some are already intoxicated... The eyes of the immense crowd are ever being turned towards the lighted clock-face... [As] the hour approaches, the hands seem to stand still, but in one more second the hurrahing, and cheering, the hand-shaking, the health-drinking, is all kept up as long as the clock continues to ring out the much longed-for midnight hour...[After,] the crowds slowly disperse, the much intoxicated and helpless ones being hustled about a good deal, the police urging them on out of harm's way. The first-footers are off.

As with many other days over the Solstice period, the traditions of Mummer plays or guising also takes place on New Year's Eve in Scotland. (Christmas is called in Gaelic *An Nollaig Mhor*, Big Yule and New Year's Day, *An Nollaig Bheag*, Little Yule.) Here the players are referred to as "The White Boys of Yule" from the fact that all wear white except for the single black-clad villain, Beelzebub.

In Shetland they used to dress in coats made of straw, an ancient reference to the turning of the year. The hero is sometimes called Goloshan, sometimes Galgachus, an interesting point as this is the name of an early Scottish hero who successfully resisted the Roman Legions. The players send one of their number ahead to announce their coming:

Rise up, goodwife, and shake your feathers,
Dina think that we are beggers;
We are bairns that come to play
and for to seek our hogmanay.

This night was the night when everything that could be was tidied up, cleaned, washed or pol-

ABOVE: *The celebration of Hogmanay, or New Year's Eve, is said to be Druidic in origin*

ished. As F. Marian McNeill points out in her wonderful collection of folk-customs, *The Silver Bough*:

The house received a mini spring-cleaning. Slops and ashes, which are usually removed in the morning, are carried out. Debts must be paid, borrowed articles returned, stockings darned, tears mended, clocks wound up, musical instruments tuned, pictures hung straight; brass and silver must be glittering; fresh linen must be put on the beds. Even in the slummiest houses... brooms and pails, soap, polishing rags and darning-needles emerge from neglected cupboards and drawers, and the bairns receive a thorough scrubbing in honor of the New Year.

Unfinished Business

All of these things reflect the importance of the New Year, which is a new beginning in every way. Clearing up unfinished business, of whatever kind, is still a good notion, and blowing away the cobwebs from the old year that has passed is no bad thing either. In parts of Scotland this was accomplished by the juniper and water rite.

After sunset on Hogmanay people went out to gather branches of juniper and buckets of fresh water from a well or stream. The branches were then placed by the fire to dry out. In the morning the head of the household took a first drink of the water and then went around the house sprinkling everyone with a few drops.

This done, all doors and windows were closed tight and the branches of dried juniper were set alight and taken though the house until everything was thoroughly fumigated. This almost certainly dates back to a very old rite in which the sacred juniper was burned at fireplaces to ensure the gifts of the New Year were properly celebrated. We can still do this today, since there are numerous kinds of incense made from juniper, or if we are adventurous enough, we can make our own. Taken through the house this leaves a pleasant aroma and gives us a sense of new beginnings.

ABOVE: *Any gifts brought into the house on New Year's Eve should be welcomed with ceremony, as they will bring good fortune on the house.*

First Footing

New Year's Eve is traditionally a time for assessing the past twelve months and for looking ahead to the New Year. Numerous customs are still retained in Europe and the United States, including the idea of kindling a new light from the old. This can be achieved in a number of ways, including the following simple ceremony.

At a few minutes to midnight, put out all of your lights except for a single candle or a lantern (it's important that the light be a living one rather than electric). Send someone outside (traditionally it is someone who has dark hair) with the light, which they must guard and protect from the weather. As the clock strikes twelve have that person knock on the door. Open it and welcome them in with some form of ceremonial greeting, such as:

Welcome to the light of the New Year
And welcome he/she who brings it here!

Go around the house with the candle and relight all the lights you put out. If these can be candles so much the better, but don't burn the house down! In Scotland this custom is known as "First Footing," and the person who first puts his or her foot across the door is the one who brings fortune to the whole household. Often someone in the house arranges with a friend to come to the house at the exact time and carrying a gift – called a *handsel* in Scotland, and consisting of a lump of coal, or a bottle of whisky – something that will ensure that more gifts come throughout the next twelve months.

In parts of Scandinavia, the god Yule is welcomed in much the same way, with a chair and table set up just inside the door of the house with gifts and food for Yule – the godlike representation of the Solstice.

Eggnog Forever!

And of course this is the best time to have a good, sustaining drink to share with friends and family and those who come first footing. A great American institution at this time of the year, is the wonderful drink known as Eggnog (Egg-Flip in Britain, where it is sadly less familiar). At one time, during the nineteenth century, this used to be served with free restaurant lunches during Christmas week. Everyone seems to have their own recipe for this, with varying degrees of alcohol added or subtracted according to taste. (It used to be said that any man found standing on New Year's Day would go from house to house "Egg-noging" until he was no longer vertical.)

This recipe was sent to me by a friend in Seattle – it has everything!

RIGHT: Wash your Christmas pudding down in the traditional way with a jug of Eggnog!

TRADITIONAL EGGNOG

INGREDIENTS: (Serves 30!)
12 eggs
1½ cups/12oz/350g sugar
1 quart/1.1 liter heavy cream
1 quart/1.1 liter milk
1 quart/1.1 liter bourbon whisky
(Scotch whisky or rum can be used if preferred)
1 cup/8fl.oz/250ml rum

(Make about a week before serving to allow it to mellow.)
• Separate the eggs. Beat the egg whites together until stiff, then beat in a ½ cup/4oz/100g of sugar. Beat the egg yolks until pale and light. • Add the remaining cup/8oz/250g of sugar and a ¼ teaspoon of salt.
• Combine the egg mixture with the milk and the bourbon. Beat well, then add the cup of rum.
• Pour into a jug and store in a cool place.
• Shake or stir thoroughly before serving. Ladle into small cups and sprinkle with nutmeg.

DAY 7

NEW YEAR'S DAY, THE KALENDS OF JANUARY

The Kalends will remembered be
The king's no longer dead, you see.

JOHN MATTHEWS:
THE KING RETURNS

The old year is officially dead and laid to rest and the New Year begins in a mood of hopefulness. Once, this was the time for wild and unbridled celebrations of life. In ancient Rome, as we have seen, the Kalends were a riotous outpouring of fun and festival. For us also, it can and should be a time of celebration, not just of the new beginnings that we make, but also as a glad remembrance of the old year and a feeling of gladness that we are still alive! Even though we may not always see any real change in circumstance with the dawn of the

ABOVE: *Mummers traditionally went from door to door with a Wassail bowl, containing a hot spicy brew.*

New Year, there is always something to be thankful for, if we look deeply enough, and the celebrations that follow on this day are all ones that offer the promise of better days to come. It is customary in Scotland for nothing to be taken out of the house on this day – whether it be slops, rubbish, or any of the household goods: this is to ensure that the good fortune brought in by the First Footer doesn't leave the dwelling.

Wassail! Wassail!

On this day, in many parts of Britain and the United States, the tradition of wassailing the trees in the cider orchards of the country has been going on since at least Saxon times, whence the word *wassail* – from *wase haile*, meaning "good health" derives. The practice was intended to drive away evil spirits that might attack the trees, and to ensure a good crop of apples for the coming year. It may also echo the calls made in more ancient times for the sun to return.

The oldest and biggest tree in the orchard was usually chosen to represent the rest, and in Somerset, England, this tree was invariably referred to as "The Apple-Tree Man." The wassailing usually took place around midday, when a company of people, usually representatives of the local community as well as the owners of the trees, made their way into the orchard and wassailed the tree by pouring cider on its roots and placing pieces of cake or toasted bread soaked in cider in the branches. Sometimes more pieces were hung from higher twigs to encourage the robins, who were regarded as guardian spirits of the trees. Lower branches were bent down and their ends dipped in cider. A great noise was then made, with shouting and banging tin plates or, more recently, firing shotguns into the air. Sometimes the bark was struck or even split

ABOVE: In ancient times people would call out to the sun to encourage its return.

to let out evil spirits, and songs were sung to the tree along with many toasts and cries of "Huzzah!"

Right across Britain there are variations on this pattern. Sometimes a small boy was put up the tree, where he sat shouting "Tit, Tit, more to eat" and was fed scraps of cake and cheese. He was said to represent the tom tit, or some other small bird, which protected the tree. In other places, notably Devon and Cornwall, the men of the party would bow three times to the oldest tree, an action that was said to encourage the tree to bear heavy fruit, but which probably dates back to more ancient times when apple trees were deemed especially sacred by the native Celtic people of Britain.

The songs that accompany the wassailing are remarkably consistent countrywide, despite some local variations. In Buckinghamshire the song, always sung loudly while the wassailing ceremony was in progress, went like this:

> *Here's too thee, old apple tree*
> *Whence thou may'st bud and*
> *whence thou may'st blow,*
> *And whence thou may'st*
> *bear apples enow.*
>
> *Hats full, Caps full, Bushel,*
> *bushel sacks full,*
> *And my pockets full too!*
> *Huzzah!*

The reference to blowing here probably refers to the belief that a strong wind would move the roots of the tree and thus cause it to fruit sooner. At one time the wind god Aloes was also invoked to aid in this, and in Uptown St. Leonard's, Gloucestershire, the wassailing song reflects this:

> *Blow, bear well,*
> *Spring well in April,*
> *Every sprig and every spray*
> *Bear a bushel of apples against*
> *Next New Year's Day.*

Much like the teams of mummers who went from house to house collecting money, so there was a band of professional wassails who went around with a wassail bowl, generally made from apple wood and often beautifully carved. The wassail brew was called "lambs' wool" in some parts of the county, and usually consisted of hot ale, apples, and spices with the occasional addition of cream or beaten eggs to give the effect of wool floating on the drink. The wassails collected alms in exchange for good wishes for the coming year. The song they sang again varied from place to place, but a this one is from Somerset, where interestingly the bowl is made from another sacred tree, the ash.

Wassail, to our town,
The cup is white, the ale is brown:
The cup is made of the ashen tree
And so is the ale of the good barley.

Wassailing is as good a practice today as it ever was, especially if you happen to have an apple tree or trees of your own, and if not, you may find that the ceremony is taking place somewhere in your region anyway. If so, you might wish to go along and join in the merriment, and if the custom is unknown or has died out where you live, why not revive it! The practice is already undergoing something of a revival, and for many people has become a fixture in the ritual celebration of Midwinter. Once widely celebrated in the United States from the 1900s onward, the custom fell into disregard for a time. Recently, however, in the 1960s a farmer from Washington saw wassailing take place in Somerset and took the idea home with him and reestablished the idea in his area. With the growing interest in the Revels performances across the United States, this is a custom that is beginning to find a new and enthusiastic following.

ABOVE: Plow Monday is one of many
festivals celebrating the goodness
of the land.

A WASSAIL CEREMONY

A very simple wassail ceremony might follow this pattern.

• Heat a large container of ale or beer – about 3 to 4 pints.

• Add $\frac{1}{2}$ cup/4oz/100g of sugar and $\frac{1}{4}$ cup/2oz/50g of mixed spice (cinnamon sticks and whole cloves are also excellent). Cut up 2 or 3 small sweet apples and add those.

• Add a $1\frac{1}{4}$ cup/$\frac{1}{2}$ pint/300ml of pineapple juice and the same of orange. Squeeze 2 lemons into the brew.

• Place over a slow flame; then, before it begins to boil, take off the heat and whip up some cream. Let this float on top of the brew like foam.

• Put into a suitably large bowl (the more ornate the better).

• Now go out to the tree or trees with a few friends (these don't have to be apple trees, since all can benefit from a well-intentioned blessing, but it is traditional to wassail fruit-bearing trees). Wet the roots liberally with the brew. Pass the rest around and when everyone is thoroughly warmed up sing one of the wassailing songs quoted above. Lift your glasses to the tree and shout "Huzzah!" three times as loudly as you can.

The Luck of the Year.
It is the bird-quiet hour,
The mid-day contemplation of the sun.

On this bleak day, when no sun shines,
What wraps the birds in silence,
What power blankets their song?

CAITLÍN MATTHEWS:
AN EXCERPT FROM INCANTATION FOR
PLOW MONDAY

194

ABOVE: The wassail pot, filled with a warming mixture of ale or beer, apples, and fruit juices, is used to bless the apple tree in Midwinter.

ABOVE: The struggle between the forces of dark and light,
as symbolic of the triumph of Spring over Winter,
is still re-enacted today in seasonal Mummer plays.

There are many other celebrations connected with this day. It is considered essential to note the first things one does in the morning, and to do them with care and attention. In Scotland the first water drawn from the well was considered lucky and was called "The Flower o' the Well." This probably goes back to ancient rites concerning the worship of wells, which were considered both as gateways to the Otherworld and as the dwelling places of powerful spirits.

"Well-Dressing" still goes on in England and Ireland, though it is more associated with Easter and the May Day celebrations. In coastal areas, "The Flower o' the Shore" was the first seaweed and driftwood gathered to put on the fires at home. If you happen to have a fireplace you may still practice this, thinking as you do so that you are echoing the rites of your ancestors who acknowledged the gift of the newly risen sun in this way.

New Year's Day is also a good time to practice divination, looking forward to the future and whatever it may bring. In the Highlands of Scotland divining what the year had in store from observing the weather was traditional. According to which way the wind blew in the morning, the pattern of the months to come was observed. Throughout the Celtic world the winds were assigned their own colors, and according to the direction from which they blew they could bring good news or bad. The wind that blew on Hogmanay was called *Dar-an-coil*, "the night of the fecundating of the tree," a name that derives from very ancient times. A Highland weather rhyme says:

> *Wind from the West,*
> *fish and bread;*
> *Wind from the North,*
> *cold and flaying;*
> *Wind from the East,*
> *snow on the hills;*
> *Wind from the South,*
> *fruit on trees.*

Also in Scotland was the practice of divining from the Trash Chenille, the Candlemas Bull. In this, small passing clouds that might resemble, however vaguely, the shape of a bull, used to be eagerly looked for before daylight faded on New Year's Day. According to its position in the sky, and the nature of the cloud, many things could be divined. If it lay to the North, or was densely black, or had a soft, frosty appearance, it promised a year of plenty. If it lay to the East, the year would be good enough. If it lay to the South there would be enough straw but not much grain. If sighted in the West, the year would be dull and unproductive. In this we may note the importance of North as a bringer of good luck, perhaps a dim memory of the powerful deities who sent their spirits to watch over the newborn earth at this time.

LEFT: With the defeat of the Turkish Knight the restoration of light and goodness are assured.

*ABOVE: Legend has it that Midwinter snow is really the feathers
that have been shaken from Mother Holle's bedspread.*

*ABOVE: Christmas is a time for
indulgence, but remember to
give thanks for all you receive.*

DAY 8

SNOW DAY

*When icicles hang by the wall,
And Dick the shepherd blows his nail,
And Tom bears logs into the hall,
And milk comes frozen home in pail...*

SHAKESPEARE: LOVE'S LABOUR'S LOST

On this day we pay our respects to snow. No depiction of Christmas and Midwinter celebration is complete without it. Snow has so many qualities and so many aspects that it is not surprising that the Inuit people have literally hundreds of words that describe its variety of colors and texture. So today let us devote ourselves to the contemplation and honoring of the million small crystals that drift across the lands of the Northern hemisphere at this time of the year. And, if we have no snow to look at and celebrate, let us at least remember it in all its fine whiteness, cancelling out the darkness of Midwinter and transforming even the grayest and bleakest of scenes into a place of magic.

SNOW REFLECTIONS

Make your own snowflake crystals by folding small squares of paper into half and then in half again. Cut out notches from the folded and edge ends and hang them over your shrine. The following words from John Greenleaf Whittier's poem *Snowbound* make an appropriate invocation to the Winter's whiteness.

*The sun that brief December day
Rose cheerless over hills of gray,
and, darkly circled, gave at noon
A sadder light than waning moon...*

*A night made hoary with the swarm
And whirl-dance of the blinding storm,
As zig-zag wavering to and fro
Crossed and re-crossed the winged snow...
And 'ere the early bed-time came
The white drift piled the window-frame,
And through the glass the clothes-line posts
Looked in like tall and sheeted ghosts*

DAY 9

EVERGREEN DAY

Sing lustily of Christmas folly,
Sing of ivy, bay and holly,
Banish each his melancholy,
And evermore be merry.

A CHRISTMAS GLEE

We have heard in Chapter 4 of the many traditions associated with the Winter Solstice that involve trees and greenery. On this day then, which again has no festival associated with it, let us take time to contemplate the evergreens that bring their powerful presence into our homes at this time of year. From the earliest times trees have been worshiped and many are sacred to the gods and goddesses of the ancient world. We have read of the Druids' love for the oak tree, from which they took the sacred mistletoe at the time of the Solstice. We have learned how, during the Kalends of Midwinter, garlands of yew and juniper were used to decorate the houses of ancient Rome. During the Middle Ages an old play was performed at this time that told the story of the Paradise Tree, a scion of the original Tree of Knowledge, which Adam carried forth from Eden and planted in the outer world, where it grew to a great height and was, according to later tradition, used to make the cross on which Christ was crucified.

Since the nineteenth century we have been erecting pine trees in our homes – especially after the publication in 1845 in America of a children's book called *Kriss Cringle's Christmas Tree*, after which the custom spread like wildfire throughout most of the continent. But the evergreen had older stories told of it among the native peoples of the United States. In particular I love this story from the Cherokee tribe.

ABOVE: *The oak tree was sacred to the Druids, and was carrier of the all-important mistletoe.*

The following poem is an Italian benison from the sixteenth century. Recite it in celebration of the ninth day:

A SOLSTICE SALUTATION

I salute you!
There is nothing I can give you which
you have not.
But there is much, that while I cannot give,
you can take.
No heaven can come to us, unless our hearts find
rest in it today.
Take heaven!
No peace lies in the future which is not
hidden in this present instant.
Take peace!
The gloom of the world is but a shadow.
Behind it, yet within our reach, is joy.
Take joy!
And so at this Christmastime, I greet you,
With the prayer that for you, now, and forever,
The day breaks, and the shadows flee away!

TAKE JOY! THE TASHA TUDOR CHRISTMAS BOOK
(WORLD PUBLISHING CO., CLEVELAND, OH)

Why There Are Evergreens

When the Great Mystery was creating all the trees and plants he wanted to give a gift to each of them. But he could not decide which gift was appropriate to which tree, and so he held a contest to find out. He told the young trees that he wanted them all to keep watch over the earth for seven days and seven nights.

The trees were very excited to be given such an important task and for the first night they had no difficulty in staying awake. But on the second night it was harder, and some of them fell asleep. By the third night even more were unable to remain awake, even though they whispered to themselves for hours. On the fourth night even more fell asleep.

Finally, by the seventh night, only a handful were still awake: the pine, the cedar, the spruce, the fir, the holly, and the laurel. "What great endurance you all have!" cried the Great Mystery. "To you I shall give the gist of remaining green forever. You shall guard the forest even in the dead of Winter when all your brothers and sisters are sleeping." Ever since then the rest of the trees lose their leaves in Winter and sleep until the Spring; but the evergreen trees are always awake, and always watching.

ABOVE: The Major Oak in Sherwood Forest, Nottinghamshire, figures in many of the Robin Hood tales and is significant of the importance placed on trees in myth and legend.

THE·VISIT·FROM·THE·FATES

might well have been seen as gloomy occasion, was made into something of a romp, with young men attempting to set fire to the flax or hemp the women had set ready for spinning, while the women retaliated by throwing buckets of water not only over the torches but those who carried them! The poet Robert Herrick, who recorded so many old customs in his works, describes the fun as follows:

DAY 10

St. Distaff's Day

*Some say that ever gainst
that season comes wherein
our Saviour's birth is celebrated,
the bird of dawning
singeth all night long.*

SHAKESPEARE: HAMLET

*Partly work, and partly play
Ye must on St. Distaff's day:
From the plough soon free your team,
Then come home and fother them.
If the maids a spinning go,
Burn the flax and fire the tow...*

*Bring in pails of water, then
Let the maids bewash the men:
Give St. Distaff all the night
Ten bid Christmas sport goodnight:
And next morrow every one
To his own vocation.*

HESPERIDES

A mong the village women of the pre-industrial world this day was known as St. Distaff's Day (or sometimes, more obscurely, as Rock Day) because it was more often than not on this day that they had to return to the humdrum working world after the great Midwinter festival. Before the coming of mechanized industry, women were constantly spinning wool and flax into thread. They had to produce all the cloth needed for their families, and for even the simplest garment miles of thread had to be spun. But the day, which

In the long dark days of Midwinter any excuse for fun and games was seized upon, and soon after St. Distaff's Day the men had their own festival – Plough Monday, which was once again an occasion for Mummers and guisers to entertain the village with their plays about the death and resurrection of the harvest. The cast of the Plough Monday Mummers or "The Fool's Plough" as it was also called, included a king and a male queen, a fiddler, a purser to take up the collection, a couple of wardens wearing top hats and sprigs of greenery, and a team of boys who carried a plough and were jokingly referred to as "plough bullocks." But the most significant figure was the fool, who according to a nineteenth-century description was "almost covered with skins, a hairy cap on his head, and the tail of some animal hanging down his back."

In later times the plough was blessed by the parish priest, though we may imagine that it was once done by the local Druid. In some places the "plough jag", as it was called, would send out the pursers to collect money and, if it was sufficient, they would plough a symbolic furrow and then perform a solemn and grotesque dance around it. If, however, they failed to get as much money as they thought right, they would plough up the nearest piece of ground wherever they stood – even if it was the middle of the road!

Though Plough Monday now falls upon the 8th of January, after Twelfth Night, it must once have been part of the Winter festivities. It seems to have its origins with the Roman Compitaline festival, held where four estates joined. Here a little shrine was built, open to four directions, and a plough set up on each of the four altars in this shrine along with a wooden doll for every freemason in each household. The ceremonial breaking of the earth was then solemnly observed, with priests to oversee and bless the proceedings.

In parts of Britain, Plough Monday is still followed by Straw Bear Tuesday, in which a man dressed as a bear is carried through the town collecting gifts along the way. This is accompanied by a haunting tune which may indeed be very old, like that played by the Abbot's Bromley Horn Dancers *(see Chapter 5)*.

On this day then we celebrate the beginning of the return to normal time and normal acts after the feast. Though there are still several days to go before Twelfth Night, it is still appropriate to look ahead at this point and to begin considering what the New Year may bring. In many parts of the Northern world these days are given over to divining

CASTING THE FUTURE

For this you need a little lead such as the sticks provided for use in soldering. Place a small piece of this in an old spoon and hold it over a hot flame until it melts. Then, thinking of the question you want answered, toss the molten lead into a metal bucket filled with water. This produces a satisfying cloud of steam and when the lead is fished out it will have taken a strange shape in which all kinds of things can be read. If the shape provides no clear conclusion, then it can be held up in front of a candle and the shadow thrown on the wall can be further studied. In Finland this is still carried out regularly and horse-shoe shaped ingots and special ladles can be found in market places at this time of year.

RIGHT: Candles and fire are not only warm and atmospheric, but an important symbol of Light and Life in the darkness of the Winter Solstice.

*ABOVE: The night before Christmas is a magical time in
many ways, and this is kept alive today in the stories of Santa Claus.*

the future. One method, which may still be practice with reward, is lead pouring.

DAY 11

EVE OF EPIPHANY, FESTIVAL OF THE THREE KINGS

This morn I met the train
Of the three great kings of the East:
This morn I met the train
Of the kings on the wide high road.

OLD CAROL OF PROVENCE

This is the day when, traditionally, the Magi found their way to the stable at Bethlehem and gave their gifts to the Child of Wonder. In the Eastern Orthodox Church Epiphany is still celebrated as the Nativity of Christ. As we have seen (*see Chapter 2*) the identity of the Three Kings is no more certain than their number. The great seventeenth-century writer Sir Thomas Browne cast doubt upon their veracity in his *Pseudodoxia, or Enquiries into Vulgar and Common Errors* (1646):

> *A common conceit is of the three Kings...*
> *conceived to be the wise men that travelled*
> *unto our saviour by direction of the Star.*
> *But although we grant they were kings, yet*
> *we cannot assured they were three. For the*
> *scriptures make no mention of any number;*
> *and the number of their presents, Gold,*
> *Myrrh, and Frankincense, concludeth not*
> *the number of their persons; for these were*
> *the commodities of their Country, and such*
> *as probably the Queen of Sheba in one*
> *person brought unto Solomon.*

Whatever the truth of these figures, their importance remains undisputed. Recently they have been described as members of a secretive sect whose knowledge and understanding of the inner life of the world is far greater than we realize. In parts of France throughout the Middle Ages and into the succeeding centuries, it was customary to re-enact their journey as a reminder of that older time. The Provencal writer Frederic Mistral (1830–1914) gives an unforgettable account of one such occasion:

> *With hearts beating in joyful excitement,*
> *eyes full of visions, we sallied forth on the*
> *road to Arles, a numerous company of*
> *shock-headed urchins and blond-headed*
> *maidens with little hoods and sabots,*
> *bearing our offerings of cakes for the kings,*
> *dried figs for their pages, and hay for the*
> *camels.*
>
> *The daylight waned... We strained our eyes*
> *as far as they could see, but in vain... Then*
> *we met a shepherd... He asked whither we*
> *were bound so late in the day. We enquired*
> *anxiously had he seen the kings, and were*
> *they still a long way off. Oh, the joy when*
> *he replied that he had passed the kings not*
> *so very long since – soon we should*
> *meet them. Off we set running with all*
> *speed... Then, just as the sun disappeared*
> *behind a great dark cloud and the bravest*
> *among us began to flag – suddenly, behold*
> *them in sight!*
>
> *A joyful shout rang from every throat as the*
> *magnificence of the royal pageant dazzled*
> *our sight. A flash of splendour and gorgeous*
> *color shone in the rays of the setting sun,*
> *while the blazing torches showed the gleams*
> *of gold on crowns set with rubies and*
> *precious stones. The Kings! The Kings! See*
> *their crowns! See their mantles – their flags,*
> *and the procession of camels and horses...*
> *[as] we beheld at last the three kings:*
> *Gaspard, with is crimson mantle...*

*Balthazar, with his cloak of blue, and above
and beyond all, the Moorish king.'*

TRANS. C.E. MAUD

On this day of days it is appropriate to
honor the Magi who, whatever their religion
and beliefs, set out on a journey similar to
that which so many of us make in search of a
truth that has no name, and which here, on this
occasion, happened to take the form of the Child
of Wonder. Figures representing the Kings, easily
available in most stores at this time of year, can
be arranged to form a small shrine, and with a
single candle placed beside each one, we may
thus remember the quest for knowledge and
understanding that they represent.

Giving the Gift

*You shall receive whatever
gift you may name,
as far as wind dries,
rain wets, sun revolves;
as far as sea encircles
and earth extends.*

CULHWCH AND OLWEN
TRANS. CAITLÍN MATTHEWS

Even the giving of gifts can be a ceremony all
of its own. In Sweden and Germany there was
a tradition until recently of the *julknap*, a gift
wrapped in layers of paper or cloth. The person
bringing the gift would knock at the door and
when it was opened fling the package into the
house before running off. This was sometimes
used as a means of making a marriage proposal
or declaration of love, in which case a golden
heart or a letter (or even the person making
the proposal) was hidden within.

On one occasion in the United States a
certain Major Jones of Georgia decided to
follow this custom. He climbed into a meal
sack suspended from a hook in the porch of

his true love's house and spent the night
there. However, he forgot the wind – it blew
all night and caused the sack to swing to and
fro like the swaying of a ship. As well as sea-
sick tablets he had also forgotten dog repellent
and, unfortunately, the house dog paid him
close attention throughout the night!

Considering the Gifts

Although we will probably have given all our
carefully selected gifts by now, this is still a day
on which to consider the whole nature of gift
giving and receiving. At a time when the com-
mercial Christmas has a tendency to swamp
the sacredness of the season, we ask and are
being asked, "What do you want this year?'
There are certainly things that we would quite
like, things that we hope will be brought for us,
but these are not the same as our wants. True
wants are not small things satisfied by prettily
wrapped parcels: they are the immense needs
of inner space that can be overwhelmed by all
our little wants and yearnings. To consider our
real needs – the things we lack in our lives – is
often too frightening, opening up an abyss of
need that calls our very existence into question.

Our real wants eat holes in us: never
resting, never loving, never greeting, never
finding, never seeking, never ever being satisfied deep down. These ravenous wants define
our treasures so truly. They create a Christmas list that no store could supply: time to
stop and really enjoy, in a space of quietness
and contentment, all the things we were put
on earth to do.

Space to give and receive love reciprocally.
The grace to seek and find our spiritual joy.
Freedom from the tyranny and burden of
other's expectations, of what others think.
Acceptance of ourselves as we truly are. The
list could go on and on once we begin to set
down our true needs.

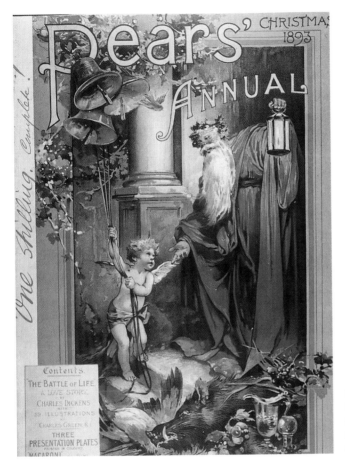

LEFT: The commercialism of Christmas can be overpowering, but with some thought gift giving can still be a fulfilling act.

LISTENING TO YOUR NEEDS

Make a list of the real wants and needs that you have within you. Consider the whole nature of gift giving and the appropriateness of the things you yourself have given and received this year. Then, if you can, make a present to yourself of one of one of the things you listed – give yourself more time, speak out about the desire for recognition of the person you really are. And, next time you give a gift, whatever the occasion, put more of yourself into it, make something with your own hands if you can, create your own wrapping paper and tie it up with wool instead of ribbon – make the gift a true giving of yourself. And say, or inscribe, some special words to go with the present. Here is a suggested formulae, though you will certainly want to find your own words as well:

BLESSING ON GIVING A GIFT

> *Take, and welcome joy within you:*
> *Showers, flowers, powers,*
> *Hatfulls, capfulls, lapfulls,*
> *Treasures, measures, pleasures,*
> *All be yours to enjoy!*

CAITLÍN MATTHEWS: A CELTIC DEVOTIONAL

DAY 12

EPIPHANY – TWELFTH NIGHT

Ceremony upon Candlemass Eve
Down with the Rosemary, and so
Down with the Baies, & Mistletoe:
Down with the Holly, Ivie, all,
Wherewith ye drest the Christmas Hall.

That so the superstitious find
No one least branch there left behind:
For look how many leaves there be
Neglected there (maids trust to me)
So many Goblins you shall see.

So the poet Robert Herrick wrote in 1670, and it has indeed been the custom for generations that on this day the decorations come down and are ceremonially consigned to the fire. If one failed to do so, as Herrick notes, every spine on the holly could turn into a mischievous goblin! But there is a deeper reason for all this. It is time to end the festivities and lay aside the branches and leaves that have bedecked the house over the holidays. And, traditionally, the final flare of celebration was often the brightest, with more feasting, more drinking, more dancing – as if to say that we don't really want it all to end, but if end it must let us celebrate in style! The Victorian artist Leigh Hunt summed it up.

Christmas goes out in fine style with Twelfth Night. It is a finish worth of the time. Christmas day was the morning of the season; New Year's Day the middle of it or noon; Twelfth Night is the night, brilliant with the innumerable plates of Twelfth Cakes. The whole island keeps court; nay, all Christendom. All the world are Kings and Queens. Everybody is somebody else; and learns at once to laugh at, and to tolerate, characters different from is own by
enacting them. Cakes, characters, forfeits, lights, theatres, merry rooms, little holiday-faces, and, last but not least, the painted sugar on the cakes – all conspires to throw a giddy splendour over the last night of the season.

HADFIELD: THE TWELVE DAYS OF CHRISTMAS

We can still celebrate the end of the Solstice festival with a last triumph. Traditionally, a cake was baked for this day, and a bean hidden somewhere in the mixture and baked along with it. Whoever received the piece of cake with the bean was appointed King or Queen Bean for the night and lead the company in songs and games. Here is a recipe for Twelfth Night cake, and two games to play on this merry night.

TWELFTH NIGHT CAKE

INGREDIENTS:

1 cup/8oz/225g butter	1½ cups/8oz/225g sultanas
1 cup/8oz/225g sugar	3 tbsp/35ml brandy
2 cups/8oz/225g flour	3 tbsp/35ml honey
4 eggs	¼ cup/2oz/50g candied cherries
1½ cups/8oz/225g currants	pinch cinnamon
1½ cups/8oz/225g raisins	1 dried bean

- Grease a 12in/30cm cake tin.
- Cream the butter and sugar together and stir in the well-beaten eggs and the brandy.
- Sift the flour with a little cinnamon and fold into the mixture, then stir in the dried fruit.
- Add the bean.
- Pour the mixture into the tin and bake for three hours 150°C/300°F/Gas Mark 2.
- Allow to cool for 30 minutes before turning out.
- Melt the honey and glaze the top of the cake, and decorate with the cherries.

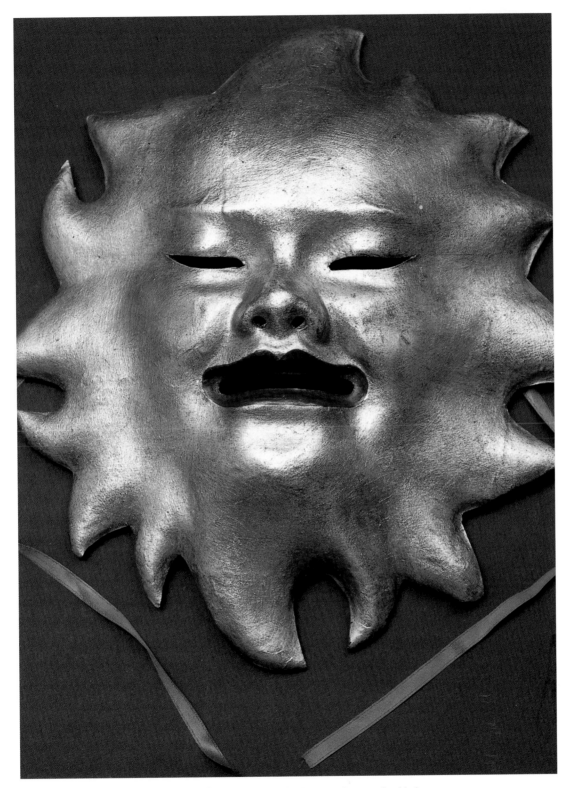

ABOVE: Remember, the welcoming of the returning sun should always feature in your festivities over the Twelve Days of Christmas.

GAMES AND SPORTS

This game used to be played in Scotland until quite recently. It is less dangerous than it seems, though care should always be taken.

SNAPDRAGON

• Fill a large shallow dish with raisins (muscatels for preference) and pour a few spoonfuls of brandy over them.

• Put out the lights then set light to the brandy and while it is still going snatch one of the raisins from the flames.

• As you put the raisin in your mouth, make a wish. It will be granted in the next twelve months they say!

ABOVE: Say farewell to the Solstice by making a wish for the coming twelve months.

The Twelve Days of Yule

The following is a variation on the famous song about the twelve Days of Christmas from Scotland. Gather a few friends around the fire. Have one of them say or sing the first verse aloud. Then have everyone repeat it, the same with the next verse and so on. As the verses get longer, whoever makes a slip in repeating the lines pays a forfeit – any small object they possess such as a candy or a nut. (Note also the 13th day of Yule – a sure sign of an ancient origin.)

The King sent his lady on the first Yule day
A papingo-aye; (an exotic parrot)
Who learns my carol and carries it away?

The king sent his lady on the second Yule day
Three partricks (partridges), a papingo-aye,
Who learns my carol and carries it away?

The king sent his lady on the third Yule day
Three plovers, three partricks, a papingo-aye;
Who learns my carol and carries it away?

The king sent his lady on the fourth Yule day
A goose that was grey
Three plovers, three partricks, a papingo-aye;
Who learns my carol and carries it away?

The king sent his lady on the fifth Yule day
Three starlings, a goose that was grey
Three plovers, three partricks, a papingo-aye;
Who learns my carol and carries it away?

The king sent his lady on the sixth Yule day
Three goldspinks, three starlings,
a goose that was grey
Three plovers, three partricks, a papingo-aye;
Who learns my carol and carries it away?

The king sent his lady on the seventh Yule day
A bull that was brown, three goldspinks,
Three starlings, and a goose that was grey
Three plovers, three partricks, a papingo-aye;
Who learns my carol and carries it away?

The king sent his lady on the eighth Yule day
Three ducks a merry laying,
A bull that was brown,
Three goldspinks, three starlings,
A goose that was grey
Three plovers, three partricks, a papingo-aye;
Who learns my carol and carries it away?

The king sent his lady on the ninth Yule day
Three swans a-merry swimming,
Three ducks a-merry laying,
A bull that was brown, three goldspinks,
Three starlings, a goose that was grey
Three plovers, three partricks, a papingo-aye;
Who learns my carol and carries it away?

The king sent his lady on the tenth Yule day
An Arabian baboon,
Three swans a-merry swimming
Three ducks a-merry laying,
A bull that was brown,
Three goldspinks, three starlings,
A goose that was grey
Three plovers, three partricks, a papingo-aye;
Who learns my carol and carries it away?

The king sent his lady on the eleventh Yule day,
Three hinds a-merry hunting,
An Arabian baboon,
Three swans a-merry swimming,
Three ducks a-merry laying,
A bull that was brown,
Three goldspinks, three starlings,
A goose that was grey
Three plovers, three partricks, a papingo-aye;
Who learns my carol and carries it away?

The king sent his lady on the twelfth Yule day,
Three maids a-merry dancing,
Three hinds a-merry hunting
An Arabian baboon,
Three swans a-merry swimming,
Three ducks a-merry laying,
A bull that was brown,
Three goldspinks, three starlings,
A goose that was grey
Three plovers, three partricks, a papingo-aye;
Who learns my carol and carries it away?

The king sent his lady on the thirteenth Yule day,
Three stalks a-merry corn,
Three maids a-merry dancing,
Three hinds a-merry hunting

An Arabian baboon,
Three swans a-merry swimming,
Three ducks a-merry laying,
A bull that was brown,
Three goldspinks, three starlings,
A goose that was grey
Three plovers, three partricks, a papingo-aye;
Who learns my carol and carries it away?

Farewell To The Solstice

When all is done, when the twelve days are over, we may begin to look forward to the next year. It is time to dismantle your Solstice shrine. Some things you will want to keep; the more ephemeral components can be returned to nature, to be remade next year. As you put things away in a box for another year, give thanks to every single one of the gifts of the Solstice. Let us leave the twelve days with the words of an old French Epiphany carol :

Noel is leaving us,
Sad to say,
But he will come again,
Adieu Noel.

His wife and his children
Weep as they go;
On a grey horse
They ride through the snow.

The Kings ride away
In the snow and the rain;
But after 12 months,
We shall see them again.

TRANS. R.L. GALES

FOLLOWING PAGES: *The twelve-day festival stands as a beacon of light in the darkness of Winter.*

TALES from the NORSE

With Pictures
by
Reginald L Knowles
& Horace J Knowles

Chapter 7

CELEBRATING THE SOLSTICE

Who lists may in their Mumming see
Traces of ancient mystery.
WALTER SCOTT: MARMION

In outlying towns and villages throughout Britain (and more recently in the United States) one of the most eagerly anticipated aspects of Christmas is the arrival of the Mummers – those grand and hilarious "actors" who arrive on various days throughout the Midwinter season, and perform their plays of wonder, farce, and resurrection for anyone who cares to watch. Remember to give a few coins to the company at the end of the show!

LEFT: Tales, stories, songs, and plays are all marvelous ways of celebrating the Solstice with friends and family.

The Mummers Come Calling

Both the Mummers and their plays, as we saw in Chapters 1 and 5, have played an important part in the Solstice celebrations for generations. There are so many interesting aspects to these plays. The Turkish Knight with his blackened face probably refers back to the mock king of *an Dudlach*, the Gloom, who ruled over the Midwinter celebrations in Celtic times. He became confused with the Turks sometime after the Crusades, when they were the enemies. King George is sometimes called St. George, and can be traced back to the dragon-slaying hero, and beyond that to the Hero of a Thousand Battles against the incoming tide of darkness. The presence of Father Christmas once again suggests the antiquity of this character, while the Doctor represents the "resurrection man" or tribal shaman of an even older age.

Other plays, such as that performed in Lincolnshire in 1779, have an even more extraordinary array of characters, among which are "A Fool and his five Sons," who are named Pick Henry, Blue Breeches, Pepper Breeches, Tattered Breeches, and John Allspice. The description of what takes place is given in a brief and charming song (*see box*).

Not all of us have the good fortune to live in a part of the world where these old traditions still take place. But there is no reason why we should not include one of these ancient plays as part of our own Midwinter celebration. All it requires is a few friends and a little ingenuity with a needle and thread or an old clothes box, and a Mummer play can be created out of next to nothing. The form and pattern of the play is the same everywhere and is concerned with death and resurrection, with the death of the old year and the return of the sun and the New Year with it.

These plays are still performed throughout Britain. Every region has its own version, and contemporary references are frequently added – to the delight of performers and watchers alike! So, if you are moved to continue this ancient tradition, you can easily take this example as a starting point and take it in any direction you like. Nor do you have to be a great actor to carry this through – the more knockabout the play gets, the better.

*We are come over
Mire and Moss.
We dance an Hobby Horse.
Then, a Dragon
you shall see,
And a wild Worm
for to flee.
Still we are all brave
jovial boys,
And take delight in Christmas toys.*

THE OVERTON MUMMERS' PLAY

In comes I,
little Johnny-Jack
With my wife and
family at my back.
Although my wife is but small
I have to work hard to find
Bread and cheese
for them all.

This version of the Morris play that follows was recorded by George Long in the village of Overton in Hampshire, England, around 1930, though it probably dates from around 1850 and in its original form as early as the twelfth century. It is still performed, and is still, in a sense, being written, as each year differs slightly from the previous. I have followed Long's version with the occasional addition of a few lines from other old plays to flesh out the whole and I have also made a few cuts to shorten the action. For those wishing to read the full text, as well as much more about the tradition surrounding these old plays, I recommend Long's book The Folklore Calendar *and also the excellent* English Mummers and Their Plays *by Alan Brody.*

A Tale Of Old Christmas

Dramatis Personae
Father Christmas
King George
Turkish Knight
(a brave fellow)
The Doctor
(a quack)
Twing Twang
(a fool)

(ENTER FATHER CHRISTMAS)

Father Christmas

> In comes I, old Father Christmas
> Welcome or welcome not,
> I hope old Father Christmas
> Will never be forgot.

Twing Twang

> I hope he won't be here.

Father Christmas

> Christmas comes but once a year
> When it does it brings good cheer;
> With a pocket full of money
> And a cellar full of beer.
> Roast beef, plum pudding and
> mince pie.
> Who likes them better than I?

Twing Twang

> I do!

Father Christmas

> I don't know that you do my
> little fella.
> But I want room, acres of room,
> For after me comes King George,
> with all his noble train.
> In this room there shall soon be
> a battle
> More dreadful than ever was
> known,
> Betwixt King George and the
> Turkish Knight.
> Enter in King George, and
> boldly clear the way,
> For old Father Christmas has
> only got
> A short time for to stay.

(ENTER KING GEORGE)

King George

> In comes I, King George, so bold,
> so grand.
> I do appear, with my old tribes
> and Britons
> By my side. I am come to close
> this year.
> Here is England's rights, here
> England's wrongs,
>
> Here's England's admirations.
> When I pull out my old trusty
> rapier,
> Is there a man before me can
> stand
> That I can't knock him down
> With my created hand?

(ENTER TURKISH KNIGHT)

Turkish Knight

> In comes I, the Turkish Knight,
> Just come from Turkey Land old
> England for to fight.
> I'll fight thee King George,
> That valiant man of courage bold,
> Let the blood be never so hot
> I'll shortly draw it cold.

King George

> 'Twas I that fought the fiery
> dragon
> And brought him to his slaughter,
> And by that fight I hope to win
> The Queen of Egypt's daughter.
> If any man dare to enter this hall
> I'll cut off his head and kick it
> about like a football!

(KING GEORGE AND THE
TURKISH KNIGHT BATTLE AND
THE TURKISH KNIGHT FALLS DEAD)

Father Christmas

> King George, King George, what
> hast thou done?
> Thou has ruined me by the
> killing of my son.
> Oh, is there a Doctor to be found,
> To heal this noble Turk a-bleeding
> on the ground?

(ENTER DOCTOR)

Doctor

> Oh Yes, Oh Yes, there is a Doctor
> to be found
> To cure this noble Turk a-bleeding
> on the ground.

FATHER CHRISTMAS

What can you cure, Doctor?

DOCTOR

I can cure the itch, the stitch, the palsy and the gout,
The raging pain within and the raging pain without.
If the devil's in a man, I'll fetch him out.
Give me an old woman, four score and ten,
With scarce a stump of a tooth in her head,
I will make her young and plump again.
More than this. If she falls downstairs and breaks her neck,
I'll settle and charge nothing for my fees.
Recollect I'm not like one of those bony quack doctors
Who runs from door to door telling a pack of lies,
I will shortly raise the dead before your eyes.

KING GEORGE

Where have you been learning all these things, Doctor?

DOCTOR

I've been to England, Ireland, Scotland and Dover,
I've traveled the wide world over.

KING GEORGE

What is your fee, Doctor?

DOCTOR

Ten guineas is my fee. Thee being a poor man,
Half of that I'll take of thee.

KING GEORGE

(HANDING HIM SOME MONEY)
Take that and cure him.

DOCTOR

I've a little bottle in the waist-band of my belt
Called "The Golden Frosty Drop"
A little to the eye, a little to the thigh,
A little to the string bone of the heart,
Rise up, thou noble Turk, and try to stand.
See the time of day.
After you've one, put out your tongue,
And let's hear what you can say.

(THE DOCTOR ADMINISTERS A LARGE DOSE OF HIS CONCOCTION, AT WHICH THE TURKISH KNIGHT JUMPS UP ALIVE AGAIN.)

FATHER CHRISTMAS

Well done, my little man.
Thee aren't like those old quack doctors.
Thee does the work all right my lad.
Will thee have the money now
Or stop here till thee get's it?

TURKISH KNIGHT

Now see, King George, I've risen again.
How long have I been on that old floor?
I've been hurried and scurried,
I've been dragged from door to door.
Pick me up a stranger,
Knock me down a blow,
Wherever I'd have been if the ground hadn't caught me
I do not know.

SOMEONE THEN PARADES AROUND THE SPECTATORS WITH A BOX, AND THE COMPANY JOINS IN SINGING

ALL

Good Master and Mistress,
As you sit by the fire,
Remember us poor ploughboys
That run through mud and mire.
The mire it is deep,
And we travel far and near,
We will thank you for a Christmas Box
And a mug of your strong beer.

The Sun in the Greenwood

The celebration of the Solstice has always been about ritual, whether this takes the form of the ancient dancing, guising, and mumming that offered gifts to the gods, or the more recent celebration of the birthday of the Child of Wonder. In the brief contemporary (and culturally non-specific) ritual that follows, and which can be performed either by a small band of friends, or read as a solitary meditation, we find gathered together some of the characters we have met throughout this book. Here are Santa Claus himself, the Green Man, Mother Carey, St. Lucy, the Mabon – all the great Pagan and Christian characters, celebrating the rich and glorious medley that is Midwinter.

THE SUN IN THE GREENWOOD

A ritual for Midwinter by John and Caitlín Matthews

Dramatis personae

SAINTS
St. Nicholas
St. Lucy
St. Thomas
St. Stephen

ANIMALS
The Wren
The Horse
The Deer
The Bear

DEITIES
Mabon
Modron
Elen
Herne

CHARACTERS OF FOLK-LORE & LEGEND
Green Knight
Green Lady
Mother Carey
Father Christmas

NORTH
EARTH
◯
THE COURT OF HOLLY
Mother Carey & Father Christmas
Bear

NORTH-WEST
◯
ST. NICHOLAS

NORTH-EAST
◯
ST. LUCY

WEST
MOON
◯
THE COURT OF MISTLETOE
Herne the Hunter
Elen of the Ways
Reindeer

EAST
SUN
◯
THE COURT OF YEW
Mabon & Modron
Wren

SOUTH-WEST
◯
ST. STEPHEN

SOUTH-EAST
◯
ST. THOMAS

SOUTH
STAR
◯
THE COURT OF IVY
Horse
Green Knight & Green Lady

ABOVE: *Plan of the ritual*

THE ROOM IS DECORATED WITH GREENERY AND CANDLES. PLACES ARE SET AT THE FOUR QUARTERS FOR THE COURTS, AND SEATS FOR THOSE WHO WILL STAND BETWEEN.

THE COMPANY ARE WELCOMED IN BY THE SAINTS, WHO STAND IN PAIRS ON EITHER SIDE OF THE DOOR. THE MAIN PARTICIPANTS THEN ASSEMBLE OUTSIDE AND AWAIT THEIR CUE TO ENTER. WHEN ALL ARE SETTLED, THE SAINTS TAKE UP THEIR POSITIONS AT THE CROSS QUARTERS.

BELLS ANNOUNCE THE BEGINNING OF THE CEREMONY, AT WHICH POINT THE COMPANY STAND UP.

ST. NICHOLAS

We are met here at the still point of the turning year, in a space between the worlds, at the heart of the greenwood, where the Midwinter sun reigns in splendor, to celebrate the Solstice mysteries. I hold in my hands a bag of good things, the largesse of the year, gifts for the giving, this Solstice tide.

BELLS

ST. LUCY

We welcome all who come here with glad hearts to celebrate the passing of the old year and the birth of the new, the turning of the wheel one notch further, the re-enactment of the age-old mystery of the sun in the greenwood, the eternal battle for the year's renewal. I carry upon my

head the crown of candles, to crown your endeavors with the Midwinter light.*

BELLS

ST. THOMAS

We call upon all here present this day to enter the time before time, when we shared the earth with gods and spirits and spoke the languages of bird and beast, when we danced on the greensward and sang the songs of creation and remembering. I hold the spear that finds the deepest darkness and releases the living light of wisdom.

BELLS

ST. STEPHEN

Back through the years, across the bridge of time, we call out to the rulers of the four courts of Winter to come forth and to join us in this celebration. Come, bright lords and ladies, creatures of fur and feather, horn and hide; come bird and beast, come sun and star; come rainbow and come green dancing tree and bright shining flower. I carry away the stone of all that burdens your hearts this Wintertime, that you may be able to receive the gift of joy.

BELLS

THE FOLLOWING PROCESSIONS CAN TAKE PLACE TO SUITABLE MUSIC FOR EACH ENTRY.

ENTER THE COURT OF YEW: THE WREN, MODRON AND MABON. THEY MOVE SLOWLY AROUND THE ROOM ONCE AND THEN STAND IN EAST.

ENTER THE COURT OF IVY: THE HORSE, GREEN LADY AND KNIGHT. THEY MOVE SLOWLY AROUND THE ROOM ONCE AND THEN STAND IN SOUTH.

ENTER THE COURT OF MISTLETOE: THE DEER, ELEN AND HERNE. THEY MOVE SLOWLY AROUND THE ROOM ONCE AND THEN STAND IN WEST.

ENTER THE COURT OF HOLLY: THE BEAR, MOTHER CAREY AND FATHER CHRISTMAS. THEY MOVE SLOWLY AROUND THE ROOM ONCE AND THEN STAND IN NORTH.

THE FOUR SAINTS TOGETHER

Here at the gateway of the year May we strive to make good cheer. In our revels shall joy abound And sorrow be cast underground.

ST. LUCY

Who stands in the east, in the court of the yew?

THE WREN

The yew, that most ancient of trees, stands guard in the eastern quarter. I am the wren, the king of all birds, who dies every year but comes back again, who flies so high that I can see all seekers on the path of the heart's wisdom.

222

MODRON

*Modron am I, also called by
some the mother of all living. I
sought my son, taken from me
when scarcely three nights old,
throughout the length and
breadth of the land. Now I seek
the bright blessing of the
newborn sun, when all that is
immanent is seeded in the heart
and in the head, and the
promise of the old year bears
fruit at last. I am the mother
who welcomes all her children to
her hearth and who teaches
them the wisdom of the heart.*

MABON

*Mabon am I, whom my mother
sought and whom heroes and
creatures, working together,
found and set free. I am the
young sun who rises with the
morning and who shines down
my light through the new day.
At night I journey in other
lands, leaving my task to my
cousin the moon. I am the
watcher at the gates of dawn,
who guides and guards the way
of those who seek the greater
light, who look to the new sun
for inspiration and courage.
Now I represent the New Year,
whose bright rays reach out to
all created things in the still
moment between the old year
and the new.*

ST. THOMAS

*Who stands in the south in the
court of ivy?*

THE HORSE

*The ivy that hangs by the door
opens the way between the
worlds. I am the horse who can
carry you across the threshold
and into the Otherworld itself.
Worshiped for my speed and
grace, I have been with you from
the oldest time. Remembered as
the Mari Llwyd, my riddles challenge all who seek the wisdom of
the ancient ways. I call upon the
Lord and Lady of this court to
name themselves.*

GREEN LADY

*The Green Lady am I, queen of
the wildwood and of all growing
things. I stand in the place of the
star, where the light rises to illu-
minate those who seek the
wisdom of the bright ones who
sing all together to welcome in
the newborn year. In my train
come all those who wander the
pathless ways of the forest and
who seek the strength of the
earth. I challenge all comers to
face their hidden fears and go
beyond them.*

THE GREEN KNIGHT

*I am the Green Knight, the lord
of the beasts, the terrible challenger who came to the court of
King Arthur on Christmas Eve
to bring a draft of Winter into
that place. Of all who seek the
way through the woods, I ask
that they acknowledge the
wisdom of the animals, and that
if they answer my challenge they
should do so in the spirit of the
errant knight, who goes in
search of adventure and who
expects nothing save what fate
brings. I challenge all who walk
this path to meet with me in the
green chapel and there discover
what they will.*

ST. STEPHEN

*Who stands in the west in the
court of mistletoe?*

THE DEER

*Honored by the druids, the
mistletoe, oldest of the sacred
plants, offers the deep dreaming
way into the waters of the west.
The deer am I, who runs beside
Herne the Hunter at the rising of
the morn. My antlers brush the
stars and my cloven hooves have
walked the roadways of the
Underworld from the start of
time. My cousins, the reindeer,
draw the sleigh of the old wise
man Sinta Claus.*

ELEN

Elen of the ways am I named. I keep the paths between the many worlds and wind the strands of time and place around the souls of those who travel on these ancient tracks. Those who seek the wisdom of the spirit, who are drawn thither by their dreams, must first encounter me at the gates of the Solstice. Then, if they pass the tests I set before them, they may proceed, deeper and yet deeper into the mystery of the Winter harvest.

HERNE

Herne the Hunter am I. I have run through the deepest and darkest places in the forest from the beginning of time, and I have danced in the morning and the evening on this old green earth. My antlers are my living crown, and my shining gaze can pierce the depths of the night and the heart of thought. When my horn is blown, all the creatures of the earth answer and gather close by my feet. To all who venture in the court of mistletoe I offer this challenge: come, dance with me and run with me, and feel the thunder of the blood in your heart and in your head.

ST. NICHOLAS

Who stands in the north, in the court of holly?

THE BEAR

Holly bears the berry, red as any blood, and thorns to pierce the souls of men who seek the Winter mystery, that runs deep as time itself. I am bear. I have walked the uplands and the heartlands of this earth since time immemorial, and I know the hearts of men as well as I know my own. In the caves of time and space I lie and dream, and in my dreams I hear the song of Winter. Ice and snow wrap up the earth in bands of iron; yet beneath beats the steady heart of creation, just as it beats in the hearts of all who set forth in search of the solstice revels. I call upon the Lord and Lady of this court to name themselves.

MOTHER CAREY

Mother Carey am I, also known as Holle, she who keeps the old stories you love to tell. When I shake my pillow the snow falls, and I ride the wild winds of change and forgetting. I can turn your dreams inside out or upside down, or gather you under the wings of my stormy petrel and send you forth in search of fresh wisdom along the wind's keen ridge. Whenever you see or hear me you will know that wonder is near – the wonder of Winter's darkness and the light it hides inside.

FATHER CHRISTMAS

As many names have I had as months in the year: Old Saint Nick, Sinta Claus, Old Sir Christemas, Woden, but mostly just plain Santa. I first climbed the great tree when mankind slept in caves, bringing back gifts from the Otherworld. Later I became the bringer of jollity, the bearer of the wassail bowl, the leader of the merry dance from Christmas Day to Twelfth Night. You all know me, and in your hearts you still believe. Remember, when you see me next I'll have a blessing for each of you, and a gift for the new year to be.

THE SAINTS

Now the Solstice courts are established.

ST. LUCY

The sun rises in the court of yew.

ST. THOMAS

The star shines over the court of ivy.

ST. STEPHEN

The moon shines over the court of mistletoe.

ST. NICHOLAS

The earth abides in the court of holly.

ALL

The courts of the greenwood are established. Let the Winter games begin!

ALL THE COURTS AND SAINTS TOGETHER

Set your teeth the wind to face,
Beat the snow down, tread the
frost,
All is gained when all is lost!

FATHER CHRISTMAS

I reach into my sack – a sack
that has no bottom and holds
gifts for everyone – and pull
forth a story – a jest that tells
of Midwinter and the mystery
of the turning year.

ENTER THE MUMMERS, WHO PERFORM
THEIR PLAY WITH MUSIC AND DANCE AND
MAXIMUM MUMMERFICATION. AT THE END
THEY SING THEIR CLOSING SONG TO THE
SPIRITS OF CHRISTMAS AT THE FOUR COURTS.
THE MUMMER PLAY INCLUDED ABOVE MAY
BE USED, OR A NEW ONE WRITTEN!

FATHER CHRISTMAS

We have heard the story, seen
the dance, sung the song! Now is
the time for gifting. Gifts I have
for everyone, and from them
everyone shall learn and grow.
But the greatest gift of all is the
gift of the old year to the new,
the gift of peace and the mystery
of true giving. Let us now cele-
brate and honor the newborn
year – and let some of us reveal
ourselves in other guises!

THE WREN

In the east the year is young. It
is known as the Mabon, the
mother's own dear son. Let all
who would, come forward.
There are gifts to be given and
blessings to share.

MABON AND MODRON REMAIN WHERE THEY
ARE (SITTING), WHILE REPRESENTATIVES OF
THE THREE OTHER COURTS APPROACH. THE
GREEN KNIGHT IS HANDED A SPRIG OF IVY
BY THE GREEN LADY AND COMES FROM THE
SOUTH AROUND THE CIRCLE TO THE EAST.
HERNE IS HANDED A SPRIG OF MISTLETOE
BY ELEN AND APPROACHES ROUND THE
CIRCLE FROM THE WEST. FATHER CHRISTMAS
COMES FROM THE NORTH, HAVING BEEN
HANDED A SPRIG OF HOLLY BY MOTHER
CAREY. EACH GIFT IS A TOKEN OF THEIR
GREEN POWER. EACH ONE OFFERS THEIR
GIFT TO THE MABON WITH SOME BRIEF
WORDS OF THEIR OWN DEVISING. THEN THE
FOUR ANIMALS COME FORWARD, STARTING
WITH THE WREN, TO OFFER THEIR OWN
PLANETARY GIFTS. THIS SHOULD ALL BE
DONE SLOWLY AND WITH GREAT REVERENCE.

FATHER CHRISTMAS

Thus is the New Year honored.
But the gifting is not yet done.
All who have come on this long
road to the turning of the year
shall receive a gift and a bless-
ing. First the blessing. Let all
who would, come now to the
Mabon and the Modron.

THE COMPANY APPROACH THE MABON AND
MODRON SINGLY TO RECEIVE A BLESSING
THAT IS GIVEN IN WHATEVER WORDS THEY
FEEL ARE MOST APPROPRIATE.

FATHER CHRISTMAS

You have received the gifts of the
Mabon and the Modron. Now it
is time to receive a gift from me!

FATHER CHRISTMAS PROCEEDS AROUND
CIRCLE GIVING OUT GIFTS TO ALL

MOTHER CAREY

Good people all, let us now com-
plete our celebration of the
Solstice with merriment and the
passing of the wassail bowl!

FATHER CHRISTMAS AND MOTHER CAREY
BRING FORWARD THE WASSAIL BOWL AND
INSTALL IT IN THE CENTER ON A SPECIALLY
PREPARED ALTAR THAT IS CARRIED TO THE
CENTER BY ONE OF THE OFFICERS. THE
SPIRITS OF CHRISTMAS FROM THE FOUR
COURTS NOW COME FORWARD AND BLESS
THE BOWL IN THEIR OWN WAY. IT IS THEN
PARADED AROUND THE ROOM TO THE
SINGING OF "THE SOMERSET WASSAIL".
THE BOWL IS THEN MOVED OUT TO THE
NEAREST TREE, WHICH IS WASSAILED, AND
THEN ALL THE COMPANY DRINK FROM THE
BOWL AND DEPART TO THE WORDS OF
FATHER CHRISTMAS.

FATHER CHRISTMAS

I bid you all depart in merriment
and joy! May the New Year bring
you all your hopes and wishes,
and may King Sinta Claus bring
you all you desire on Christmas
Day in the morning! Wassail!
Wassail! Nowell! A blessing to
all who serve!

SATURN AND THE DRAGONS OF THE SOLSTICE

A Mystery Play by
Martin Ludgate

This modern ritual drama beautifully captures the spirit of the Solstice, with its blend of comedy and breathless wonder. It is easily performed by eleven people, or fewer by doubling up some of the parts. It is an ideal way to celebrate the mystery of Midwinter as a group, and have a lot of fun in the process.

Speakers

SATURN

THE DRAGONS OF THE QUARTERS OF THE WINTER SKY

  AIR DRAGON

  FIRE DRAGON

  WATER DRAGON

  EARTH DRAGON

THE LADIES WHO DWELL ON THE HILL OF TOMORROW

  DAME DAY

  DAME DUSK

  DAME DARK

VOICES OF WISDOM AND LOVE IN THE EAST

  FIRST VOICE

  SECOND VOICE

  THIRD VOICE

The Voices in the East may be spoken by two or even one, if numbers are low; if the overall number of participants is greater than eleven, then these three parts may be divided and allocated as appropriate.

PROPERTIES

• A lit candle may be held or placed on an altar in the east.
• A cup of wine or punch and a loaf of bread are required for the sharing.
• Some incense (frankincense and myrrh are appropriate) may be set fuming on a windowsill. These are the minimum requirements for this piece.

Participants may attire themselves in such extravagant garb as seems appropriate for the work; the dragons may wish to create eccentric headgear or spangled masks for their adornment.

PRELIMINARY POSITIONING AND SUBSEQUENT SHIFTING

Saturn is in the west, and remains there until he joins the procession led by the Dragons. After the procession, he effectively returns to his starting position in the west. He moves to the east to acknowledge the light and subsequently returns to his place where it is indicated in the text, near the end of the work.

The Dragons begin in the cross-quarters. When summoned by Saturn they move into the center, to draw the chariot of the solstice. They lead the procession through the "sky" to find the birthplace of the light. After the procession, they range themselves in the south. They also move to the east when it is their turn to acknowledge the light.

The ladies begin in the north and remain there until they join Saturn and the Dragons in the procession. After the procession they return to their positions in the north. As with the others, they move to the east when it is their turn to acknowledge the light.

The voices remain in the east throughout the work.

There follow five invocations – one to each of the four quarters and the center. Participants are requested to volunteer to perform these invocations. The themes for the quarters and the center are as noted below. They are exemplars of the hope that sustains us through the dark season of the year.

Eastern Quarter invokes the Bright Child – the promise of the season and the coming year.

Southern Quarter invokes the Warmth of Goodwill – lights of friendship exchanged in visits and greetings.

Western Quarter invokes the Outpouring of Love – familiar and reassuring words and music.

Northern Quarter invokes the Hearth, the Home and All That's Past – including food and fond memories.

Center invokes, at the hub of all seasons, the Earth, the Star and Human Hearts.

When the invocations are ended, all should go to their appointed places, and a chime should be struck or bells jingled to indicate the commencement proper.

Saturn and the Dragons of the Solstice

ALL [TOGETHER]
*When the chill skies are gray
And the nights have grown long
We'll send sorrow away
As we sing an old song -
A song that was uttered
When Winter was King,
And strong dragons fluttered
Above, on the wing.*

VOICE 1
*Cold Winter now has truly come;
The sky is sick, the earth is dumb.*

DAY
I have seen him walking through the leafless wood – a mist of whispers and a white rash of rime.

SATURN
Cold Winter has come, with a mouth of grizzled gums, swallowing the sun.

DUSK
I have heard him whistling on the unprotected hill – a song of silence and clouds full of snow.

DRAGONS [TOGETHER]
Cold Winter has come, in a cloak of locked doors, crooking his neck.

DARK
I have smelled him in the frost-crusted fields, stripping perfume from the hedgerows and the hunting grounds of the bee.

VOICE 1
Cold Winter has come, with an empty basket on his shoulder, chuckling at children struggling through the stinking ditches.

VOICE 2
I have touched his unmerciful hand in the justice of his season, and my breath has broken in the baleful chill of his eye.

VOICE 3
Cold Winter has come, wearing crowns of bitter splendor.

SATURN
But I have tasted the closely-wrapped delights in his sackful of sweetness – precious gifts, jewels of sensation.

DAY
Stories like sugar-plums of memory.

DUSK
Carols like ribbons of starlight in a sparkling heaven.

DARK
Friendship and greetings and a gentle peace.

ALL [TOGETHER]

The weather is dire
And the year has grown old,
But with cows in their byre
And with sheep in their fold,
And food and a fire
To ward off the cold –
Our sorrows we'll shrive
Now that Winter is here,
While our hearths are alive
With good will and good cheer!

For with kith and with kin
And the kindness of friends,
All strangers we'll win
And with foes make amends –
So that good will comes in
As the Ageing Year ends!

Soon we'll wish you a hale
And a Happy New Year,
But we'll first tell a tale
While King Winter is here!

VOICE 1

Once upon a time …

VOICE 2

Long, long ago …

VOICE 3

Far, far away ….

SATURN

But not so long and not so far.

VOICE 1

There dwelt a farmer in
a fertile land.

VOICE 2

And sometimes things were good, and
sometimes they were not so good.

VOICE 3

The year turned – each Summer
chased the Spring; each Fall toddled
after Summer.

VOICE 1

And Winter always shuffled in with
a promise of a holiday, when the
weather would be too wilful and the
ground too hard for working.

SATURN

In the season of the long nights of the
year, the farmer would visit his
neighbors or welcome them to his
homestead, and eat and drink with
them and enjoy good cheer.

DRAGONS [TOGETHER]

"This is the Feast of Saturn," his
neighbors would say. "Let us be
merry in the lap of Winter!"

SATURN

And the farmer would smile, and
raise his glass to his lips and offer
them a friendly toast and a Happy
New Year.

VOICE 1

The Golden Age had passed long
since, but echoes of that blessed time
came again to the earth at Midwinter
– echoes of the days when Saturn was
King of the Gods. In that happy
time, the earth had fruited and fed
humanity without stinting. But at
the end of the Golden Age, Saturn
withdrew from his former glory.
Somewhere, somehow, he set the first
clock ticking, and the changing
seasons came into being.

SATURN

As a boon to humankind, Saturn
created agriculture – the work appro-
priate to each season.

DAY

Harrowing the fields and plowing –
Every task its tide allowing.

DUSK

Sowing 'neath a growing moon;
Cropping after plenilune.

DARK

Winter horses fed on hay
We gathered on Midsummer Day.

DAY AND DUSK [TOGETHER]

Grain from harvest for our bread –
Fall's great bounty keeps us fed
Till the warming springtime rain,
When the earth grows green again.

DAMES [TOGETHER]

Green and gold and silent ground –
Thus the wheeling year goes round,
Slowing only when folk bide Near
their hearths at Solstice tide.

VOICE 1

One deep and starry night near the
Dark Gate of the Year, Saturn looked
about him – the skies were clear – the
air was still.

SATURN

This is good weather for going for a
ride. I could make a trip to the house
on top of the Hill of Tomorrow. It
must be a year and a day since I last
saw Dame Day and Dame Dusk and
Dame Dark.

VOICE 2

So out of the coach house he rolled his
great chariot of lapis lazuli, with its
wheels of polished ebony, and glitter-
ing lanterns of sapphire.

VOICE 3

And he called to the Dragons of the
Winter Solstice to come and draw the
chariot.

CHIME STRUCK AGAIN, OR JINGLE OF BELLS
AGAIN

SATURN

Dragons hide where no-one looks,
Deep inside old storybooks;
But they'll hear my invocation,
And soon appear from
imagination.
Dragon of breath and dragon of
flames,
Come from the quarters that echo
your names!
Dragon of flood and dragon of stones,
Come from the quarters my calling
intones!
Dragon of air, on a wind of the east,
Help me to journey to a
Midwinter feast!

AIR

I am the laughter in the Winter
wind, falling like snow in the streets;
tumbling sparks of whiteness in the
bitter wildness.

The Dragon of the Eastern Sky –
Who knows the winds as well
as I?

SATURN

Dragon of Fire, from southern
burning,
Help me to journey – for New Year
I'm yearning!

FIRE

I am the song in the Solstice hearth,
flaring like Summer buds in splendid
gardens; garlands of warmth in a
curtained room.

The Dragon of the Southern Flame –
What burns as strong as my true
name?

SATURN

Dragon of Water, in the seas of the
west,
Help me to journey in this season so
blest!

WATER

I am the punch in the cheering bowl,
flowing like love into every willing
heart; fruits breaking into liquid
sweetness in every mouth.

The Dragon of the Western Sea –
What waters flow as deep as me?

SATURN

Dragon of Earth, rolling out of the
north,
Help me to journey – here's three;
make a fourth!

EARTH

I am the earth abiding its hour, incu-
bating the green fevers of Spring;
certainty and rest.

The Dragon of the Northern Stone –
Who knows the earth but I alone?

DRAGONS [TOGETHER]

We are the power of imagination,
invincible and boundless.
We Dragons love Midwintertide,
And, joyful, join your jolly ride!

VOICE 1

Without even being asked, they
picked up the traces of the chariot,
and Saturn hopped aboard, and all
of a sudden they were running –
leaping – flying – off into the wonder
of the Winter sky!

AT THIS POINT THE DRAGONS, IN FORMA-
TION, MAY GAMBOL AROUND THE ROOM,
WITH SATURN IN TOW.

VOICE 2

*The Dragons sang as they raced
through the heavens.*

DRAGONS [TOGETHER]

*O listen to us, and we'll tell you no
lie –
Great Saturn, with twinkles alive in
each eye,
In his chariot of blue lapis lazuli
Led by four dragons, goes merrily by!*

*The feast of Midwinter is now
drawing nigh –
The New Year must wake and the
Old Year must die!*

VOICE 3

*On they went, northward, dodging
cloudbanks, cresting high places with
consummate ease, shouting cheery
greetings to the fish in the seas and
the goats on the mountains!*

VOICE 1

*But there was a new star in the fir-
mament that night – a star with tails,
like an arrow speeding toward the
east. It crossed the path of the
Dragons as they neared the Hill of
Tomorrow, and startled them.*

SATURN

*It flashed in my face!
It scorched my new hat!*

DRAGONS [TOGETHER]

*Yet it blazed with true grace!
Whatever was that?*

VOICE 2

*There was no time for an answer, for
they were almost at the Hill of
Tomorrow.*

VOICE 3

*And in a house on top of the hill
lived three wise women.*

DAY

*Dame Day, who carded and spun the
wool of the hardy mountain sheep,
and dyed it in all kinds of colors – so
that her bespattered gown looked like
a broken rainbow.*

DUSK

*Dame Dusk, who knitted and wove
the wool into patterns and pictures,
and sewed the pieces together for
clothes and cloaks and blankets – so
that she always seemed to be wearing
a multitude of illustrations.*

DARK

*And Dame Dark, who knotted and
snipped the loose ends, and beaded
and spangled the
garments and coverlets – so that her
robe appeared to be jeweled with
riches.*

DAMES [TOGETHER]

*Three women of wisdom, of cunning
and skill,
They lived in a house on the top of a
hill –
A hill that was higher than over-
stretched hopes,
For the Northern Aurora illumined
its slopes!*

VOICES [TOGETHER]

*And the beansticks they set in the
garden now lie
Toppled by tails of that star passing
by.*

*The Dragons and Saturn come safely
to land,
And in a small group by the gatepost
they stand.*

SATURN

*I can see a light shining through the
little window – they must be in. Now,
mighty Dragons of Midwintertide, let
them know we're here!
Take your time from me –
One, two, three!*

DRAGONS [TOGETHER]

*Clang, clang, clang
At the garden gate!
Hear us tintinnabulate!
In the silent snow a-falling,
Sturdy Dragons come a-calling!*

DAY

*O my sisters, did you hear someone
clanging at the gate?
O who would come a-clanging so
insolently late?*

DARK

Tis a drunkard homeward ganging,
On the hinges helpless hanging,
Swinging back and forth and
banging –
If we'd only locked the gate!

DRAGONS [TOGETHER]

Knock, knock, knock
At the big front door!
What can we be knocking for?
Though the weather is appalling,
We are Dragons come a-calling!

DUSK

O my sisters, did you hear someone
knocking at the door?
O who would come a-knocking in
weather wild and hoar?

DARK

Some droll mummer full of mocking,
Come with nuts to fill your stocking –
The prospect seems quite shocking!
Turn the key and bolt the door!

DRAGONS [TOGETHER]

Tap, tap, tap
At the window pane!
Tapping twice and then again
Enthusiastic and enthralling
Thrilling Dragons come a-calling!

DARK

O my sisters, did you hear someone
tapping at the pane?
O who would come a-tapping in
snow and sleet and rain?

DAY

It is just a rook a-flapping,
Or some spirit rudely rapping Such a
deed deserves a slapping!
Pull the blind across the pane!

DRAGONS [TOGETHER]

Rattle, rattle, rattle
At the rusty latch!
Our persistence none can match!
The Chariot of the Solstice hauling,
Cheery Dragons come a-calling!

DUSK

O my sisters, did you hear someone
rattling at the latch?
O who would come a-rattling, their
death of cold to catch?

DARK

Through such bitter weather battling,
Only gossips geared for prattling,
With a thirst for tittle-tattling,
Would be rattling at the latch!

DRAGONS [TOGETHER]

Sing, sing, sing
For admittance here,
While the echoes cling
To the summits sheer!
While dreams our weary world are
shawling,
Daring Dragons come a-calling!

DAMES [TOGETHER]

O my sisters, do you hear someone
singing just outside?
Now who would come
a-singing upon a Solsticetide?
To the winds all caution flinging,
To this mountain fastness winging,
Some small music sweetly
bringing?
Tis the dragons! Come inside!

CHEERS! GREETINGS! DAMES GREET THE
DRAGONS AND SATURN EFFUSIVELY!

DARK

Heavens above, and gracious me!
We couldn't think who it could be
Loudly landing here and so
Rowdy in the hushing snow!

SATURN

Although 'twas not our purposed
care
In traveling so far,
I'll ask if you have seen the flare
That trailed the Solstice Star.

DUSK

We have indeed! Such flashes
The laws of physics flout!
It burned our bin to ashes,
And singed each Brussels sprout!

DAY

A comet in conception –
Not circling round the sun,
But seeking a connection
With some much brighter One.

DRAGONS [TOGETHER]

*It sounds just like a stellar hero
Seeking for a lover.
We won't find out by staying here
Let's follow and discover!*

VOICE 1

*And then and there, that is what they
did! The Dragons returned to the
traces of the chariot. Dame Day and
Dame Dusk and Dame Dark tucked
themselves into mantles and tippets
and cozy boots. They bundled some
bread and wine into a basket, and
boarded the chariot with Saturn.*

VOICE 2

*They could see the Solstice Star in the
East. It seemed to beckon them, and
a nimbus of loving warmth appeared
around it as the Dragons, the chariot,
and its occupants rose majestically
into the sky.*

VOICE 3

*As they went, the Dragons sang new
words to an old song. And Saturn
and the Wise Women joined in!*

MUSIC: THE SONG OF THE DRAGONS IS
SUNG TO JOHN HENRY HOPKINS' OLD TUNE,
FAMILIAR TO US AS "WE THREE KINGS OF
ORIENT ARE."
DURING THIS, THE DRAGONS, SATURN AND
THE DAMES SHOULD WALK DEOSIL IN PRO-
CESSION AROUND THE ROOM.

SONG OF THE DRAGONS

*We are Dragons, swooping along
Kings of story, monarchs of song,
Glowing, gleaming,
Beasts of dreaming,
Born to be sage and strong.*

*O – Dragons in the starry night,
Legends manifest in flight,
Stern as thunder,
Winged with wonder,
Seeking truth and love and light.*

*Pale with air and potent with fire,
Proud of all the songs we inspire,
Four combined
In single mind
Pursuing our one desire.*

*O – Dragons helmed with gem and
horn,
Children of a timeless dawn,
Deft, discerning,
Ever yearning
For the place where light is born.*

*Over crest and mountainous scree,
Over spring and fountain and sea,
Racing gale
And comet's tail
To where the new light must be.*

*O – Dragons, free from all disguise,
Wilful, witty, deeply wise,
Time's defenders,
Scaled with splendors,
Flying through the winter skies*

*Wild as love and mighty as earth,
Salt as tears and vital as mirth,
Rising, roaring,
Swiftly soaring,
Seeking the light's new birth.*

*O – Dragons, Dragons, trailing cheer,
Headlong through the midnight clear,
Aye expressing
Endless blessing
Every day in every year!*

DURING THE LAST VERSE, SATURN AND THE
WISE WOMEN RETURN TO THEIR STARTING
POSITIONS. THE DRAGONS RANGE THEM-
SELVES IN THE SOUTH. THERE IS NOW A
CIRCLE OF PEOPLE ALL AROUND THE ROOM.

VOICE 1

*The Star had settled in the sky ahead
of them, directing its beams onto a
distant
range of hills.*

VOICE 2

*Their journey in the chariot did not
seem long, and they speedily arrived
at the spot on which the Star was
shining.*

VOICE 3

*The Dragons, Saturn and the Wise
Women landed in
the stillness of a small hill-town one
of those out-of-the-way places where
nothing ever seems to happen.*

VOICE 1

Directly under the Star stood a ram-shackle building that appeared to be held up solely by the belief of those who saw it. Swallows glided in circles above the fragmentary roof, like a great garland of wings.

VOICE 2

Dogs and cats and mice sat and stead-fastly gazed at the presence of the Light new-born.

VOICE 3

Ox and ass knelt down in the loving brightness.

VOICE 1

A lamb from the hillside and a lion from the mountain lay companion-ably beside one another.

VOICE 2

And a dirty white foal from the fields, with the gleam of a star on its brow, stood wondering in the silence of the wide doorway.

DRAGONS [TOGETHER]

"It is the birthday of the Child," whispered the Dragons. "But we have brought no presents with us. What shall we give him?"

DAMES [TOGETHER]

"We shall give him what we can," said the Dames.

IN TURN, THE DAMES, THE DRAGONS, AND SATURN COME FORWARD INDIVIDUALLY AND KNEEL BEFORE THE LIGHT IN THE EAST. AFTER EACH GIFTING, EACH

SPEAKER RETURNS TO HIS OR HER POSITION. DRAGONS RETURN TO THEIR POSITIONS IN THE SOUTH.

DAY

Infant new-born, to help on your way,
I bring you a gift – the bright hope of day.

... AND THE SPEAKER ADDS TO THIS WHATEVER DAME DAY THINKS IS APPROPRIATE

DUSK

The bloom has a scent, and the lover has musk,
But here is true fragrance – the sweet rest of dusk.

... AND THE SPEAKER ADDS TO THIS WHATEVER DAME DUSK THINKS IS APPROPRIATE.

DARK

Unnumbered stellations, unmatched is the sight;
Receive now my gift – the wonder of night.

... AND THE SPEAKER ADDS TO THIS WHATEVER DAME DARK THINKS IS APPROPRIATE.

AIR

No tone-deaf pedant this gift shall rescind:
Birdsong and music, and the hymn of the wind.

... AND THE SPEAKER ADDS TO THIS WHATEVER AIR DRAGON THINKS IS APPROPRIATE.

FIRE

Here's perpetual flame to enliven endeavor,
And love to keep you warm forever.

... AND THE SPEAKER ADDS TO THIS WHATEVER FIRE DRAGON THINKS IS APPROPRIATE.

WATER

All kisses kind-hearted, and tears never vain;
The refreshment of water and amiable rain.

... AND THE SPEAKER ADDS TO THIS WHATEVER WATER DRAGON THINKS IS APPROPRIATE.

EARTH

The gift of great goodness abiding is mine:
The sustainment of earth and bread and wine

... AND THE SPEAKER ADDS TO THIS WHATEVER EARTH DRAGON THINKS IS APPROPRIATE.

SATURN

May the turning year always fulfil every need –
Bud and blossom and fruit and seed

... AND THE SPEAKER ADDS TO THIS WHATEVER SATURN THINKS IS APPROPRIATE.

AFTER PRESENTING THEIR GIFTS, THEY
RETURN TO THEIR POSITIONS AT THE
BEGINNING OF THIS SECTION — THAT IS,
WITH THE DRAGONS IN THE SOUTH. THIS IS
AN APPROPRIATE POINT FOR ALL (EXCEPT
THE VOICES) TO PUT DOWN THEIR SCRIPTS
AND JOIN HANDS, IN PREPARATION FOR THE
CONTEMPLATION.

CONTEMPLATION

MUSIC BEGINS. THE PIECE OF MUSIC USED
HERE BEGINS WITH THE MELODY OF AN
AUSTRIAN CAROL, THE ENGLISH NAME OF
WHICH IS "THE DARKNESS IS FALLING" THE
VOICES MAY EITHER SPEAK THE VERSE
BELOW SOFTLY OVER THE MUSIC, OR SING
ALONG WITH THE CAROL.

VOICES [TOGETHER]

The Bright Child's awoken
With blessing for you.
His promise is spoken –
That Love is your due.
And here, for a token,
A symbol that's true –
The darkness is broken;
The light comes anew!

AT THIS POINT, THE VOICES PUT DOWN
THEIR SCRIPTS AND JOIN HANDS WITH THE
OTHERS FOR THE CONTEMPLATION. THE
MUSIC CONTINUES, AND THE MELODY
CHANGES TO A FAMILIAR ONE.

AFTER THE MUSIC FOR THE CONTEMPLA-
TION HAS ENDED, WE MOVE ON TO THE
SENDING.

THE SENDING

VOICE 1

Turn out now to the world.
Send out the Light.

PARTICIPANTS RELEASE EACH OTHERS'
HANDS AND TURN OUTWARD. AFTER DEDI-
CATIONS HAVE BEEN MADE, AND AN
APPROPRIATE AMOUNT OF TIME HAS
PASSED, PARTICIPANTS TURN INWARD
AGAIN.

SHARING

VOICE 1

Receive now the manifest gifts of the
Light.

VOICE 2

BLESSES THE BREAD EXTEMPORE, AND
THEN DISTRIBUTES IT TO THE COMPANY

VOICE 3

BLESSES WINE SIMILARLY, AND
DISTRIBUTES IT. MUSIC CAN BE PLAYED
DURING THE SHARING. WHEN EVERYONE
HAS RECEIVED BREAD AND WINE, AND THE
MUSIC HAS FINISHED, WE MOVE ON TO THE
CLOSING.

THE CLOSING

THE CENTER AND THE QUARTERS ARE
CLOSED IN REVERSE ORDER BY THOSE WHO
OPENED THEM. THE CLOSING EVOCATIONS
SHOULD BE RELATED IN THEME TO THE
INVOCATIONS AT THE BEGINNING.

Notes for Participation

The urge to instigate seasonal celebrations is strong in us as the Winter Solstice approaches. There are many thoughts and suggestions throughout this book on how we can engage with the feelings and perceptions that living through the depths of Winter evoke in us. These are suggestions, not hard and fast customs or ceremonies. Our preconceived ideas of ceremony tend to see such celebrations as rather solemn events that have to be performed in rather straight-laced, traditional ways. Remember that all ceremony and celebration arises from need to express our feeling of the spiritual and numinous, our heartfelt response to the things, events, and archetypes which communicate a deeply moving understanding of how the natural world and all the species within it are part of a greater embrace. Our own rituals and celebrations don't have to be theatrical, ceremonial, or churchy – but they can express our intimate love, our perceptive insight, our human joy.

One of the first challenges that faces anyone thinking about celebrating the Solstice for him or herself or with friends, family, and community is the fact that we each suddenly become the celebrant of the ceremony. The fact that we have been doing this for generations is often forgotten: each householder has enacted domestic rituals through the years with little thought of their own sacred role, or has shared sacred celebrations in the community. We may feel that this is not something we

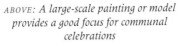

ABOVE: A large-scale painting or model provides a good focus for communal celebrations

are cut out for: preparation and planning are one thing, but a sense of unworthiness holds some back. We are living in a time when people are rediscovering authority in their spiritual lives and are finding out what it is to be, not a member of a congregation, but the instigator and celebrant of ceremony as an expression of their own sacred journey.

The celebrations in this book may be considered as approaches to exploring the sacred dimensions of Solstice without always or only seeing them through a Christian focus. There is no monopoly on this season: you have read in these pages of the many traditions worldwide that regard Winter as a particularly sacred time, an opportunity for communing with the gifts of the Solstice. The mantle of the year wraps its many colors about everyone's shoulders: no-one is excluded from these celebrations. If you have a firm belief, then you will find that celebratory aspects of your spiritual tradition draw upon Solstice customs. If you have no fixed belief, you can discover sacred pathways that lie within Winter's gift. If you look toward the ancestral and native traditions of the world, you will already know the sustaining hospitality of personal spiritual celebration and community customs.

There are several suggestions in this book about making a shrine. A shrine is a nexus point, a place where the everyday meets the sacred. It can become a focus for our sacred dedication, a crucible of our desires, an incubator of hopes. We all have shrines: the family photograph shelf; the certificates of educational merit; the swimming medals or sporting trophies; even the film-stars and pop-singers' posters on the wall in the teenager's bedroom. For most people, the sacred heart of the home, the central shrine, is the hearth. Each householder is the keeper and guardian of the hearth: the flame at the heart of the household shrine is the flame of love, devotion, and commitment with that we each inspirit our dwelling. We would not be without such shrines.

Some shrines are temporary, open to change or to be dismantled after the proper season. We may consider the Christmas Crib in this light: when Epiphany is over, the Crib comes down until next year. Your Winter shrine-making will be of this order. When you are preparing your shrine, you are making a place where your sacred aspirations are affirmed and witnessed by both passers-by and by the holy ones who live in the unseen realms. Shrines are meeting-places for the seen and unseen, for the manifest and the withdrawn, for the human and the divine. There is a natural respect for such shrines: we do not put coffeecups upon them, for example, or treat them as mundane places. Shrines like to be visited and kept immaculate. They are visual reminders of a spiritual dimension that lies all about us. Shrines can be indoors or out. Outdoor shrines, or mobile shrines in the branches of trees, can be very

ABOVE: *This imposing costumed figure shows what can be done when performing a ritual play.*

powerful places. Shrines within the home need not be ostentatious: a candle, a picture, and vase of greenery will not offend anyone with whom you may be sharing a house.

You may wish to create an integral Solstice Shrine, upon which all the different components of your Winter celebration can be focused. This might be the top of a dresser or shelf, by your hearth, or somewhere outdoors in your yard. Your Solstice Shrine may be

LEFT: *Performing your own Mummer play with music and costumes is an immensely satisfying experience.*

very simple or it might resemble a mini-landscape of Winter in which different things are placed. Be sensitive to what wants to go onto it, and how it is arranged. If you are meditating over the season, you may like to sit where you can contemplate it.

You may be performing your celebrations alone. If this is so, then you can have a very special rapport with the gifts of Solstice. One of the challenges of lone celebration is of making it real. It is very easy to read a book and celebrate in your head: but to take the suggestion off the page and into action is another matter. Uttering words aloud or making gestures may seem pointless if you are alone, but remember that the creation of celebration arises in our deep imagination and needs to be performed in our own realm. Do not doubt that it will be witnessed by the holy ones who maintain the universe, by the ancestors and descendants who have lived and will live their lives upon this holy Earth, by the spirits of creatures, trees, and the elements themselves. The ceremonies and celebrations that we perform alone are enacted for the benefit of all beings; we also witness to the sacred gifts of season for all

those who cannot or will not ask for those gifts, for all who yearn to be included but for whom Winter means only cold, emptiness, and darkness. When we become celebrants of the Solstice, we kindle a light in that darkness and share the gift.

The celebrations suggested in these pages need to be brought to life by your engagement and performance. You can read them over and begin to envisage what you'll need to make them work for you in your personal circumstances. Will you be indoors or out? What preparations need to be done? What will you need to take? Will those celebrating with you need any special thought? No communal celebration or ceremony should last longer than about an hour – children get fractious, the elderly need to sit or rest, guests want refreshment, animals need their exercise.

If you are using this book in order to enable communal celebrations with family or friends, adapt the celebrations to your needs. The major thing is that everyone should feel welcome and no-one be excluded. People of differing spiritual backgrounds may need consideration: if it is Christmas or Hannukah for them, then your celebrations should also remember and respect that fact. Including everyone can be fun, if you have made your preparations well. If you're outside, don't forget the warmth factor: do you have a place where a bonfire can be made safely? It would make a good gathering place. Is it going to be dark? Then bring lighted lanterns and torches. Will everyone be cold afterward? Don't forget to have hot food and drink ready when people come back in. Give everyone something to involve them: young children are usually the most enthusiastic to join in the game of celebration, but don't forget the shy guest, the difficult relative, or the laconic friend. If you're going for a full Winter ceremony, ensure that there is a song everyone can sing or a simple dance that everyone can join in with.

Groups of people naturally congregate in circles, unless the group is very big indeed. Invite everyone to stand in a ring, so that the sight-lines are good for everyone. Don't let anyone sit out behind: there's nothing more disconcerting at a celebration than someone who doesn't want to join in but still wants to watch. Invite retiring guests to stand or sit with the rest. You don't all have to hold hands, just to be present together. Extend the welcome of the circle to everyone present and give the people assembled a sense of purpose and engagement.

State clearly to those assembled why you are gathering. Stress the inclusive factors of your ritual: turning toward light at a time of darkness, being together and of one heart, being at peace with the whole of creation. If you're doing a meditation together, keep it short, with a time of silence somewhere within it for personal revelation and spiritual refreshment. Give clear instructions about what is expected next, so that people celebrating with you are not embarrassed or left

uncertain: for example, "and now let's sing the song at the bottom of the page," or " Ted, will you pass round the candle now? Let's all light our tapers as he goes round, remembering the returning sun." Before you conclude your celebration, always remember those who are not present, those in need, particular situations in the world at that time or events that are close to your community: invite everyone to share a moment of silence to remember these things or to speak them aloud all together so that they are witnessed. Thank everyone for being present and maybe invite everyone to give a short blessing or statement of thanks to their spiritual inspirers.

If you're with friends with whom you frequently celebrate round the year, you will have a much more intimate and spontaneous way of arriving at your celebration. You may want to discuss it together beforehand, decide a rough shape to proceedings and delegate different people to bring or prepare different things: for example, one to bring a song, one to be responsible for making a fire, one to bring greenery from their yard, and so on. When you're all gathered, you may have a period of silence wherein you each attune to the purpose of the celebration: then the whole thing may unfold with natural grace and easy spontaneity.

If you're outside and are approached by neighbors or passers-by, invite them to join in, if appropriate: let them know that you're enjoying a seasonal celebration or custom. Don't be ashamed or secretive: this is a time for sharing the gifts of Solstice, not for exclusive and excluding ceremonies.

The creation and performance of celebration need not be an over-dressed event. Simple ceremony is always effective and meaningful if our hearts and intentions are allowed to follow through.

THE PATTERNS OF THE SOLSTICE

A GUIDE TO THE CELEBRATIONS IN THIS BOOK

The Solstice tide stretches from just before the night of Midwinter itself (December 20/21st) to just after Twelfth Night or Epiphany (January 6th). In between these two dates are a number of significant highs and lows that together make up the flow of the solstitial period. These form a pattern that is the basis for a cycle of celebration and ceremony that can easily be followed by anyone seeking to discover for themselves the deeper significance of Midwinter:

ABOVE: *The changing tides provide the rhythmic patterns that govern the winter solstice.*

1
PREPARING FOR THE SOLSTICE
December 1st – 21st

From the beginning of December to the Solstice night itself is a period of preparation for the return of the Midwinter Sun. Such preparations include cleansing the self and the home in readiness to welcome in the New Year and take our leave of the old. It is a time of letting go of old thoughts, ideas, and things, of decorating the home, buying or making gifts for the upcoming season of Christmas, and of celebrating the manifold aspects of the season and our own relationship to the natural and supernatural worlds that surround us. Throughout the book will be found various suggestions for accomplishing this, while the whole of Chapter 6 is given over to the celebration of the Twelve Days of Christmas. Activities that are particularly appropriate for this first period are :

* **MAKING A SOLSTICE ALTAR** (*see above*)
* **CELEBRATING THE DIRECTIONS** (Chapter 1)
* **INVOKING THE OLD ONE** (Chapter 1)
* **LITANY OF THE WINTER SOLSTICE** (Chapter 1)
* **HONORING THE EVERGREEN** (Chapter 3)
* **INVITING IN THE CREATURES OF THE SOLSTICE** (Chapter 5)
* **RENEWAL OF THE SOLSTICE** (Chapter 1)

2

CELEBRATING THE SOLSTICE
December 21 – 22nd

Over the night of the Solstice itself there are a number of ways to acknowledge the return of the Midwinter Sun. Those that are particularly relevant to this period are:

- **A PLACE FOR ALL**
  (Chapter 4)
- **THE SUN IN THE GREENWOOD**
  (Chapter 7)
- **SATURN AND THE DRAGONS OF THE SOLSTICE**
  (Chapter 7)
- **THE GIFTS OF THE SOLSTICE**
  (Chapter 4)
- **THE WISHING TREE**
  (Chapter 3)

3

PREPARING FOR CHRISTMAS
December 23rd – 25th

The period from the Solstice itself to Christmas Day is a time of preparation on every level for the events of the Nativity. While the prime focus of this time is on the birth of Jesus, we can also remember other Children of Wonder born on December 25th. It is also a time to spend with our own children, talking about the significance of the Solstice with them, and selecting and making gifts together. At this time also we concentrate on last-minute preparations – final touches of decoration, putting up the Christmas Tree, bringing in the Yule Log, making special dishes for the Christmas table. Suggestions for this period include:

- **THE YULE CANDLE**
  (Chapter 3)
- **YULE LOG CEREMONY**
  (Chapter 3)
- **THE BIRTHDAY OF WINTER: MAKING A SHRINE**
  (Chapter 2)
- **CONSIDERING THE GIFT**
  (Chapter 6)
- **A SHRINE TO OLD CHRISTMAS**
  (Chapter 4)

4

FROM CHRISTMAS TO NEW YEAR
December 26th – 31st

From the high spot of Christmas to the high spot of the New Year is a period of great activity, with each of the days leading up to the end of the Old Year (new style calendar) being filled with possibilities for celebration and contemplation. Contemplation, that is, of the old and the new, of things to be let go of and the new intentions we hope for in the months to come. Suggestions for this period are as follows:

- **OBSERVING THE SOLSTICE**
  (Chapter 1)
- **GUISING TODAY**
  (Chapter 5)
- **HONORING THE CHILDREN**
  (Chapter 6)
- **HONORING THE MOTHERS**
  (Chapter 6)
- **DOING SOMETHING FOOLISH**
  (Chapter 6)
- **EGGNOG FOREVER**
  (Chapter 6)

5
NEW YEAR REVELS
December 31st – January 1st

This is always a period for intense celebration. But woven into the secular round of parties are other, equally ancient customs: First Footing, Wassailing, divining the path the New Year will take, reading the oracle of the hearth-fires.

- **WASSAILING ALL**
  (Chapter 6)
- **FIRST FOOTING**
  (Chapter 6)
- **SHAPES IN THE FIRE**
  (Chapter 6)
- **UNFINISHED BUSINESS**
  (Chapter 6)
- **MAKING A BOAR'S HEAD**
  (Chapter 6)
- **A TALE OF OLD CHRISTMAS:**
  THE OVERTON MUMMER PLAY
  (Chapter 7)

6
THE NEW YEAR TIDE:
TWELFTH NIGHT
January 1st – 6th

The quiet days that follow the noisy celebrations of the New Year are a time for contemplation, for considering the patterns of the Old Year and the hoped for patterns of the New. This is a time to think of New Year resolutions, of looking inward at the self and outward at the world and seeing how these match up. Suggested activities for this period will be found in the following sections:

- **12TH NIGHT CAKE**
  (Chapter 6)
- **CONSIDERING THE GIFTS**
  (Chapter 6)
- **GAMES AND SPORTS**
  (Chapter 6)
- **ON TWELFTH NIGHT**
  (Chapter 3)

These six periods of time, many of that flow into one another, provide a basis for a complete celebration of the Solstice tide. You may not wish, or be able, to do everything suggested here, but if you ring the changes, and follow the dictates of your own heart, you should be able to celebrate the Winter Solstice for many years to come, building up and adding to a growing yearly pattern from your own store of ideas.

This is a period that takes place largely outside time; if you take advantage of the sacred season to ponder the patterns of life and becoming, and to celebrate those things that are eternal, you can discover so much more than you ever though possible about yourself and your relationship to the wondrous creation that surrounds you on every side.

RESOURCES AND FURTHER READING

BOOKS

A vast number of books have been written about the Winter Solstice and the history of Christmas. There follows a list of those books, recordings, and other resources that I have found most helpful.

Bancroft, Anne,
Origins of the Sacred,
London: Arkana, 1987

Banks, M.M.,
British Calendar Customs,
London: Kegan Paul, Trench, Tubner, 1937-41

Baker, Margaret,
Discovering Christmas Customs and Folklore,
Princes Risborough: Shire Publications, 1994

Brennan, Martin,
The Stars and The Stones,
London: Thames & Hudson, 1983

Brody, Alan,
The English Mummers and Their Plays,
London: Routledge & Kegan Paul, 1970

Budge, Wallis,
The Book of the Cave of Treasures,
London: The Religious Tract Society, 1927

Burland, C.A.,
Echoes of Magic,
Totowa, New Jersey: Rowman & Littlefield, 1972

Burton, Tim,
The Nightmare Before Christmas,
New York: Hyperion Books, 1993

Cawte, E.C.,
Ritual Animal Disguise,
Cambridge: D.S. Brewer, 1978

Chambers, E.K.,
The Medieval Stage,
New York: Dover Publications, 1996

Clancy, Joseph P.,
The Earliest Welsh Poetry,
London: Macmillan, 1970

Coffin, Tristram Potter,
The Book of Christmas Folklore,
New York: The Seabury Press, 1973

Cooper, J.C.,
The Aquarian Guide to Festivals,
London: The Aquarian Press, 1990

Count, Earl W., and Alice Lawson,
4000 Years of Christmas,
Berkley, CA: Ulysses Press, 1997

Crichton, Robin,
Who is Santa Claus?,
Edinburgh: Canongate, 1987

Danaher, Kevin,
The Year in Ireland,
Dublin: Mercier Press, 1972

Dawson, W.F.,
Christmas, its Origin and Associations,
London: Elliot Stock, 1902

Dearmer, P., R. Vaughan Williams, and Martin Shaw (Eds.),
The Oxford Book of Carols,
London: Oxford University Press, 1928

Duchesne-Guillemin, J.,
'Jesus, Trimorphism and the Differentiation of the Magi,' in E. Sharp and J. Hinnells (Eds.),
Man and His Salvation,
Manchester: Manchester University Press, 1973

Eckenstein, Lina,
Comparative Studies in Nursery Rhymes,
London: Duckworth, 1906

Eisen, Armand,
The Story of Santa Claus,
Atlanta, FL: Turner Publishing Inc., 1993

Evers, Larry, and Molina Felipe S. (Eds.),
Yaqui Deer Songs: Maso Bwikam,
Tucson: Sun Tracks and the University of Arizona, 1987

Ferguson, John,
The Religions of the Roman Empire,
London: Thames & Hudson, 1970

Fideler, David,
Jesus Christ, Son of God,
Wheaton, IL: Quest Books, 1993

Foley, Daniel J.,
The Christmas Tree,
New York: Chilton Co, 1960

Gaarder, Jostein,
The Christmas Mystery,
London: Phoenix House, 1996

Ginzburg, Carlo,
Ecstasies,
London: Hutchinson Radius, 1969

Godwin, Joscelyn,
**Mystery Religions
in the Ancient World,**
London: Thames & Hudson, 1981

Green, Joyce Conyngham,
**Salmagundi: Being a
Calendar of Sundry Matters,**
London: J.M. Dent, 1947

Green, Marian,
A Calendar of Festivals,
Shaftesbury: Element Books, 1991

Gribbin, John,
Blinded by Light,
London and New York: Bantam
Press, 1991

Grimm, Jakob and Wilhelm,
**Grimm's Tales for
Young and Old,**
Trans. by Ralph Manheim, London:
Gollancz, 1978

Guinn, Jeff (Ed.),
**The Autobiography
of Santa Claus,**
Fort Worth, TX: The Summit Group,
1994

Hadfield, Miles and John,
The Twelve Days of Christmas,
London: Cassell, 1961

Hampson, R.T.,
Kalendars of the Middle Ages,
London: Henry Kent Causton, n.d.

Harrison, Jane,
**Prologomena to the
Study of Greek Religion,**
London: Merlin Press, 1961

Heinberg, Richard,
Celebrate the Solstice,
Wheaton, IL: Theosophical
Publishing House, 1993

Hottes, Alfred Carl,
**1001 Christmas Facts
and Fancies,**
Dodd, Mead & Co., 1959

Houston, Jean,
**Manual for the Peacemaker:
An Iroquois Legend to
Heal Self and Society,**
Wheaton IL: Quest Books, 1995.

Hughes, David,
The Star of Bethlehem Mystery,
London: J.M. Dent & Sons, 1979

Hutton, Ronald,
**The Rise and Fall
of Merry England,**
Oxford: Oxford University Press,
1995

Hutton, Ronald,
**The Stations of the Sun:
A History of the Ritual Year
in Britain,**
Oxford: Oxford University Press,
1996

Hyde, Walter,
**Paganism to Christianity
in the Roman Empire,**
Philadelphia: University of
Pennsylvania Press, 1946

James, E.O.,
Seasonal Feasts and Festivals,
London: Thames & Hudson, 1961

Jones, Julia, and Barbara Deer,
**Catten Cakes and Lace:
A Calendar of Feasts,**
London: Dorling Kindersley, 1987

Karas, Sheryl Ann,
The Solstice Evergreen,
Boulder Creek, CO: Aslan
Publishing, 1991

Kennedy, Peter (Ed.),
Folk-Songs of Britain & Ireland,
London: Cassell, 1975

Kightley, Charles,
**The Customs & Ceremonies
of Britain,**
London: Thames & Hudson, 1986

King, John,
The Celtic Druid's Year,
London: Blandford Press, 1996

Koontz, Dean,
Santa's Twin,
San Francisco and London: Harper
Prism, 1996

Krythe, Maymie R.,
All About Christmas,
New York: Harper Bros., 1954

Langstaff, Nancy and John,
**The Christmas Revels
Songbook,**
Boston: David R. Godine, 1985

Lehane, Brendan,
The Book of Christmas,
Amsterdam: Time Life Books, 1986

Lipsanen, Anneke,
The Finnish Folk Year,
Helsinki: Otava Publishing Co. Ltd.,
1987

Lonsdale, Steven,
**Animals and the
Origins of Dance,**
London: Thames & Hudson, 1981

Long, George,
The Folklore Callendar,
London: Philip Allen, 1930

Macrobius,
**Commentary on the
Dream of Scipio,**
Trans. by W.H. Stahl, London and
New York: Columbia University
Press, 1952

McNeill, F. Marian,
**The Silver Bough:
A Calendar of Scottish
National Festivals**
(4 vols.), Glasgow: William Maclellan,
1961

Matthews, Caitlin,
The Celtic Book of Days,
New Alresford: Godsfield Press, 1995

Matthews, Caitlin,
Celtic Devotional,
New Alresford: Godsfield Press, 1996

Matthews, Caitlin,
Elements of the Celtic Tradition,
Shaftesbury: Element Books, 1996

Matthews, J.,
A Bardic Source-Book,
London: Cassell, 1998

Matthews, J.,
A Celtic Reader,
London: HarperCollins, 1995

Matthews, J.,
A Druid Source-Book,
London: Cassell, 1997

Matthews, J.,
**Robin Hood:
Green Lord of the Wildwood,**
Glastonbury: Gothic Image Publica-
tions, 1996

Matthews, J.,
**Taliesin: Shamanism
and the Bardic Mysteries in
Britain and Ireland,**
London: Thorsons, 1991

Mayfield, Beatrice,
Apple Games and Customs,
London: Common Ground, 1994

Metcalf, Edna,
The Trees of Christmas,
New York: Abingdon Press, 1969

Meyer, Marvin W.,
**The Ancient Mysteries:
A Sourcebook,**
San Francisco: Harper & Row, 1987

Miles, Clement A.,
**Christmas in Ritual
and Tradition,**
London: T. Fisher Unwin, 1912

Murphy, G.R. (Trans.),
The Heliand: The Saxon Gospel,
Oxford: Oxford University Press,
1992

Nissenbaum, Stephen,
The Battle for Christmas,
New York: Random House, 1966

O'Brien, Tim,
Light Years Ago,
Dublin: The Black Cat Press, 1992

Pennick, Nigel,
The Pagan Source Book, London:
Rider, 1992

Phelps, John,
The Prehistoric Solar Calendar,
Baltimore, MD, 1955

Pool, Daniel,
Christmas in New York,
New York: Seven Stories Press, 1997

Rae, Simon (Ed.),
The Faber Book of Christmas,
London: Faber & Faber, 1996

Restad, Penne L.,
Christmas in America,
Oxford: Oxford University Press,
1995

Reid, Bill,
The Raven Steals the Light,
Seattle: University of Washington
Press, 1984

Sawyer, Ruth,
The Long Christmas,
London: The Bodley Head, 1994

Skelton, Robin, and Margaret
Blackwood,
Earth, Air, Fire, Water,
London: Arkana, 1990

Simek, Rudolf,
**Dictionary of Northern
Mythology,**
Cambridge: D.S. Brewer, 1993

Sibley, Brian,
**A Christmas Carol:
The Unsung Story,**
Oxford: Lion Books, 1994

Spence, Lewis,
**Myth and Ritual in Dance,
Game and Rhyme,**
London: Watts & Co., 1947

Sunson, William,
A Book of Christmas,
New York: McGraw Hill, 1968

Toulson, Shirley,
The Celtic Year,
Shaftesbury: Element Books, 1993

Toulson, Shirley,
The Winter Solstice,
London: Jill Norman & Hobhouse,
1981

Trevelyan, M.,
**Folk-Lore and Folk-Stories
of Wales,**
London: Elliot Stock, 1909

Uttley, Alison,
Plowmen's Clocks,
London: Faber & Faber, 1952

Uttley, Alison,
**Recipes from an
Old Farmhouse,**
London: Faber & Faber, 1966

Uttley, Alison,
Stories for Christmas,
London: Faber & Faber, 1977

Van Renterghan, Tony,
When Santa Was A Shaman,
St. Paul, MN: Llewellyn Publications,
1995

Vermaseren, M.J.,
Mithras, the Secret God,
London: Chatto & Windus, 1963

Walwin, Peggy C.,
St. Nicholas, Our Santa Claus,
Gloucester: Albert E. Smith, 1971

Whitlock, Ralph,
**In Seach of Lost Gods:
A Guide to British Folklore,**
Oxford: Phaidon, 1979

Williamson, Duncan,
Tell Me A Story for Christmas,
Edinburgh: Canongate, 1987

RECORDINGS

There are countless numbers of recordings of Christmas music, though this tends to be primarily concerned with the Christian celebration. However, several albums have appeared over the past few years which draw on a wider range of material. A recording specially compiled to accompany this book, and performed by Martin and Jessica Simpson and Lisa Ekströn, will be shortly available on Red House Recordings. It is called **Beautiful Darkness: Celebrating the Winter Solstice.** In addition the best alternative selection of Solstice music is contained in a set of four CDs compiled and performed by Nancy & John Langstaff, whose Revels programs (see below) have become a feature of life in many parts of the United States, and whose work is gradually becoming better known in Europe.

Over the past few years the Paul Winter Consort, with a wide variety of guest artists and friends, have been presenting a celebration of the Winter Solstice in the Cathedral of St. John the Divine in New York. Once again, as with the Revels, this offers a unique opportunity to celebrate the return of the Midwinter Sun in a spectacular setting with evocative performance. A live recording of the celebration is also available: **Solstice Live! A Celebration of the Winter Solstice** by the Paul Winter Consort with special guests (Living Music, LD0024).

Christmas Day in the Morning: A Revels Celebration of the Winter Solstice
Revels Records CD1087

The Christmas Revels: Traditional and Ritual Carols, Dances, and Processionals
Revels Records CD 1078

Wassail! Wassail! Early American Christmas Music
Revels Records CD 1082

Sing We Now of Christmas: Six Centuries of European Christmas Music
Revels Records CD 1091

To Drive the Dark Away: Traditional Songs & Dances for the Winter Solstice
Revels Records CD1098

There is also a book,
The Christmas Revels Songbook: Carols, Processionals, Rounds and Ritual, and Children's Songs in Celebration of the Winter Solstice
Boston: David R. Godine, 1985

IN ADDITION WE WOULD RECOMMEND THE FOLLOWING ALBUMS:

A Celtic Christmas I-III: Wyndham Hill Samplers
Wyndham Hill 01934-11178-2, 01934-117689-2, 01934-11233-2

To Drive the Cold Winter Away
by Horselips
Horselips Records, Moo 9

To Drive the Cold Winter Away
by Loreena McKennitt
Quinlan Road Productions No.102

La Fete de L'Ane
(The Festival of the Ass) by the Clemencic Consort.
Harmonia Mundi, HM 1036

The Night Before A Celtic Christmas
by Dordan
Narada, ND 61063

Salva Nos
by The Medieval Babes
Virgin Records CDVE935

Tapestry of Carols
by Maddy Prior with the Carnival Band
Saydisc SDL 366.

To Warm the Winter Night
by Aine Minogue.
Evergreen Music & Recordings EM-014

Winter's Turning
by Robin Williamson
Plant Life Records PLR075
(for this and other Robin Williamson recordings please write to: Unique Gravity, 196 Old Road, Brampton, Chesterfield, Derbyshire, S40 3QW U.K.)

THE REVELS

The Winter Revels, organized by John Langstaff and his company, now take place all over the U.S.A. near Midwinter. They incorporate many traditions and enact the ceremonies, sing the songs, and perform dances and plays that go with them. To see Morris dancing, Wassailing, and much more, and to take part in a wonderful celebration of the Midwinter holiday, these are a must. The following details (correct at time of going to press) will bring information on these events.

Revels Inc.
Dept R
One Kendall Sq
Bldg 600
Cambridge, MA 02139
Tel: (617) 621 0505
       (617) 621 8913
Fax: (617) 621 1709
E Mail: Productions@revels.org
Orders to above address or E Mail:
Records@revels.org

Revels North
Tel: (603) 298 8913
E Mail: jrs@aol.com

Revels Houston
Tel: (713) 688 3303
E Mail: revelshon@iapc.net

New York Revels
Tel: (212) 206 6875
       (718) 242 5370
E Mail: nkpetaja@earthlink.net

Philadelphia Revels
Tel: (610) 688 5303

Portland Revels
Tel: (503) 224 7411
E Mail: dklewis@teleport.com

San Francisco Bay Revels
Tel: (510) 452 9334
E Mail: sfbayrevls@earthlink.net

Washington Revels
Tel: (202) 364 8744
E Mail: washrevels@aol.com

Puget Sound Revels
Tel: (206) 756 1804
E Mail: psrevels@aol.com

Minnesota Revels
Tel: (612) 699 3388
E Mail: velikon@freenet.msp.mn.us

SANTA'S ADDRESSES

Every year seems to bring forth a fresh crop of web sites aimed at the Christmas holiday. Many of these do not survive to the next season, but here are two which have reappeared over two years.

www.northpole.com
www.north.pole.org/

If you want to write to Santa in the old-fashioned way, the following address will always find him and generally gets a reply as well:

Joulupukki,
96930 Napapiiri,
Finland.

COURSES

John and Caitlín Matthews give regular courses on Shamanic, Arthurian, and Celtic traditions and produce a quarterly Newsletter. For information on these and publishing news, write to:

BCM HALLOWQUEST,
LONDON,
WC1X 3XX.

enclosing eight first class stamps, or (outside the U.K.) Eight International Reply Paid Coupons (available at any post office).

ACKNOWLEDGMENTS

A number of people have helped and encouraged me in the writing of this book, in particular my wife Caitlín, who gave admirable advice and support throughout, came to my rescue (again!) at the eleventh hour, and who cheerfully allowed me to pillage her notes for a talk entitled "The Animals of the Solstice," originally delivered at Hawkwood College in 1995. Much of this was incorporated into Chapter 5 of the present work. I would also like to remember all those who joined us in celebrating the Winter Revels at Hawkwood in the same year, whose willingness to follow where we lead was, as ever, an inspiration. To ace mummer and wielder of the Billy-on-a-Stick, Marc Vyvyan-Jones, for permission to use his song "The Four Noble Trees." To Martin Ludgate, who knows more than he should about the Solstice, for letting me use his mystery play *Saturn and the Dragons of the Solstice*. To Diana Paxson for permission to use her "Invocation to Holla." To my friend Ari Berk, for drawing my attention to the Losley Papers, and for advice on Native American Solstice celebrations and Esquimaux names for snow. To Barbara Finn for making me fully aware of the network of American Revels. To my editor at Godsfield Press, Sandy Breakwell, for some great last minute amendments; and to Brenda Rosen at Quest Books, for helpful suggestions and a timely supply of information. Lastly, to David Spangler who has, over the years, manifested so many of the aspects of Father Christmas in his own life, as well as mine, that I could not help but mention his contribution, without which this would have been a poorer book. J. M.

BETWEEN DARKNESS AND LIGHT
(for Emrys)

It is within the darkness and the silence
That the magic of Christmas starts;
Somewhere between the glimmer of lights
And the first breathless moment
When children come
Stumbling like new-born angels
Into morning light.

Within the darkness and the silence
We sit, watching wonder
Evolve into form; where we
Enter the ringing silence
In which the first bells of Christmas
Sound the music of the soul;

Where the morning joy begins
With a single carol
To a half-forgotten tune.

It is here, between the darkness
And the light,
That we wait, uncertain,
Seeking the moment
That challenges us to believe
In a freshly minted miracle
Born every Christmas Day.

JOHN MATTHEWS.
Christmas, 1995.

PICTURE CREDITS

The publishers would like to thank the following for permission to reproduce copyright material.